Just the Facts

Introduction *to* Plant Science

National Agricultural Institute

© 2014 National Agricultural Institute, Inc.

ALL RIGHTS RESERVED. No part of this work covered by the copyright herein may reproduced except as permitted under Section 107 or 108 of the United States Copyright Act, without the prior written permission of the publisher.

Revised August 2015

National Agricultural Institute, Inc.
151 W. 100 S.
Rupert, ID 83350
USA
(208) 957-7000

ISBN 978-0-578-14146-6

To learn more about the National Agricultural Institute, Inc. visit:

www.national-ag-institute.org
Or visit us on Facebook: www. facebook.com/Agri101

Send comments or questions to roparker@national-ag-institute.org

Notice to the Reader

Publisher does not warrant or guarantee any of the products described herein or perform any independent analysis in connection with any of the product information contained herein. Publisher does not assume, and expressly disclaims, any obligation to obtain and include information other than that provided to it by the manufacturer. The reader is expressly warned to consider and adopt all safety precautions that might be indicated by the activities described herein and to avoid all potential hazards. By following the instructions contained herein, the reader willingly assumes all risks in connection with such instructions. The publisher makes no representations or warranties of any kind, including but not limited to, the warranties of fitness for particular purpose or merchantability, nor are any such representations implied with respect to the material set forth herein, and the publisher takes no responsibility with respect to such material. The publisher shall not be reliable for any special, consequential, or exemplary damages resulting, in whole or part, from the readers' use of, or reliance upon, this material.

Table of Contents

1 The Importance of Plants to Humans 1
    Roles of Plants 1

2 Plant Parts 5
    Roots 5
    Parts of the root system: 6
    Leaves 6
    Stems 8
    Flowers 8
    Fruit 9

3 Functions of Plant Parts 12
    Roots: Primary Functions 12
    Plant Leaf Processes 12
    Stem Functions 13
    Fruit and Seed Production 13
    Importance of Flower Reproduction 13

4 Anatomy of Plants 16
    Plant Cell 17
    Cell Structures 17
    Tissues 21
    Anatomy of Primary Organs 24
    Primary and Secondary Growth 26

5 Importance of Soil 29
    Importance of Soil 29
    Soil and Plant Culture 30
    Soil - Medium for Plant Growth 30

6 Soil Texture and Structure 34
    Composition of Soil 34

Table of Contents

    Organic Matter 35

    Soil Profile 36

    How the Nature of the Parent Material Affects the Soil 37

    Physical Properties of Soil.. 37

7 Influence of Texture on Soil 41

    Soil Separates 41

    Soil Classification According to Texture 43

    Soil Profile 43

    Components of a Soil Profile 44

    Characteristics of the Four Horizons 44

    Soil Profile Color Significance 45

    Importance of Soil Profile in Determining Crop Production 45

    Soil Testing 45

    Collecting Soil Samples 46

8 Soil Erosion and Conservation 49

    Erosion 49

    Types of Soil Erosion 49

    Cultural Practices Contributing to Soil Erosion 50

    Results of Erosion 51

    Soil Conservation Practices for the Control of Soil Erosion 51

9 Introduction to Irrigation 55

    History of Irrigation 55

    Irrigation Systems 56

    Ditch Maintenance 59

    Scientific Irrigation Scheduling 59

    Irrigation System Advantages and Disadvantages 60

10 Irrigation Terminology 63

    Water 63

    Irrigation Terminology 64

11 Irrigation Practices 68

Table of Contents

    Irrigation Practices 68
    Selecting Land for Irrigation 68
    Obtaining Water 69
    Water Quality 69
    Drainage 70

12 Knowing When to Irrigate 72
    Knowing When to Irrigate 72
    Degree of Moisture Feel Percent of Field Capacity 74
    Other Methods for Determining When to Irrigate 75
    Crop Water Requirements 76

13 Water Measurement and Soil Capacity 78
    Water Measurements and Soil Capacity 78

14 Transpiration 82
    Transpiration 82
    Environmental Factors Affecting Transpiration 83

15 Translocation 85
    Translocation 85
    Other Functions of Translocation 86

16 Nutrients Essential to Plant Growth 88
    Introduction 88
    Sixteen Essential Elements 89
    Functions of Plant Elements Metabolism and Their Deficiencies 90
    Micronutrients 92

17 Primary Plant Nutrients 95
    Sources of Plant Nutrients 95

18 Signs of Nutrient Deficiencies 99
    A Key to Nutrient Deficiency Signs 99

19 Plant Growth Requirements 102
    Plant Growth Requirements 102

20 Fertilizer Labels and Calculations 108

Table of Contents

Fertilizer Labels 108
Nutrient Content of Commercial Fertilizers 109
Calculating the Best Buy 110
Determining How Much Fertilizer to Apply to get Recommended Nutrient Amounts   110
Fertilizing Crops for Production 111
Determining Fertilizer Need 112
Determining Crop Production Goal 112
Determining Yield Goal 113
Soil Reserve 113
Crop Residue 113
Common Commercial Fertilizers 114
How Much (N) to Feed Plants 114

21 Fertilizer Applications 118

Methods of Fertilizer Application 118
Pre-plant Applications: Broadcast or Injection 119
At-Planting Applications 120
Post-Emergence Applications: Side or Top Dressing 121
Water-Run Applications: Open or Closed Systems 122
Foliar Applications 122
Fertilizer-Pesticide Mixtures 123
Calibration of Fertilizer Spreaders 123

22 Photosynthesis 127

Importance of Photosynthesis 127
Process of Photosynthesis 129

23 Respiration 133

Respiration Process 133
Factors Affecting Respiration 136
Importance of Respiration to Agriculture 136

24 Mitosis 139

Mitosis 139

Table of Contents

    Steps of Mitosis 140

    Assessment 142

25 Vegetative Growth 144

    Annuals 144

    Biennials 145

    Perennials 145

26 Plant Propagation by Seed 148

    Plant Propagation by Seed 148

    Seeds 149

    More about Seeds 150

27 Starting Plants from Seed 152

    Propagation from Seed 152

    Seedbed Preparation and Planting 153

    Planting in Flats 153

    Factors Causing Poor Seed Germination 154

    Transplanting 155

    Care of Young Plants 156

28 Plant Propagation by Vegetative Means 159

    Vegetative Reproduction 159

    Eight Common Types 159

29 Introduction to Plant Pests 165

    Introduction to Plants Pests 165

    Weeds 166

    Invertebrates 167

    Vertebrates 167

    Disease Agents 167

    Challenges of Pests 168

30 Damage Caused by Plant Diseases 170

    Damage Caused by Plant Diseases 170

    Disease-Causing Organisms 171

Table of Contents

31 Cultural Methods of Plant Disease Control ... 174
- Cultural Methods of Plant Disease Control ... 174
- Cultural Disease Control ... 174

32 Chemical Methods of Disease Control ... 179
- Disease Control Chemicals ... 179
- Foliage Sprays and Dusts ... 180
- Seed Treatment ... 180
- Controlling Postharvest Diseases ... 180
- Soil Treatment ... 181
- Disinfestation of Warehouses ... 181
- Controlling Insect Vectors ... 181
- Treating Tree Wounds ... 182
- Resistance and Hazards ... 183

33 Biology of Insects ... 185
- Biology of Insects ... 185
- Insect Body ... 186
- Life Cycle ... 187

34 Insect Control ... 190
- Damage Caused by Insects ... 190
- Insect Control ... 191

35 Pesticide Safety: High Toxicity ... 195
- Pesticide Safety - High Toxicity ... 195
- Protective Equipment ... 196

36 Pesticide Safety: Low Toxicity ... 199
- Pesticide Label Information and Low Toxicity Pesticides ... 199
- General Rules ... 201
- First Aid ... 202

37 Insect Collections ... 205
- Insect Collecting ... 205

38 Weed Identification ... 208

Table of Contents

    Weeds 208
    Weed Collections 210
    Life Cycles of Weeds 210
    Identification 210

39 Weed Control 215
    Importance of Weed Control 215
    Weed Control 215
    Controlling Weeds with Herbicides 216

40 Workplace Safety 219
    Workplace Safety 219
    Common Accidents and Identifying Prevention Procedures 220
    Safety 221

41 Genetic Engineering and Biotechnology 225
    Biotechnology 225
    Genetic Engineering of Plants 226
    Purposes of Biotechnology 226
    Examples of Biotechnology on Production Agriculture 227
    Tissue Culture, a Biotechnology – Advantages and Disadvantages 228
    How Tissue Culture Works 228
    Steps in Tissue Culture 229
    New Words from Biotechnology 230
    Public Awareness 231

42 Fiber Crops 234
    Fiber Crops 234
    Cotton 234
    Cotton Description and Growth 235
    Adaptation and Distribution 235
    Management 236
    Planting 236
    Pest Management 236

Table of Contents

    Weed Management 237

    Protection from Insects and Fungal Diseases 237

    Fertilization 237

    Tissue Analysis 237

    Irrigation 238

    Harvesting 238

    Grading and Processing Cotton 238

43 Cereal Grains 241

    Five Criteria for Selecting a Grain Crop 241

    Cultural Practices for Major Grain Crops 242

44 Forage Crops 247

    Forage Crops 247

45 Oilseeds 250

    Oil Crops 250

    Soybeans - Most Important Oil Crop in the United States 251

46 Sugar Crops 255

    Sugar Crops 255

    Growing and Harvesting Sugar Cane 256

    Extracting Sugar from Cane 257

    By-products of Sugar Cane 258

    Growing and Harvesting Sugar Beets 258

    Extracting Sugar from Beets 258

    By-Products of Sugarbeets 259

47 Vegetable Crops 261

    Economic Importance of Vegetables to U.S. Agriculture 261

    Importance of Vegetables in Human Nutrition 263

    Environment Affects Growth 264

    Important Techniques in Producing a Vegetable Crop 265

    Pests Negatively Affect Growth and Production 265

    Biotechnological Advances Can Aid in Increasing Vegetable Production 265

Table of Contents

    Marketing of Commercially Grown Vegetables 266

48 Specialty Crops 269

    Specialty Crops 269

    USDA Involvement 275

    Production Practices to Successfully Grow These Crops 276

    Soil Tillage Requirements 277

    Crop Fertilization 277

    Pest Management 279

    Disease Control 279

49 Fruits 282

    Cultural Practices for Fruit Crops 282

    Harvest or Post-Harvest Methods for Fruit and Nut Crops 283

50 Nut Production 285

    U.S. Nut Production 285

    Selecting Nut Trees 286

    Some Nut Varieties 286

    Cultural Practices for Nut Crops 287

    Disease and Pest Control 287

    Harvest or Post-Harvest Methods for Nut Crops 288

51 Flowers and Foliage 290

    Value of Floriculture 290

    Flowering Herbaceous Perennials (common and *scientific* names) 291

    Growing Perennials 292

    Flowering Annuals (common and *scientific* name) 292

    Annual Bulbs 295

    Flowering Houseplants 300

52 Sod Production 303

    Value of Turf 303

    Functions of Turf 304

    Turfgrass Maintenance Practices 304

Table of Contents

Turfgrasses (common and scientific names) 304

Sod Production Practices 305

Marketing and Selling Sod 308

53 Organic Production 311

Organic Farming 312

International Organic Standards 313

Claims of Organic Production 314

Crop Nutrition 314

Manure 315

Best Management Practices 319

Composting 319

Characteristics of Well-prepared Compost 321

Green Manures 321

Cover Crops 321

Choice of Crops 322

Crop Rotations 322

Weed Control 323

Pest and Disease Control 324

Genetic Diversity 325

Use of Water 326

Animals and Organic Growing 326

Sustainable Agriculture 326

54 Hydroponics/Aquaponics 329

Hydroponics 329

Plant Growth Requirements 331

Common Vegetable Crops Suitable for Hydroponics or Aquaponics 332

Glossary 334

Appendix 355

National Agriculture, Food and Natural Resources (AFNR) Career Cluster Content Standards 355

    Purpose 355

Table of Contents

Process 355
Alignments and Crosswalks 356
Availabiltiy 356

Preface

This textbook, Introduction to Plant Science, is one in a series of *Just the Facts (JTF)* textbooks created by the National Agricultural Institute. This is a bold, new approach to textbooks. These textbooks present the essential knowledge in outline format. This essential knowledge is supported by a main concept, learning objectives and key terms at the beginning of each section. Content of the books is further enhanced for student learning by connecting with complementary PowerPoint presentations and websites through QR codes (scanned by smart phones or tablets) or URLs. Each textbook is available in print and electronic formats.

The time is now for a new mindset about textbooks. Textbooks for the future need to take advantage of both print and digital technology, while keeping costs down.

Just the Facts series of textbooks provides a synergistic textbook model - print and digital working together to be better than either one alone. Moreover, in a time of increasing costs for textbooks, print copies of Just the Facts textbooks are $50 or less per book.

The first of these new textbooks also includes:

- *Just the Facts: Introduction to Agriculture*
- *Just the Facts: Introduction to Biology*
- *Just the Facts: Introduction to Soil Science*
- *Just the Facts: Introduction to Animal Science*
- *Just the Facts: Introduction to Food Systems Science*

Other titles scheduled for release as a part of the *Just the Facts* textbook series includes: *Introduction to Agribusiness; Introductory Food Science; Introduction to Sustainable Agriculture; Introduction to Aquaculture Science;* and *Introduction to Equine Science*.

Just the Facts textbooks are a project of the National Agricultural Institute, Inc. created, written and assembled by:

Rick Parker, PhD, President
Marilyn Parker, Vice President
Karen Earwood, Administrative Assistant
Miriah Pace, Administrative Assistant

1 The Importance of Plants to Humans

Major Concept
Plants play a major role in sustaining and enriching life.

Objectives
- Identify two important contributions plants make to all other living things
- List three products from plants
- Name three by-products from plants

Link to Standards
PS.01. Develop and implement a crop management plan for a given production goal that accounts for environmental factors.

Key Terms
- Energy

Roles of Plants
- Because of their photosynthetic processes, green plants form the base of the food chain and thus the beginning of the energy flow through an ecosystem.
  - Only important organisms able to receive inorganic elements and incorporate them into organic compounds in living tissues.
  - **Energy**, not used directly by the plant in carrying out its life processes, goes into the production of new tissues or biomass.
    - ✓ Other organisms, including humans, use this as a food source.
- Provide oxygen to all living organisms:
  - Plants in the world's forests and rangelands provide oxygen (O_2) globally.

- Edible Plants
  - Edible concentrated portions of various plants such as seeds, fruits and tubers are used as a food source not only for the human population, but also for livestock.
  - Fixing of nitrogen (N) by legumes to enrich the soil.
    - ✓ Bacteria on roots put atmospheric nitrogen into the soil.
  - Most important food plants are grains of the grass family, examples include:
    - ✓ Wheat
    - ✓ Rice
    - ✓ Maize (corn)
    - ✓ Sorghum
    - ✓ Barley
  - Certain plants also provide the major beverages of the world, including:
    - ✓ Coffee
    - ✓ Tea
    - ✓ Fruit juices
- Industrial Uses
  - Scarcely a product exists in which plants have not played some important role, either as a component, an implement in its construction or at least as the energy source (fossil fuels) of its production.
  - Many textile fibers are derived from plants, including:
    - ✓ Cotton
    - ✓ Flax
    - ✓ Hemp
  - The wood of trees is used to make tools, furniture and houses.
    - ✓ Turpentine, acetic acid and methanol are also obtained from trees
- Medicinal Uses
  - Anti-malarial quinine from cinchona bark.

- - Heart-stimulant digitalis from foxglove leaves.
  - Antispasmodic atropine from belladonna (nightshade).
  - Rauwolfia tranquilizers from the plants of the genus *Rauvolfia*.
- Oils
  - Oils are stored as food reserves in the seeds and fruits of many plants.
  - Most are used as human food but some are used for industry.
  - The most significant oil plant is soybean.
  - Also important are the coconut, sunflower, peanut, cottonseed and rapeseed.
- Provide Protection for the Environment
  - Shade
  - Windbreaks
  - Erosion control protection for watershed
  - Beautification

Summary

Plants are essential to humans in many ways such as oxygen, food, fiber and shelter. Plants can be used to modify the environment. Plants also produce many other important products and by-products such as medicines that are useful to humans and animals.

Resources

Free complementary PowerPoint:
http://www.tagmydoc.com/dl/1ZgxiK/gk67

Parker, R. 2010. Plant and soil science: Fundamentals and applications. Clifton Park, NY: Delmar Cengage Learning. (Pgs. 6-9).

Food and Agriculture Organization of the United Nations
http://faostat.fao.org

Why Plants are Important
http://www.bgci.org/plantconservationday/whyplantsimportant/

Biology of Plants
http://www.mbgnet.net/bioplants/earth.html

Assessment

1. T or F? Plants provide oxygen to all living organisms.

2. One of the by-products plants produce?
   a.) turpentine   b.) leaves   c.) grass   d.) more plants

3. T or F? Plants produce shelter only for other plants.

4. Plants provide _____ in legumes to enrich the soil.
   a.) oxygen   b.) nitrogen   c.) phosphorous   d.) potassium

5. One of the medicinal products plants provide?
   a.) calcium   b.) penicillin   c.) resin   d.) glue

Take the assessment online here:

http://tinyurl.com/PlntSci-1

Hint: When the answer is incorrect, you will see: "Wrong answer! Go Back!"

Notes

2 Plant Parts

Major Concept
Become familiar with specific parts and functions of plants.

Objectives
- Identify plant parts including, roots, leaves, stem, fruit and flower
- Describe the general function of each of the listed plant parts

Link to Standards
PS.02. Apply principles of classification, plant anatomy, and plant physiology to plant production and management.

Key Terms
- Aggregate fruit
- Anther
- Apex
- Base
- Blade
- Complete flower
- Compound leaf
- Dehiscent
- Drupe or Pome
- Fibrous root
- Filament
- Imperfect flower
- Incomplete flower
- Indehiscent
- Internode
- Margin
- Meristem
- Midrib
- Multiple fruit
- Ovary
- Ovule
- Petiole
- Pistil
- Root cap
- Root hairs
- Sessile
- Stamen
- Stigma
- Stomata
- Style
- Taproot

Roots
- Two basic plant root types/systems are:

  1. The **fibrous** root system, such as in corn or beans in which the roots branch from the bottom of the plant.

  2. The **taproot** where a long tapering root such as in the carrot, dandelions and mesquite, develops.

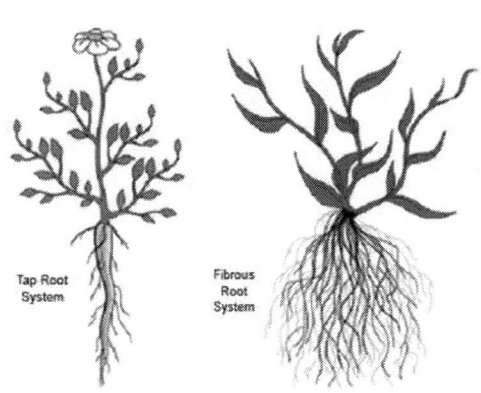

JTF: Introduction to Plant Science 5

Parts of the root system:

- **Root hairs** carry on absorption.

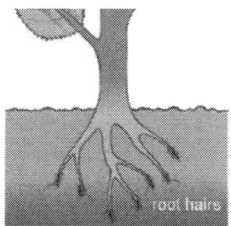

  - The **root cap** and **meristem**, which are involved in growth, are the conducting tissue.

    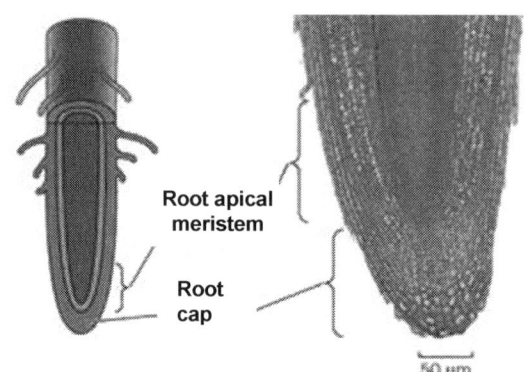

    ✓ They conduct moisture and nutrients to the plant.

    ✓ The root system develops the primary root and then branches into secondary roots.

Leaves

- The leaf is the food manufacturing factory of the plant which performs photosynthesis and contains the green pigment chlorophyll which makes the process possible.

- The leaf is composed of seven parts.

  1. The **stomata** are small openings usually on the underside of a leaf which help cool the plant through the transpiration of water.

  2. The **blade** is the main body of the leaf.

  3. The **petiole** is the stem which attaches the blade to the stem.

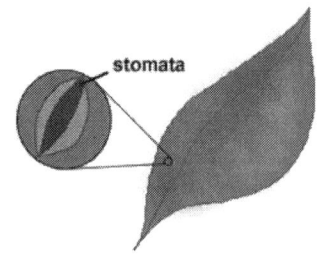
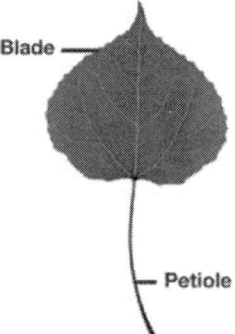

4. The **midrib**-like structure is the large central vein down the middle of the leaf.

5. The **apex** is the tip of the leaf.

6. The **base** is the bottom of the leaf and attaches to the petiole, or if a petiole is absent, directly to the stem. A leaf with no petiole is said to be **sessile**.

7. The **margin** is the edge of the leaf.

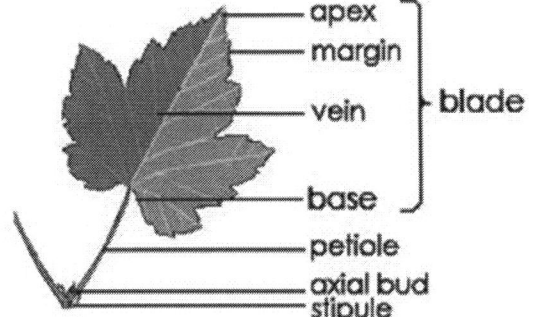

- Leaf types include:

    o Simple leaves – No division of parts.

    o Compound leaves – Having a number of leaflets on a single stalk.

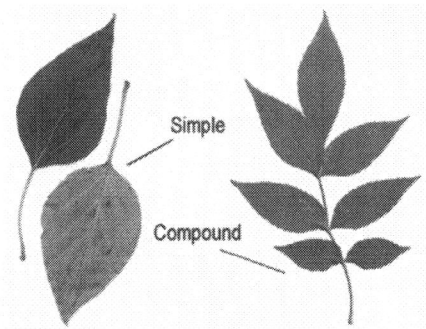

    o Needle leaves - A needle leaf is a narrow, compact leaf such as a pine or fir needle.

- The leaf functions as the food factory.

    o The leaf captures solar energy, converting it into chemical energy in the form of sugars and starch and is transferred up the food chain.

Stems

- The stem contains buds found in the area referred to as the node. Stems are the central support structure of the plant.

- External Anatomy

    o Areas between the buds are called the **internodes**.

    o Other important parts of the stem are the bark lenticels, leaf scars and scale scars.

    o Terminal growth of a plant occurs at the tips of stems with terminal buds.

- Internal Anatomy

    o Inside the stem, under the sapwood, contains xylem, phloem, cambium, sapwood, heartwood and pith.

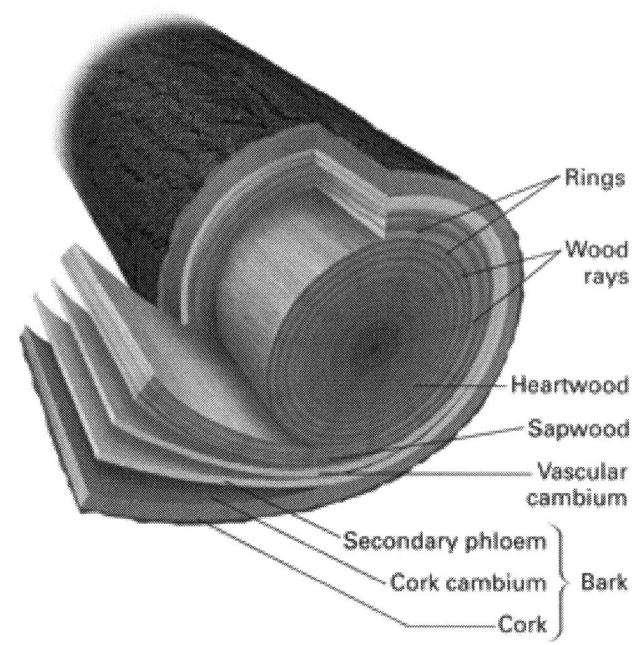

    o Inside the tree are the xylem and the cambium, then phloem, sapwood, heartwood and in the center of a tree is the pith.

    o Herbaceous plants have a different structure consisting of epidermis, cortex, pith and a series of vascular bundles.

Flowers

- Flowers of plants usually contain four main parts: sepals, petals, stamens and pistils.

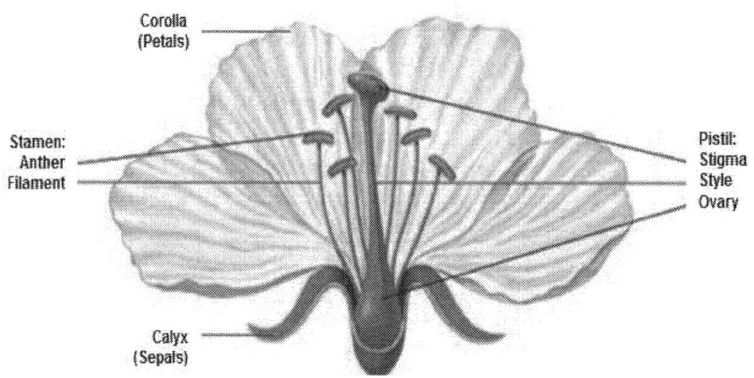

- o A flower with all four parts is called a **complete flower**.
- If the flower is missing any of the four primary parts it is said to be an **incomplete flower.**
  - o A flower with a **stamen** and **pistil**, the male and female reproductive structures, is said to be a **perfect flower**.
    - ✓ In a perfect flower, the pistil is the female part of the flower and is often in the center.
    - ✓ If it is missing the stamen or pistil it is said to be an **imperfect flower.**
- The pistil is composed of 3 primary parts – stigma, style and ovary.
  1. The pollen collecting structure at the top is called the **stigma.**
  2. The support structure below the stigma is the **style.**
  3. The enlarged part is the **ovary** containing the ovules or eggs.

  - o The pistil is surrounded by the male stamens which contain the pollen-bearing **anther**.
  - o The anther sits on top of the **filament** (holds pollen sacs) and acts as a stalk to support the anther.

Fruit

- The fruit of a plant is actually a ripened ovule. In most plants, the **ovule** or egg is fertilized by the sperm from the pollen and the ovary matures into the fruit.
- Fruits are classified by their structure, number of ovules and by dry or fleshy.

- Simple fruits, fleshy or dry, develop from a simple ovary. A fleshy example is a tomato or cranberry.
  - A simple fruit with fleshy tissue is classified as a drupe or pome.
    - A **drupe** has a stone in the center of the fruit which is its seed. Examples of drupes are olives, coconuts and peaches.
    - **Pomes** do not have a stone but have several seeds usually within a chamber. Examples of pomes are apples and pears.
- Simple fruits which are dry are classified as indehiscent or dehiscent.
  - **Indehiscent** fruits do not split open and release seeds when ripe. Examples are buckwheat, corn and wheat. Also peaches, plums and cherries.
  - **Dehiscent** fruits split open when ripe and release seeds. Examples are sweet peas, poppy and honeysuckle.
- Fruits can be classified as aggregate or multiple fruit.
  - **Aggregate fruits** are developed from a single flower with many ovaries. Examples are strawberries and blackberries.
  - **Multiple fruit** is a classification of fruit with flowers that are separated but closely clustered such as in mulberry, fig and pineapple.

Summary

Parts of a plant can be identified by their functions. The roots of a plant can be two basic types. The leaf is the food manufacturing factory of the plant which performs photosynthesis and contains the green pigment chlorophyll making the process possible. The stem contains buds found in the area referred to as the node. The stems are the central support structure of the plant. Flowers usually contain four main parts: sepals, petals, stamens and pistils. The fruit of a plant is actually a ripened ovule. In most plants the ovule or egg is fertilized by the sperm from the pollen and the ovary matures into the fruit.

Resources

Free complementary PowerPoint:
http://www.tagmydoc.com/plantparts

Parker, R. 2010. Plant and soil science: Fundamentals and applications. Clifton Park, NY: Delmar Cengage Learning

University of Illinois Extension: The Great Plant Escape
http://urbanext.illinois.edu/gpe/case1/c1facts1a.html

Botany: Plant Parts and Functions
http://ag.arizona.edu/pubs/garden/mg/botany/plantparts.html

Assessment

1. The two basic root types are taproot and _____.
   a.) stigma   b.) indehiscent   c.) perfect   d.) fibrous

2. The stomata are small _____ usually on the underside of a leaf which help cool the plant through the transpiration of water.
   a.) hairs   b.) openings   c.) vines   d.) flowers

3. A flower with a missing stamen or pistil, the male and female reproductive structures, is said to be a/an _____ flower.
   a.) imperfect   b.) incomplete   c.) complete   d.) simple

4. A drupe has a stone in the center which is its _____.
   a.) root   b.) seed   c.) stem   d.) internode.

5. T or F? Aggregate fruits are developed from a single flower with many ovaries.

Take the assessment online here:

http://tinyurl.com/PlntSci-2

Hint: When the answer is incorrect, you will see: "Wrong answer! Go Back!"

Notes

3 Functions of Plant Parts

Major Concept

Each plant part performs an important function.

Objectives

- Identify the functions of the root, leaf, stem, fruit and flower

Link to Standards

PS.02. Apply principles of classification, plant anatomy, and plant physiology to plant production and management.

Key Terms

- Cambium
- Meristem
- Ovule
- Phloem
- Xylem
- Zygote

Roots: Primary Functions

- The root carries out five primary functions:

    1. Takes in oxygen during respiration.

    2. Absorbs and translocates water and nutrients to stem.

    3. Stores food in form of starch.

    4. Anchors plant in stable position.

    5. Gives off CO_2 during respiration.

- The roots of legumes have nodules which contain nitrogen fixing bacteria.

Plant Leaf Processes

- Four functions of the leaf include:

1. Photosynthesis, the conversion of light energy into chemical energy
2. Transpiration cools the plant.
3. Stores food, which can be transferred to other areas of plant.
4. Asexual or vegetative propagation, in some cases.

Stem Functions

- Four functions of the stem include:

    1. Translocate nutrients from roots to leaves in vessels of xylem and phloem.
    2. Supports leaves of plant.
    3. Provides for growth in meristem of terminal bud.
        - ✓ Cell division occurs in the meristem.
        - ✓ **Cambium** layer provides diameter growth in stem.
    4. Can be used for vegetative propagation.

Fruit and Seed Production

- Fruit is a ripened **ovule** or egg together with associated parts and often protects the seeds.
- Dry dehiscent fruit splits open to help disseminate seeds.
    - Some actually hurl the seeds out as the seed surface explodes.
    - Others have wings or other ways to float or be carried by air.
- Fruit can provide nutrients to the soil and to a newly germinating seedling.
- Fruit also disseminates seeds by providing food for animals.

Importance of Flower Reproduction

- Colorful or fragrant flowers attract insects and birds for pollination.
    - The flower is often a biotic partner with the animals which obtain food from the flowers and in exchange help fertilize it.

- Pollination starts fertilization of ovules.
    - Producing a **zygote** or fertilized egg which becomes the seed.
- Specialized Flowers
    - Venus Fly Trap and Pitcher plant trap insects.
        - ✓ Once insect is trapped, it is digested by plant for food.

Summary

The root stores food, takes in water and oxygen and gives off CO_2. The leaf carries on photosynthesis, transpiration and stores food. The stem translocates nutrients and provides support for the leaves. The flower attracts insects and birds for pollination for continuance of the species and the fruit carries out the process of seed production and in some cases dissemination.

Resources

Free complementary PowerPoint:
http://www.tagmydoc.com/dl/1TSFmG/gk8x

Botany: Plant Parts and Functions
http://ag.arizona.edu/pubs/garden/mg/botany/plantparts.html

Plant Structure and Function
http://www.uic.edu/classes/bios/bios100/labs/plantanatomy.htm

Qld Science Teachers: Functions of Plant Parts
http://www.qldscienceteachers.com/junior-science/biology/functions-of-plant-parts

Assessment

1. Roots give off CO_2 during _____.
   a.) ovulation   b.) pollination   c.) respiration   d.) transpiration

2. Where does cell division occur?
   a.) cambium   b.) xylem   c.) phloem   d.) meristem

3. T or F? Stems can be used for vegetative propagation.

4. What starts fertilization of ovules?
   a.) transpiration   b.) wind   c.) pollination   d.) zygotes

5. The process of seed production is carried out by the _____.
   a.) flower   b.) meristem   c.) birds   d.) root

Take the assessment online here:

http://tinyurl.com/PlntSci-2a

Hint: When the answer is incorrect, you will see: "Wrong answer! Go Back!"

Notes

4 Anatomy of Plants

Major Concept

An understanding of plant growth begins with an understanding of plant anatomy – biochemicals, cells, tissues and organs.

Objectives

- Define a cell
- List the basic chemical composition of cells
- Identify the parts of a plant cell and their function
- List the two generalized types of tissues in plants
- Name the four categories of meristems
- Identify four types of permanent tissue
- Recognize the function of xylem and phloem
- Name the types of cells found in xylem and phloem
- Identify plant tissues and describe how they are organized
- Identify the anatomy of the primary root, stems, and leaves
- Define primary and secondary growth

Link to Standards

PS.02. Apply principles of classification, plant anatomy, and plant physiology to plant production and management.

Key Terms

- Cells
- Cell wall
- Chloroplasts
- Cristae
- Cytoplasm
- Endoplasmic reticulum
- Epidermis
- Eukaryotes
- Golgi apparatus
- Leucoplasts
- Meristems
- Microtubules
- Mitochondria
- Nucleus
- Organelles
- Palisade cells
- Parenchyma
- Peroxisomes
- Phloem
- Plasmolemma
- Protoplast
- Ribosomes
- Sclerenchyma cells
- Sieve tube cells
- Tissue
- Tonoplast
- Tracheids
- Vacuoles
- Vesicles
- Xylem

Plant Cell

- **Cells** are the basic structural and physiological unit of crop plants, within which chemical reactions of life occur, providing metabolites for plant life and for human use.

- Plant cells are **eukaryotes**.

    - Cells with a nucleus, where the genetic material is surrounded by a membrane.

- Cell composition

    - Ninety percent fluid (cytoplasm) and consists of free amino acids, proteins, glucose and numerous other molecules.

    - Contents of the cytoplasm and the nucleus affect the gene expression/regulations.

- Molecules that make up the cell include:

    - 50% protein

    - 15% nucleic acid

    - 15% carbohydrates

    - 10% lipids

    - 10% other

Cell Structures

- Includes cell wall, plasma membrane, protoplasts and organelles.

- Organelles include plastids, mitochondria, microfilaments, endoplasmic reticulum, nucleus, vesicles, vacuoles and Golgi apparatus.

- **Cell walls** are made of hemicellulose and secondary cell walls are made of cellulose, lignin, suberin and cutin.

- Plasma membrane, also known as the **plasmolemma**, or cytoplasmic membrane made of a phospholipid bilayer membrane.

- **Protoplast** refers to the inside of the cell or the cellular contents.

- **Cytoplasm** is the liquid matrix of the protoplast.

- o Includes water solutes, proteins, and so forth that stream through the protoplast.

- **Organelles** are the internal structures within the protoplast.

- **Leucoplasts** are for the storage of oil, starch, and proteins.

- **Chloroplasts,** double-membrane plastids with chlorophyll, used in photosynthesis, storing starch, and contain genetic information (DNA).

- **Mitochondria** are double-membrane bound and are the site of respiration and the production of respiratory energy, converting foods into usable energy—production of adenosine triphosphate (ATP)—through aerobic respiration.

  - o Inner membrane shapes differ between different types of cells and it forms projections called **cristae**.

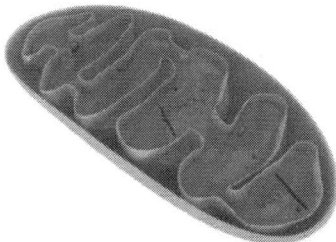

- **Nucleus** is contained in the double-membrane nuclear envelope and it contains the chromosomes, which are long strands of deoxyribonucleic acid (DNA).

  - o DNA provides the genetic code.

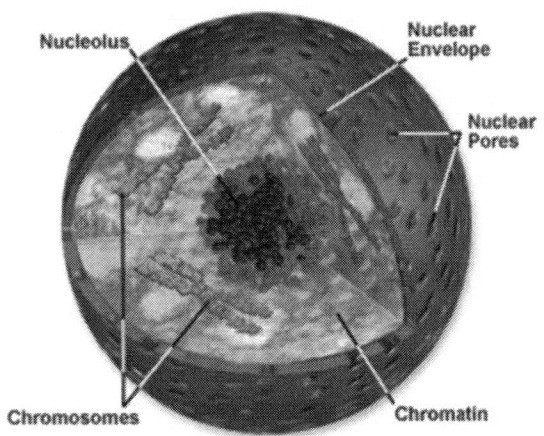

- **Vacuoles** surrounded by the **tonoplast,** occupy the major volume of the cell and contain water solution and dissolved substances—sugars, organic acids and pigments.

    o Storage reservoir for water, sugars, salts and other biochemicals.

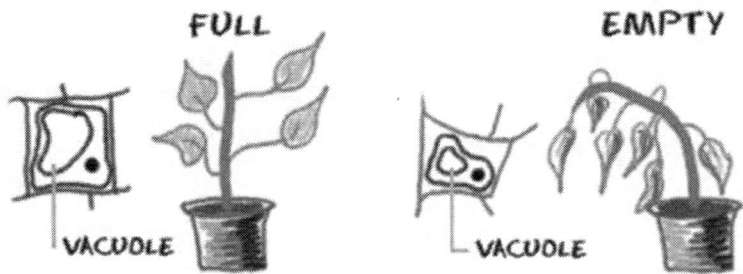

- **Endoplasmic reticulum** (ER) is important for protein synthesis.

    o Two types: rough and smooth.

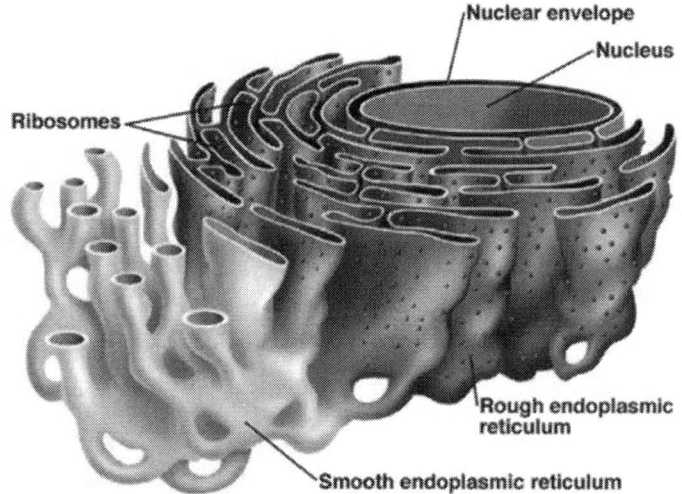

- **Ribosomes** translate the RNA into proteins.

- **Golgi apparatus** is important for glycosylation and secretion.

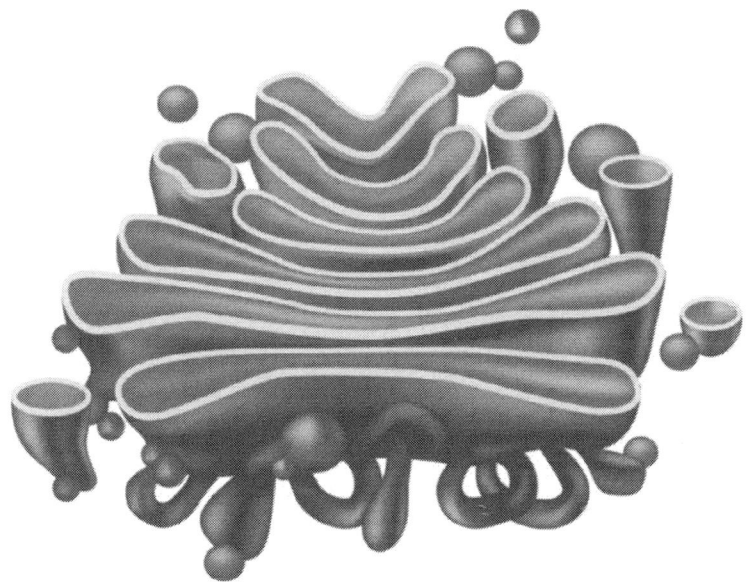

- **Peroxisomes** use oxygen to carry out catabolic reactions.

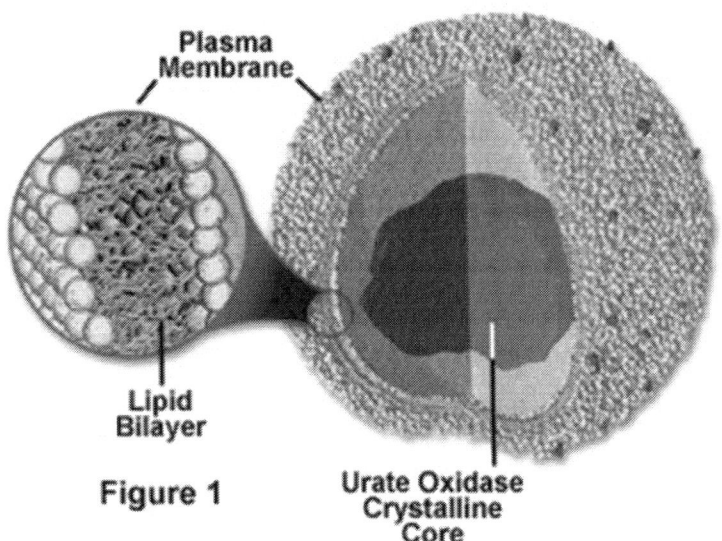

Figure 1

- Centrioles and cilia are composed of microtubules made from tubulin.

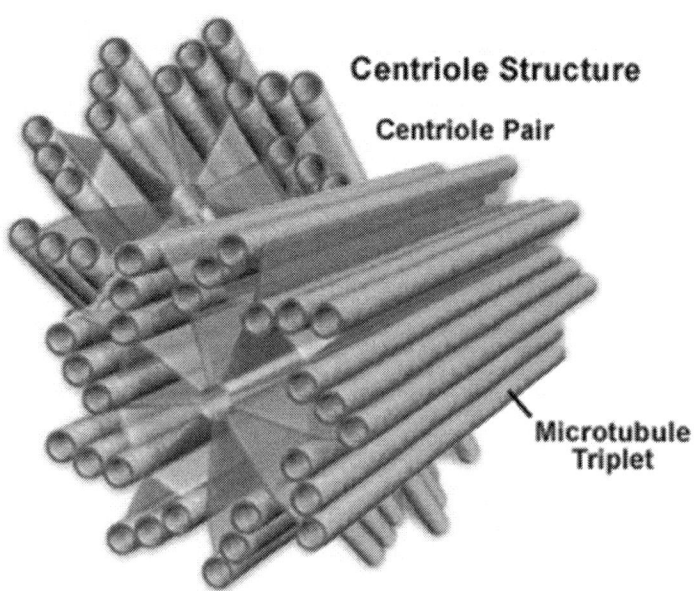

Tissues

- **Tissues** are the large groups of organized cells of similar structure that perform specific functions in the plant.

- Two generalized types of tissues: meristematic and permanent

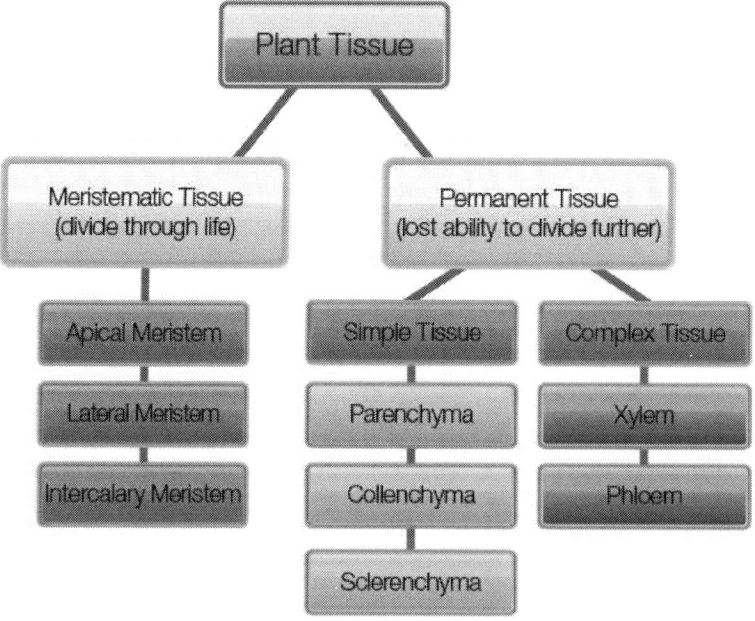

- **Meristems** contain actively dividing cells that form new tissues; found in root and shoot tips, at nodes and in the cambium.

  o Four categories of meristems:

    1. Apical

       o Apical meristems: shoots or root (at the apex or tip); produce new buds, leaves, or modified leaf parts such as flower structures in shoots, and produce new root extension in roots.

         ✓ Permanent tissues form at meristems, including the epidermis, xylem, phloem, leaves and shoots.

    2. Subapical (below)

    3. Intercalary

       o Intercalary meristems: Separated by zones of mature tissues just above the node or at the base of leaves in many monocot species such as grass; not found in the dicots.

    4. Lateral/cambial

       o Lateral meristems: found laterally along shoots; cylinders of actively dividing cells forming the conductive tissue of plants and the protective bark (cork) covering; form the vascular cambium, capable of producing new conductive tissue of xylem and phloem.

Classification of meristematic tissue according to position

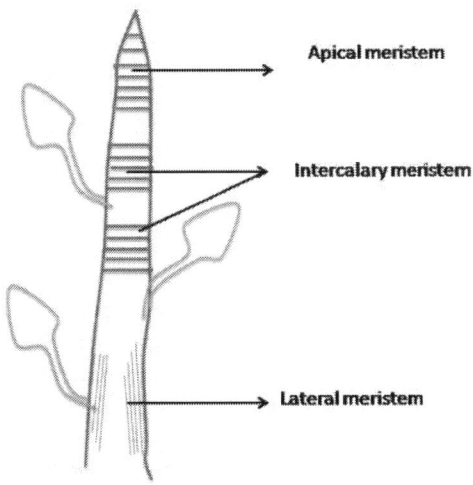

- Permanent Tissues

  o May be simple or complex.

  o Simple permanent tissues are uniform - have only one type of cell structure includes: epidermis cells, parenchyma cells and schlerenchyma cells.

  o **Epidermis** cells: a single layer (sometimes two or three layers) of cells on the exterior of stems, leaves, flowers and fruits, and depending on the origin, roots.

    ✓ Usually contain no pigment, except in the stomata guard cells and the apple epidermis with anthocyanin.

    ✓ Sometimes the cells elongate to form pubescence or hair-like structures, such as root hairs on roots or trachoma's on leaves.

  o **Parenchyma**: made of cells that have thin cell walls and large vacuoles; found in cortex of shoots or fruits; the area between phloem. In leaves, parenchyma cells contain chloroplasts for photosynthesis.

  o **Sclerenchyma cells**: thick cell walls, which make plant fibers.

  o Complex permanent tissues: include the conductive tissues, the xylem, and phloem which move water and solutes around the plant.

  o **Xylem** conducts water and dissolved nutrients, amino acids, proteins, and remobilized sugars from roots to aerial portions of the plants.

    ✓ Types of cells in xylem include vessels, tracheids, fibers, and parenchyma cells. Vessels are joined end-to-end, and the end cell walls dissolve for conduction of water.

    ✓ **Tracheids** are elongated, conductive cells, the contents of which are non-living.

    ✓ Fibers are thick support cells.

  o **Phloem** conducts soluble sugars and metabolites such as proteins, hormones, dissolved minerals, and salts from leaves to other portions of the plant.

    ✓ Cell types in phloem include sieve tube cells, companion cells, phloem parenchyma, and phloem fibers.

    ✓ **Sieve tube cells** are long, slender tubes with porous ends (occur only in angiosperms).

- ✓ Companion cells associated with sieve tube elements and provide energy to sieve tube cells and aid in the conduction and movement of solutes into and out of the sieve tube cells.

- ✓ Phloem parenchyma provides short and long-term storage for solutes moving through the phloem.

- ✓ Phloem fibers provide support.

Anatomy of Primary Organs

- Tissues are found in the roots, stems and leaves.

- Structure of Primary Roots

    o Root systems may consist of one major root (taproot) or of a profuse mass of similar-sized branches.

    o Penetration into the soil is accomplished by cell division, largely by the elongation of cells just behind the tip.

    o Protective cap covers the tip.

    o Tremendous combined surface areas of the myriad root hairs are responsible for absorption.

- Structure of Primary Stems

    o Support is provided by various thick-walled cells found in the xylem or in strands outside the xylem.

    o Water and minerals transported in the xylem, and manufactured food transported in the phloem.

    o Monocot stems, the conducting tissues occur in separated, usually scattered, bundles.

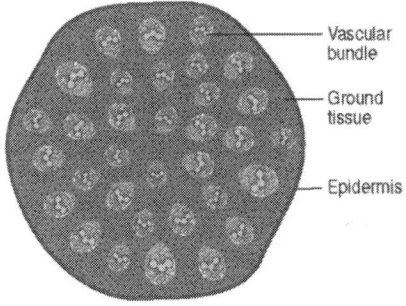

- Dicot stems, the vascular tissues arranged in a ring, with the primary xylem on the inside, the primary phloem on the outside, and a layer of dividing cells, called the vascular cambium, between them.

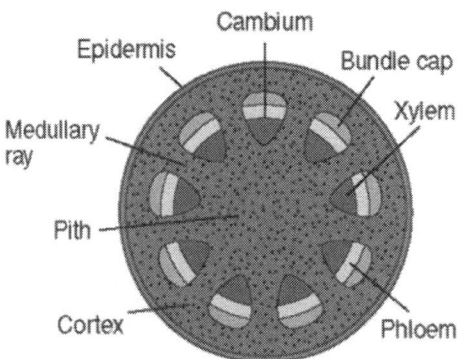

- Wood in its commercial sense refers to secondary xylem.

    ✓ Secondary xylem produced by the vascular cambium inward toward the center of the stem between itself and the primary xylem, increasing the thickness of the stem.

    ✓ Yearly production of secondary xylem usually forms a ring around that of the previous year, and these rings can be used to determine the age of a tree.

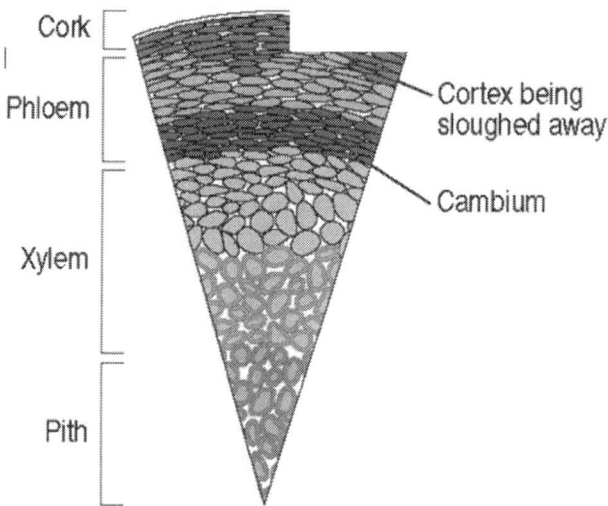

- Structure of Leaves

    - A flat, broad, thin structure gives more surface area for light interception and penetration.

    - Intake of carbon dioxide and release of oxygen occurs through small pores (stomata) in the leaf lower surface.

- Cells within the leaf may be formed into two layers, the upper, tightly packed with elongated **palisade cells**, and the lower, loosely packed with spongy tissue.

- Photosynthesis occurs mostly in the palisade cells.

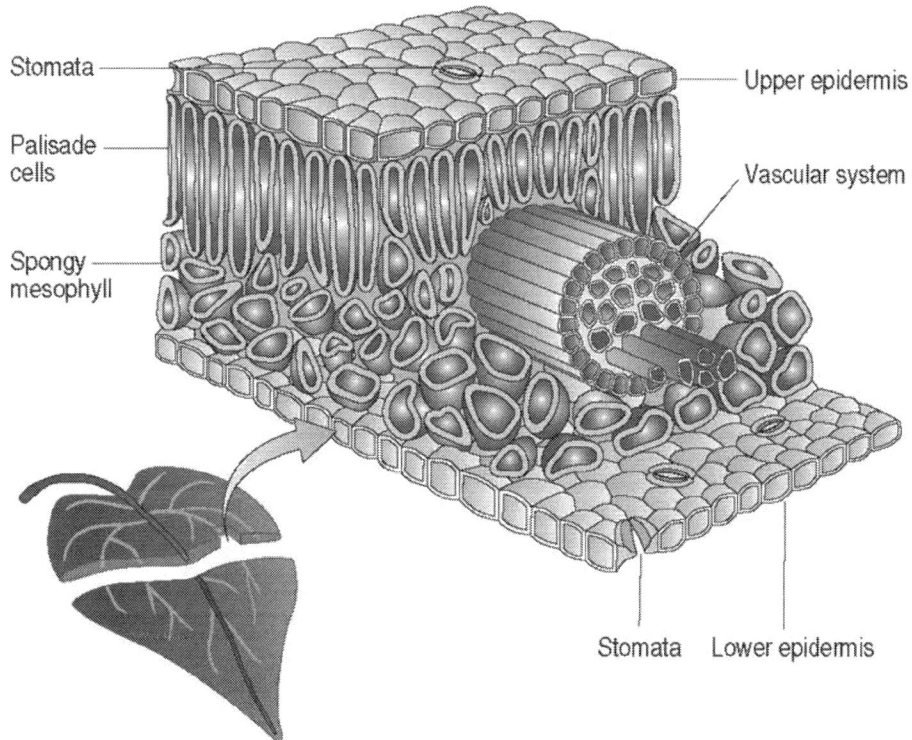

Primary and Secondary Growth

- Plants tend to grow continuously throughout their lives.

- Growth serves to increase a plant's size and to provide a limited means of movement and orientation for placing itself in a more favorable position with regard to light, nutrients, reproduction and dispersal.

- Growth involves both the production of new cells and their subsequent enlargement.

    - Following enlargement, a cell undergoes differentiation to become a part of a specific tissue.

- Primary growth takes place in young, herbaceous organs, resulting in an increase in length of shoots and roots.

- Secondary growth follows primary growth in some plants and results in an increased girth as layers of woody tissue are laid down.

- Monocots and herbaceous dicots typically exhibit only primary growth.

Summary

Basic structural and physiological units of crop plants, within which chemical reactions of life occur, providing metabolites for plant life and for human use. Plant cells are eukaryotes. Cell structures include the cell wall, plasma membrane, the protoplasts and the organelles. Organelles include plastids, mitochondria, microfilaments, endoplasmic reticulum, nucleus, vesicles, vacuoles and Golgi apparatus. Tissues are large groups of organized cells of similar structure that perform specific functions in the plant consisting of the meristem and other permanent tissues. Tissues are found in the roots, stems, and leaves. Monocot and dicot stems provide support by various thick-walled cells found in the xylem or in strands outside the xylem. Carbon dioxide intake and oxygen release take place through small pores on the lower surface of the leaves. Plants tend to grow continuously throughout their lives.

Resources

Free complementary PowerPoint:
http://www.tagmydoc.com/dl/15uVO0/gk95

Parker, R. 2010. Plant and soil science: Fundamentals and applications. Clifton Park, NY: Delmar Cengage Learning. (Pgs. 69-70)

Plants and Their Structure
http://www2.estrellamountain.edu/faculty/farabee/biobk/biobookplantanat.html

Plant Structure and Function
http://www.uic.edu/classes/bios/bios100/labs/plantanatomy.htm

Plant Anatomy
http://www.sci.sdsu.edu/plants/econbot/02-PlantAnatomy.pdf

Assessment

1. T or F? Molecules that make up the plant cell include protein, nucleic acid, carbohydrates, lipids and 10% other molecules.

2. Cell walls are made of _____ and secondary cell walls are made of cellulose, lignin, suberin and cutin.
   a.) hemicellulose   b.) leucoplasts   c.) cambium   d.) chloroplasts

3. T or F? Meristems contain actively dividing cells that form new tissues.

4. _____ cells have thick cell walls, which make plant fibers.
   a.) Parenchyma   b.) Epidermis   c.) Tracheid   d.) Sclerenchyma

5. T or F? Tissues are found in the roots, stems, and leaves.

6. _____ stems have the vascular tissues arranged in a ring, with the primary xylem on the inside, the primary phloem on the outside, and a layer of dividing cells, called the vascular cambium, between them.
   a.) Monocot   b.) Dicot

7. T or F? Photosynthesis occurs mostly in the palisade cells of the leaves.

Take assessment online here:

http://tinyurl.com/PlntSci-3

Hint: When the answer is incorrect, you will see: "Wrong answer! Go Back!"

Notes

5 Importance of Soil

Major Concept
Soil is a vital natural resource necessary for plant germination and growth.

Objective
- Define soil
- Name three ways soil is important for plant growth
- List six nutrients plants obtain from the soil

Link to Standards
NRS.02. Analyze the interrelationships between natural resources and humans.

PS.02. Apply principles of classification, plant anatomy, and plant physiology to plant production and management.

Key Terms
- Insoluble
- Soil
- Soil air
- Soil aeration
- Water-logged soil

Importance of Soil
- Soil forms a very thin interface between the earth's solid core and the atmosphere.
    - Atmosphere, crust and soil interact to provide plants and animals with the needed resources to live and thrive – proper temperature, water, carbon and other nutrients.

- Soil is created through a variety of processes and over long periods of time.
    - Processes include: heating and cooling, weathering and the forces of water and wind.
    - Decomposed plant and animal material add to the makeup of soil.

Soil and Plant Culture

- What is soil?

    - **Soil** is a mixture of broken and weathered fragments of rock and/or decaying organic matter, which covers the earth in a thin layer and serves as the medium for plant growth.

    - In some soils, the second layer (B horizon) is impermeable, which causes plants to be shallow rooted.

    - Soil is a storehouse and supplier of nutrients.

    - If nutrients are not stored in the soil, they are not available for plant use.

Soil - Medium for Plant Growth

- Plants depend on soil for four needs:

    1. Water
    2. Oxygen
    3. Anchorage
    4. Nutrients

- Water

    - Through the root system of the plant, soil supplies the water needed.

    - Water-holding capacity of soil is important in its agricultural use.

    - Soil provides moisture which is absorbed by the seed as the first step in germination.

    - About 500 lbs of water produces 1 lb of dry plant material.

        - ✓ About 5 lbs (or 1%) of this water becomes an integral part of the plant.

        - ✓ The remainder (the other 495 lbs) is lost through the stomata of the leaves in the course of transpiration.

    - Soil is used as germination media for a variety of seeds, providing the correct environment for seed germination: a favorable temperature and a good supply of oxygen for respiration by the seed.

- Oxygen - All living plants require oxygen.
    - Plants release oxygen during photosynthesis and consume oxygen during respiration.
    - Part of the plant above ground has the needed oxygen (21% of atmospheric oxygen).
    - Underground, plant roots and soil organism's use up oxygen and emit carbon dioxide resulting in **soil air** that has less oxygen and more carbon dioxide than the atmosphere.
        - ✓ **Soil aeration** exchanges soil and atmospheric air to maintain adequate oxygen for plant roots.
        - ✓ Well-aerated soil has an oxygen level of near 20%.
        - ✓ Saturated or **water-logged soil** is an example of poor soil aeration with an oxygen level around zero.
- Anchorage
    - Plants are firmly supported in deep soil where roots can grow freely.
        - ✓ Plants not anchored firmly in soil can be affected by above ground weathering
- Nutrients
    - Plants need 16 nutrients, 13 of which are obtained from soil.
    - Carbon (C), oxygen (O) and hydrogen (H) come from air and water.
    - Root hairs absorb plant nutrients dissolved in soil water (soil solution) by a process that moves nutrients into plant cells.
        - ✓ Nutrients from the Air
            1. Carbon (C)
            2. Hydrogen (H)
            3. Oxygen (O)

- ✓ Nutrients from the Soil
    1. Boron (B)
    2. Calcium (Ca)
    3. Chlorine (Cl)
    4. Copper (Cu)
    5. Iron (Fe)
    6. Magnesium (Mg)
    7. Manganese (Mn)
    8. Molybdenum (Mo)
    9. Nitrogen (N)
    10. Phosphorus (P)
    11. Potassium (K)
    12. Sulfur (S)
    13. Zinc (Zn)

  o Most of the essential nutrients in the soil are largely **insoluble** (do not easily dissolve in water) and are unavailable to plants until mineral weathering and organic matter decomposition takes place.

Summary

Soil forms a very thin interface between the earth's solid core and the atmosphere creating a mixture of broken and weathered fragments of rock and/or decaying organic matter, which serves as the medium for plant growth and support. Plants depend on soil for four needs: water, oxygen, anchorage and nutrients. Most of the essential nutrients in the soil are largely insoluble and unavailable to plants. Mineral weathering and organic matter decomposition must take place before it is usable to the plant. In order for seeds to geminate, the soil, as germination media, must provide the correct environment.

Resources

Free complementary PowerPoint
http://www.tagmydoc.com/dl/1bt5vG/gk8z

Parker, R. 2010. Plant and soil science: Fundamentals and applications. Clifton Park, NY: Delmar Cengage Learning. (Pgs. 133-143).

Ohio State University. www.ohio-state.edu

Why is Soil Important?
http://www.envirothon.org/pdf/CG/Why_Soil_is_Important.pdf

Assessment

1. T or F? Decomposed plant and animal material add to the makeup of soil.

2. _____ exchanges soil and atmospheric air to maintain adequate oxygen for plant roots.
   a.) Soil air   b.) Shrink-swell potential   c.) Soil aeration   d.) Water-logged soil

3. T or F? In some soils, the first layer (A horizon) is impermeable, which causes plants to be shallow rooted.

4. How many nutrients are currently considered necessary for plant growth?
   a.) 12   b.) 20   c.) 11   d.) 16

5. Soil provides _____ which is absorbed by the seed.
   a.) media   b.) minerals   c.) moisture   d.) organic matter

Take the assessment online here:

http://tinyurl.com/PlntSci-4

Hint: When the answer is incorrect, you will see: "Wrong answer! Go Back!"

Notes

6 Soil Texture and Structure

Major Concept
Understand the basics of soil texture and structure.

Objective
- List the basic types of soil texture and structure
- List the basic physical properties of soils

Link to Standards
PS.03. Propagate, culture and harvest plants and plant products based on current industry standards.

Key Terms
- Aggregation
- Immobilization
- Mineralization
- Parent material
- Subsoil
- Top soil

Composition of Soil
- Soil is composed of mineral matter that has been broken down by chemical, physical and biological action to the point where it can, when contained with decayed plant and animal life, support life.

- Many organisms are also found in the soil; these organisms include bacteria, fungi, molds, worms, insects and other kinds of very small plants and animals.

  o The more living organisms there are in the soil, the more productive the soil is likely to be.

    ✓ This increased productivity is due to larger amounts of nutrients being made available by the decomposition of organic matter.

- Soil also contains a variable percentage of water and air.

Organic Matter

- Consists of plant and animal residues in various stages of decay.

- Adequate levels benefit soil in four ways:

    1. Improves physical condition and structure

    2. Increases water infiltration

    3. Decreases erosion losses

    4. Supplies plant nutrients

- Release of Nitrogen (N)

    - Organic matter serves as a storehouse for nitrogen (N) but decays slowly so is not readily available for plants.

    - Other nutrients such as magnesium (Mg), calcium (Ca), sulfur (S) and micronutrients are also contained in organic matter. As decomposition occurs, these become available to growing plants.

        - Some nutrients such as nitrogen (N) and sulfur (S) can be temporarily tied up during the process.

        - If the organic matter being decomposed has a high carbon to nitrogen (C:N) ratio, meaning low nitrogen (N), microorganisms will use available soil and fertilizer nitrogen (N), a process called **immobilization**.

        - Eventually nitrogen (N) immobilized into the bodies of soil organisms becomes available as the organisms die and decay. This is called **mineralization**.

- Variability

    - In tropical areas, most soils are inherently low in organic matter because warm temperatures and high rainfall increase decomposition.

    - In cooler areas, where decomposition takes place more slowly, native organic matter levels can be quite high.

        - With adequate fertilization and good management practices, crop residues are produced and added to soil, maintaining or increasing organic matter levels in soils.

Soil Profile

- Arrangement and properties of the various soil layers are namely: topsoil, subsoil and parent material; horizons vary from soil to soil in thickness, texture, color and other properties.

  o **Topsoil** is the surface or very top layer.

    ✓ Usually called the A Horizon.

    ✓ Ranges from a depth of a few inches to several feet.

    ✓ Darker than other layers because it contains organic matter.

    ✓ Usually softer and more easily worked than the underlying layers.

  o **Subsoil** is the layer just under the topsoil.

    ✓ Usually called the B Horizon and may be higher in clay content.

    ✓ May be red, brown, yellow or gray in color.

    ✓ Usually lighter in color, since little or no organic matter is present.

    ✓ Usually firmer and more difficult to penetrate than the topsoil.

  o **Parent material** is the lowest layer.

    ✓ Can be the C Horizon from which the topsoil and subsoil have developed (A and B Horizons).

    ✓ Can be firm and difficult for roots to penetrate, or may be soft enough to allow root growth.

    ✓ Solid rock may exist under the C horizon.

    ✓ C horizon may form from rock, or may form in loose material (sand, silt, clay or gravel) put in place by water, gravity, glaciers or wind.

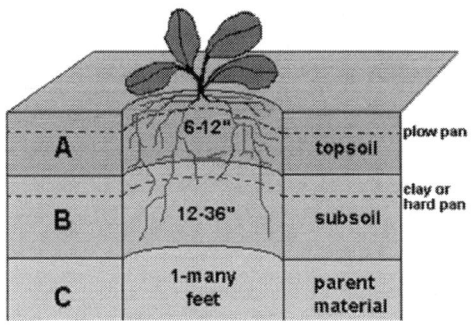

How the Nature of the Parent Material Affects the Soil

- Soils resemble the parent material from which they come.

  - The nature of the parent material will have a strong effect on the properties of young soils and will exert lesser influence on older soils.

    - ✓ Properties of the parent material that exert an influence on soil development include texture, mineral composition and degree of layering.

- The chemical and mineral composition of a soil often not only determines the effectiveness of the weathering forces, but in some instances partially controls the natural vegetation.

  - If parent material contains large amounts of organic matter, the soil will be more acidic (low pH).

    - ✓ Soil acidity encourages mineral decomposition and the overall development of the soil profile.

  - Soils formed from parent material high in limestone will be more basic (high pH).

    - ✓ Where parent materials are rich in lime, development of a soil is delayed, and it remains immature for a longer period of time.

- The degree of stratification or layering has an important influence on the properties and uses of a soil.

  - For instance, a layer of soil which is high in clay can make an otherwise useless sandy soil suitable for crop growth by adding to the water and nutrient retention of the soil.

Physical Properties of Soil

- Texture

  - Soil texture refers to the fineness or coarseness of a soil.

    - ✓ More specifically, texture is the relative proportions of the different size particles (sand, silt and clay) found in soil.

    - ✓ The texture of a soil is named after the type of particle which is predominant in the soil, i.e., a soil high in sand would be referred to as a sandy soil.

- Structure

  o Soil structure refers to the way individual soil particles are arranged to make up the mass of soil.

    ✓ It is the **aggregation** (mixture) of the first or primary soil particles into compound particles.

    ✓ Structure modifies the influence of texture in regard to moisture and air relationships, availability of plant nutrients, action of microorganisms and root growth.

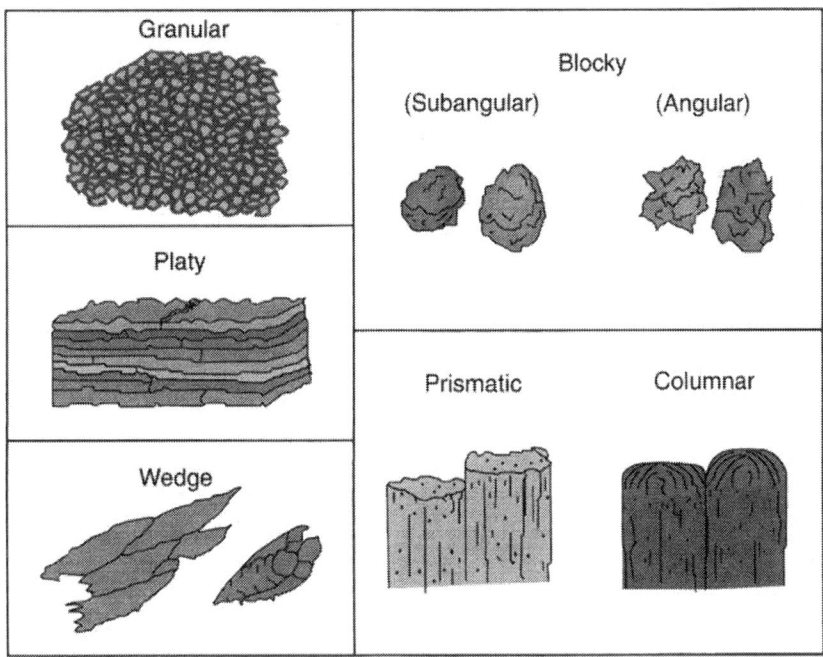

    ✓ The structure of a soil is not permanent.

    ✓ Wetting, drying, plowing or other disturbances of the soil can change its structure.

    ✓ Different structures include platy, prismatic, columnar, blocky, crumbly and granular soil.

- Depth

  o Rooting zone available to plants is restricted by the depth of a soil. This is very

  o significant to soil use and management.

- Color

    o Soil color can serve as an indicator of many soil properties.

        ✓ Organic matter content, drainage condition and aeration are soil properties related to color which are of interest to producers.

        ✓ The color of the different layers (horizons) also relates to soil history and formation.

Summary

Soil is composed of mineral matter that has been broken down by chemical, physical and biological action to the point where it can, when contained with decayed plant and animal life, support life. Organic matter consists of plant and animal residues in various stages of decay and adequate levels benefit the soil. The arrangement and properties of the various soil layers consist of: topsoil, subsoil and parent material. Degree of stratification or layering has an important influence on the properties and uses of a soil. Soil texture refers to the fineness or coarseness of a soil. Soil structure refers to the way individual soil particles are arranged to make up the mass of soil. The rooting zone available to plants is restricted by the depth of a soil and is significant to soil use and management.

Resources

Free complementary PowerPoint:
http://www.tagmydoc.com/dl/1NkMds/gk91

Parker, R. 2010. Plant and soil science: Fundamentals and applications. Clifton Park, NY: Delmar Cengage Learning. (Pgs. 112-120).

Soil and Water Conservation Society
http://www.swcs.org/

Soil Science Society of America
https://www.soils.org/

Assessment

1. T or F? The more living organisms there are in the soil, the more productive the soil is likely to be.

2. Organic matter serves as a storehouse for _____ but decays slowly so is not readily available for plants.
   a.) calcium (Ca)   b.) nitrogen (N)   c.) potassium (K)   d.) sulfur (S)

3. T or F? Soil color can serve as an indicator of many soil properties.

4. Soil formed from parent material high in limestone will be more _____.
   a.) acidic   b.) basic   c.) textured   d.) aggregate

5. T or F? The structure of a soil is permanent.

Take assessment online here:

http://tinyurl.com/PlntSci-4a

Hint: When the answer is incorrect, you will see: "Wrong answer! Go Back!"

Notes

7 Influence of Texture on Soil

Major Concept
Understand soil texture and its impact on the performance of the soil.

Objective
- Describe the components of soil texture
- Recognize the importance of soil texture to soil tilth, water use and fertility needs
- Identify the horizons in a soil profile

Link to Standards
NRS.01. Plan and conduct natural resource management activities that apply logical reasoned and scientifically based solutions to natural resource issues and goals.

PS.02. Apply principles of classification, plant anatomy, and plant physiology to plant production and management.

Key Terms
- Clay
- Horizons
- Sand
- Silt
- Soil separates

Soil Separates
- **Sand** is small coarse-grained pieces of rock.

    o Individual grains can easily be felt and seen. They have a gritty feeling and will not stick together or form clods.

    o Grades range from coarse through fine to very fine (2.00 mm - 0.05 mm in diameter).

    ✓ Because of the large size of sand particles, very little particle surface area is exposed when compared to that exposed by an equal weight of silt or clay particles.

    ✓ The part sand plays in the chemical and a physical activity of a soil is negligible.

- Since sands are inactive, their chief function in soil is to serve as a framework around which the active part of the soil associates.
- The presence of sand tends to increase the size of spaces between particles, facilitating movement of air and water.

- **Silt** is a very soft and flour-like **soil separate** (particle size).
    - Particles are so small they can be seen only with a microscope (0.05 mm - 0.002 mm in diameter).
    - Silt will form clods that crumble easily when wet.
    - Water soaks readily into silty soil, and such soil holds its moisture well.
    - Coarser silt particles are similar to the finer sands in particle surface exposed and therefore take very little part in the chemical activities of soils.
    - Finer silt has sufficient particle surface area to give it some chemical activity.
    - Silt particles have little tendency to stick together or to adhere to other particles except when combined with clay.
    - Soils with the largest water holding capacity available for plant growth are high in silt.

- Particles of **clay** (less than .002 mm in diameter) are finer than particles of silt.
    - They appear "platey" and thin in shape, and fit very closely together with little space in between.
    - Particles stick together and form clods that are difficult to break when dry.
    - Because a soil containing large amounts of clay is so hard to work, it is considered a "heavy" soil.
    - Clay soils have a much larger surface area per weight due to their small size. (Clay has thousands of times more surface area per gram than silt and nearly a million times more surface area per gram than very course sand).
    - Amount of clay in the soil has a great influence on its total water-holding capacity.
    - In addition, certain available nutrients are held on the surface of the clay particles.
    - Clay acts as the major storage reservoir for both water and nutrients.

- In summary, the more surface area that a soil separate possesses, the more attraction these particles have for water, soil nutrients and other soil particles.

Soil Classification According to Texture

- Specific soils are different combinations of sand, silt and clay; thus, each has special names and different properties.
  - When a mechanical analysis of a soil is run, a report as to the percentage of each of the separates (sand, silt, clay) is produced.
  - The soil triangle shows how the various separates combine to form the various classes of soils.
    - ✓ For example: A loam gradually merges into a silt loam or clay loam as the percentage of silt and clay increases.
    - ✓ A sandy loam is produced as the percentage of sand replaces silt and clay in the loam.

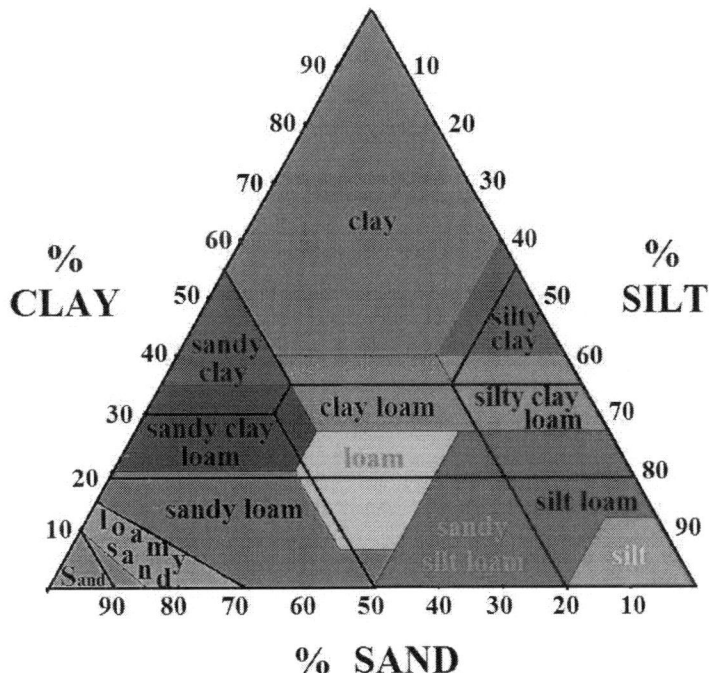

Soil Profile

- A vertical cross section through a soil.
- A succession of layers of soil material.

- These layers are called **horizons** and differ from each other in color, texture or structure.

Components of a Soil Profile

- O horizon
    - A surface layer dominated by the presence of large amounts of organic material in various stages of decomposition.

- A horizon
    - This includes the upper part of the profile in which life is most active. It is the most productive horizon because of its normally high organic matter content and granular soil structure.

- B horizon
    - This horizon is generally called the subsoil and lies below the "A" horizon topsoil.

- C horizon
    - This horizon is the parent material (which is often "rock").

Characteristics of the Four Horizons

- O horizon
    - Horizons may be divided into O1 and O2 categories, whereby O1 horizons contain decomposed matter whose origin can be spotted on sight (for instance, fragments of rotting leaves), and O2 horizons containing only well-decomposed organic matter, the origin of which is not readily visible.

- A horizon
    - May be from a few inches to a foot or more deep.
    - Usually dark colored.
    - Lighter in texture than the B horizon or C horizon.
    - More likely to have a granular structure than the other horizons.

- B horizon
    - Usually low in organic matter.

- Usually red or yellowish in color.
- Has a structure which is less desirable than that of the A horizon.
- May have a blocky or prismatic structure.
- Roots may extend into this horizon, in search of moisture and nutrients.

- C horizon
  - Deepest of the three major horizons.
  - Usually very low in organic matter.
  - Often has a coarse or rocky texture.
  - Usually considered an undesirable structure.
  - Commonly lighter in color than the A and B horizon.
  - Rarely have roots or biological activity.

Soil Profile Color Significance

- Dark brown color usually indicates organic matter.
- A gray motley color indicates poor drainage.
- Yellowish or reddish color is due to the presence of iron and indicates good drainage.

Importance of Soil Profile in Determining Crop Production

- Knowing the profile of a soil helps determine the vertical distance plant roots, water and air penetrate freely into the soil.
- If a profile shows a soil to be shallow, then a shallow rooted crop should be planted.
- The profile will also determine the water holding capacity of a soil.

Soil Testing

- Soil testing is the application of various chemical tests to a soil for the purpose of determining the nutrients in a given soil.

- Soil tests are useful in predicting whether or not a profitable response will occur when fertilizers are applied to the soil.
  - ✓ This serves as a guide to a fertilization program.

Collecting Soil Samples

- For adequate testing, approximately one pint of soil is needed from each field to be tested.

- A soil auger or tube, which takes a uniform core from the surface to the desired depth and which takes a uniform volume of soil each time, is the best tool to use for taking soil samples. (If an auger or tube is not available use a trowel or spade.)
  - The following steps should be taken into consideration when obtaining a soil sample:
    - ✓ Section off the land into fields for sampling.
    - ✓ Develop a definite pattern for sampling the field.
    - ✓ Clear away any surface trash or grass from where the core is to be taken.
    - ✓ Take at least twenty cores from each field to be tested, mix them together thoroughly in a clean container, air dry and bag or box the required amount.
    - ✓ Take the samples from normal depth of plowing (surface level to six to twelve inches deep).
    - ✓ Avoid taking samples near roadsides.
    - ✓ Avoid sampling any small areas of unusual characteristic which are not representative of the balance of the field.
    - ✓ Sample separately those areas of the field that have a different slope, color, texture or those small areas that lend themselves to separate treatment.
    - ✓ Avoid sampling such areas as dead furrows, near manure piles or under animal droppings.
    - ✓ Label all samples correctly. Information included on the label should be: your name, return address, field sample number and the desired soil test.
    - ✓ A record should be kept of where the samples were taken. This can easily be done by making a map and placing on it the sampling number from the area in which it was taken.

Summary

The more surface area that a soil separate possesses, the more attraction these particles have for water, soil nutrients and other soil particles. Specific soils are different combinations of sand, silt, and clay; thus, each has special names and different properties. A soil profile is a vertical cross section through a soil. It is made up of a succession of layers of soil material. These layers are called horizons and they differ from each other in color, texture or structure. Knowing the profile of a soil helps determine the vertical distance plant roots, water and air penetrate freely into the soil. The profile will also determine the water holding capacity of a soil. Soil testing is the application of various chemical tests to a soil for the purpose of determining the nutrients in a given soil.

Resources

Free complementary PowerPoint:
http://www.tagmydoc.com/dl/12QoIN/gk6H

Parker, R. 2010. Plant and soil science: Fundamentals and applications. Clifton Park, NY: Delmar Cengage Learning. (Pg. 111-115).

University of Hawaii - Soil Texture and Soil Structure
http://www.ctahr.hawaii.edu/mauisoil/a_factor_ts.aspx

Department of Environmental and Primary Industries - Soil Texture
http://vro.dpi.vic.gov.au/dpi/vro/vrosite.nsf/pages/soilhealth_texture

Assessment

1. Small coarse-grained pieces of rock make _____.
   a.) gravel   b.) loam   c.) sand   d.) silt

2. T or F? Silt is a soil separate.

3. Clay is considered to be a _____ soil.
   a.) heavy   b.) wet   c.) sticky   d.) soft

4. A soil profile is made up of successive layers called _____.
   a.) classes   b.) horizons   c.) levels   d.) tiers

5. In which part of the soil profile is life most active?
   a.) Surface   b.) Horizon B   c.) Horizon A   d.) Subsurface

Take assessment online here:

http://tinyurl.com/PlntSci-4b

Hint: When the answer is incorrect, you will see: "Wrong answer! Go Back!"

Notes

8 Soil Erosion and Conservation

Major Concept

Soil erosion can be controlled through conservation methods.

Objective

- List four types of soil erosion
- Describe management practices that contribute to soil erosion
- Recognize the importance of conservation tillage methods in controlling soil erosion

Link to Standards

PS.01. Develop and implement a crop management plan for a given production goal that accounts for environmental factors.

PS.03. Propagate, culture and harvest plants and plant products based on current industry standards.

Key Terms

- Crop rotation
- Cultivation on the contour
- Sod crops
- Soil erosion
- Strip cropping
- Terracing
- Water erosion
- Wind erosion

Erosion

- **Soil erosion** is the movement of soil particles from one place to another under the influence of water or wind.

Types of Soil Erosion

- **Water erosion**: Erosion by water is caused by raindrops, surface flow and gully flow. Water erosion is a selective process in which the organic matter and finer soil particles are removed first. This selective feature of soil erosion rapidly destroys productivity of cultivated lands.

    o Splashing of raindrops on bare loams, sands and sandy soils, separates organic matter, silt and clay from sand.

- These materials are then washed away by surface flow and the heavy sand is left on the field.
- This sand is turned under at the next plowing of the field or mixed with the surface layer of the soil at the next cultivation.
- In either case, a fresh supply of topsoil is brought to the surface for further action.
- Repeating this procedure over the years produces a sandier, soil, particularly in areas of severe erosion.
  - ✓ This sandier soil is less able to hold moisture and nutrients, and is therefore less productive.
- **Wind erosion**: Erosion by wind is common in dry areas where soils are often bare of vegetation and high wind velocities are common.
  - Wind catches the organic matter, lightweight silt and clay particles and then blows them away.
  - Sand and other coarse materials are left behind.
  - Organic matter, silt and clay are the most important parts of the soil, because they supply the nutrients needed by the plants. As the nutrient supply is reduced, crop production declines.

Cultural Practices Contributing to Soil Erosion

- Plowing land which is unsuitable for cultivated crops.
- Plowing soil in areas with too little rainfall to support continuous crop production.
- Breaking up large blocks of land susceptible to erosion.
- Failure to maintain crop residues on the surface while the soil is not protected by growing crops.
- Exposing soil on slopes.
- Removing natural vegetation from forest lands.
- Reducing and weakening plant growth by overgrazing.

Results of Erosion

- Loss of the most essential part of the soil - the topsoil, with its finer soil particles, better tilth, superior water-retention capacity, more plentiful mineral and organic elements and helpful bacteria.

- Reduction of crop yields.

- Need for greater use of plant and commercial fertilizers.

- Production of lower nutrients crops.

- Formation of gullies, by which erosion is speeded and farmland made impossible to cultivate.

- Covering of rich bottomlands by soils from poorer highlands.

- Destruction of road banks and removal of bridges.

- Erosion by stream banks of valuable bottomlands.

- Silting of ditches, streams, dams, lakes and reservoirs.

- Increased flood hazard because of more rapid runoff.

- Waste of water that could be used for farming and other purposes.

- Greater costs for production resulting in higher prices for consumers.

Soil Conservation Practices for the Control of Soil Erosion

- Use of thick-growing **sod crops** which cover the ground surface and fill the surface soil with fibrous roots tend to hold the soil in place and reduce erosion.

- **Cultivation on the contour** is the practice of planting and cultivating of crops following the contours of the land.

    - Effective water erosion control can seldom be obtained from contour cultivation alone.

    - Best results are obtained when contouring is used, whether with strip cropping or terracing.

- **Strip cropping** is the practice of planting two crops in alternating strips or alternately planting a strip and leaving a strip fallow on land that would otherwise be erodible.

- o Usually a cultivated crop is alternated with non-cultivated crops. The strips should be planted on the lines of contour.

- Terraces to Remove Runoff Safely

  - o **Terracing** is the practice of constructing embankments or ridges across sloping soils.

  - o The main reason for terracing in wet areas is to construct a ridge across a slope to guide surplus water off a field at an angle rather than straight down the hill.

  - o In dryland areas, terraces are constructed to increase water penetration, and reduce runoff, that it the water is "held" on the terrace rather than flowing down the hill as runoff.

- Use of Crop Rotation

  - o **Crop rotation** is the growing of selected crops in a regular order on any particular field.

  - o Principle objectives of a good rotation are to secure more economical and more consistent production of crops over a period of years and to control soil erosion.

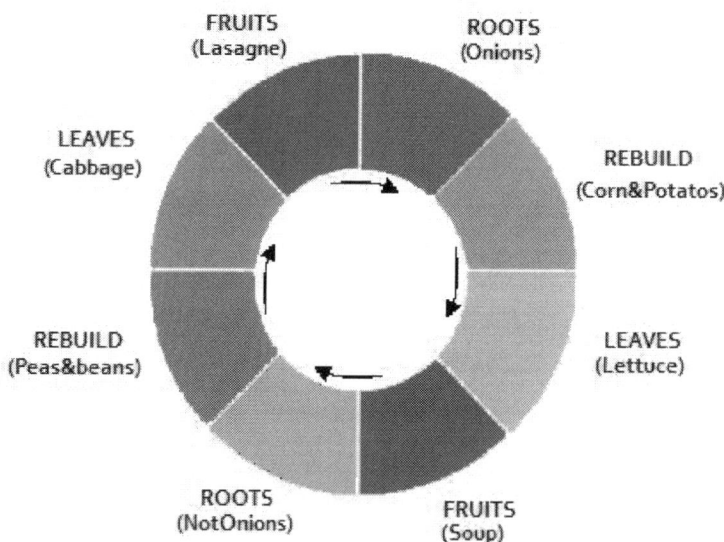

- No-till

  - o Seed is placed in a slot formed by the planter and weed control is achieved entirely by surface applied and contact herbicides.

    - ✓ When managed properly, no-till production works well on many soils.

- Cover Crops
    - Green cover protects soil during fall, winter and early spring when most prone to erosion.
        - ✓ Cover crop plowed down the following spring.
        - ✓ Winter rye and other winter crops work well for this purpose.
- Building of Ponds and Dams
    - Artificial ponds hold or impound water which otherwise would be lost as runoff, and which in the process of runoff, would carry soil with it.

Summary

Soil erosion is the movement of soil particles from one place to another under the influence of water or wind. Erosion by water is caused by raindrops, surface flow and gully flow. Erosion by wind is common in dry areas where soils are often bare of vegetation and high wind velocities are common. There are several soil conservation practices for the control of soil erosion, such as cover crops, terracing, strip cropping, etc.

Resources

Free complementary PowerPoint:
http://www.tagmydoc.com/dl/fNNGJ/gk6J

Parker, R. 2010. Plant and soil science: Fundamentals and applications. (Pgs. 155-163) Clifton Park, NY: Delmar Cengage Learning.

Ten Ways to Conserve Soil
http://greenliving.lovetoknow.com/10_Ways_to_Conserve_Soil

Assessment

1. Two types of soil erosion are water erosion and _____ erosion.
   a.) crop   b.) wind   c.) rotation   d.) contour

2. T or F? The organic matter, silt and clay are the most important parts of the soil.

3. T or F? Plowing land which is unsuitable for cultivated crops contributes to soil erosion.

4. Soil erosion increases or decreases crop yields?
   a.) Increases   b.) Decreases

5. When practicing soil erosion control, the best results are obtained when _____ is used.
   a.) contouring   b.) terracing   c.) strip cropping   d.) crop rotation

Take assessment online here:

http://tinyurl.com/PlntSci-4c

Hint: When the answer is incorrect, you will see: "Wrong answer! Go Back!"

Notes

9 Introduction to Irrigation

Major Concept

Different types of irrigation systems fit different needs when providing water to crops.

Objectives

- Name four types of irrigation systems
- List advantages and disadvantage of each type
- List three factors that influence the requirement for water
- List three advantages of Scientific Irrigation Scheduling (SIS)

Link to Standards

PS.01. Develop and implement a crop management plan for a given production goal that accounts for environmental factors.

Key Terms

- Biplane
- Border irrigation
- Check
- Drip irrigation
- Emitters
- Flood irrigation
- Furrow irrigation
- Gate
- Levee
- Siphon
- SIS

History of Irrigation

- Because a very large percentage of the earth's land mass receives less than 20 inches of rain per year, the need for irrigation is obvious.

    o Irrigation diminishes one of the greatest risks in crop production, inadequate water supply.

- Farmers have irrigated crops for over 4,000 years.

    o Records show that crops were irrigated along the Euphrates, Ganges, Nile and Tigris rivers as early as 2600 B.C.

    o Irrigation, no doubt, contributed to the founding of great civilizations.

- Even though irrigation has been practiced for so many years, modern methods were started as little as 200 years ago.

Irrigation Systems

- Water requirements vary depending on the following:

  o Crop

  o Climate

  o Season

  o Soil conditions

  o Method of application

    ✓ Selection of the right watering system can save labor and water, and assure increased crop yields.

- Basic four methods of irrigation, include:

  1. Border or flood

  2. Furrow

  3. Sprinkler

  4. Drip

    ✓ Each of these has characteristics which makes them useable in a specific situation.

- **Border** or **flood** irrigation used where the land is level.

  o Method often used for orchards and vineyards and for hay, pasture and cereal grains.

  o Land must be leveled and graded.

  o A uniform slope of 0.1 to 0.4 ft/100 ft. (0.1 - 0.4 % slope) used for most crops.

    ✓ Water enters through a head ditch or **biplane** (early type of aircraft with two pairs of wings, one above the other) and is released into the individual **checks** (areas bounded by **levees** [an embankment] running down slope) by **siphons** (tube used to convey liquid upwards), **gates** (door or valve controlling water passage) slope, or valves.

- Gated pipe can be used with flood irrigation systems to improve control over water delivery.
- Water from a lateral ditch is diverted through a screen into the gated pipe.
  - ✓ Irrigator opens or closes individual gates (often spaced about 18 inches apart) to control where water is applied, and for what length of time.
  - ✓ Initial costs may be high, and screen must be cleaned regularly.
  - ✓ Once in place, however, gated pipe allows you to customize the water delivery to the variations in the pasture.

- **Furrow irrigation** – one of the most widely used methods for crops.
  - Water runs down the **furrows** between plant rows.
  - Water moves to all parts of the soil by capillary action or gravity.
  - System is efficient in water utilization, but is expensive because of high labor costs. Costs include:
    - ✓ Forming the furrows
    - ✓ Forming and maintaining the irrigations ditches
    - ✓ Hiring help to maintain the ditches and irrigation cycle using gates, siphons, etc.
  - An advantage of furrow irrigation is uniform crop maturity, possible because water is more uniformly applied than in flood irrigation.

- Sprinkler irrigation – often used when flood or furrow systems are impractical.
  - Leveling not as critical for sprinkler irrigation.
  - More uniform wetting of the surface area possible.
  - Seed germination more uniform.
  - Salts can be washed away.
  - Less total water used, which can increase efficiency.

- Sprinklers can also be used for frost control.
- Slower rate of application of this system reduces erosion, run off and soil compaction.
  - Initial installation costs and power costs are higher than for flood or furrow irrigation systems.

- **Drip irrigation** – the latest innovation in irrigation systems.
  - Irrigation water is applied slowly, under low pressure and in precise locations through devices called **emitters**.
  - Emitters located at intervals along a lateral plastic tube which is usually laid on the soil surface.
  - Lateral lines connect to a main line that receives water from a source.
    - Water is usually applied very slowly at the rate of 1 to 2 gallons per hour per emitter under low pressure.
  - These systems are designed to reduce the waste of water from evaporation.
  - Main advantage of this system:
    - Requires less water than the other systems.
    - Delivery system is light weight, being easily moved by one person; but is normally a solid set and not moved often.
    - Fertilizers and some pesticides can be added to the water before delivery to crops.
    - Can be used on steeper slopes than other systems.
  - Disadvantages to the drip system:
    - High cost of installation
    - Increased maintenance
    - Root distribution of perennial crops changes to adjust to the new system and therefore there is a temporary loss of production.
    - Salts tend to accumulate on the soil surface and along the wetted boundaries.

Ditch Maintenance

- Irrigation ditches require regular maintenance to improve water delivery.

  - If they become overgrown with willows or other vegetation, water velocity will be reduced and water may not be delivered in a timely manner.

  - A vegetated ditch bank helps avoid erosion; however, combating weeds and maintaining a vegetated bank can be very difficult.

    - ✓ In some states, regular spring burning is used to control weeds and grasses in ditches.

    - ✓ In some areas, a ditch company will collect fees from all irrigation water rights holders on that ditch.

    - ✓ "Ditch riders" are hired to maintain ditches and operate main gates.

Scientific Irrigation Scheduling

- Saves energy, water and fertilizer costs by incorporating scientific irrigation scheduling (SIS) into the irrigation process.

- Helps irrigators know exactly when and how much to irrigate crops through a system that monitors weather and soil moisture data.

  - This process reduces energy costs for pumping water, conserves water and can reduce fertilizer use and run off.

- A process that producers can use to improve irrigation water management.

  - When used properly:

    - ✓ Provides information on when to irrigate, how much water to apply, and how to apply water to satisfy crop water requirements and avoid plant moisture stress.

    - ✓ Saves water, energy, labor and fertilizer, and in many cases improves crop yields and crop quality.

  - **SIS** uses soil moisture monitoring equipment and computer modeling to schedule irrigation of crops.

  - Over irrigation or under irrigation of crops can lead to reduced crop output and overuse of water and hence more energy consumed by pumping.

- - ✓ Can also cause the leaching of nutrients and fertilizer from the soil causing the grower to apply much more fertilizer than necessary.
  - o SIS is most beneficial to agricultural irrigation systems with a pumping capacity beyond that required to meet normal crop needs.

Irrigation System Advantages and Disadvantages

- Most often, small-acreage owners will use the method of irrigation that was in use on their property when they bought it, or the method most people in the neighborhood use.

  - o There are many methods, however, and often the choice of a different method may result in improved efficiency, more even application, or a saving in labor.

  - o Before selecting a system, you'll need to consider:

    - ✓ Proximity of the field or pasture to a water source
    - ✓ Adequate distribution system to the field (pumps, canals or pipes)
    - ✓ Amount of water required by selected crop
    - ✓ Quality of available water
    - ✓ Cost of water
    - ✓ Topography of the land
    - ✓ Soil type
    - ✓ Annual precipitation
    - ✓ Cost of irrigation supplies
    - ✓ Availability of labor to set-up and maintain irrigation system
    - ✓ Fertilization methods
    - ✓ Methods for recycling or handling excess irrigation water

  - o Irrigation systems vary in sophistication and cost to install, and each system has its advantages and disadvantages.

Summary

Because a very large percentage of the earth's land mass receives less than 20 inches of rain per year, the need for irrigation is obvious. Current irrigation systems include: border or flood, furrow, sprinkler and drip. Irrigation ditches require regular maintenance to improve water delivery. The type used depends on the water availability, land, crop and economics. Most often, small-acreage owners will use the method of irrigation that was in use on their property when they bought it, or the method most people in the neighborhood use. There are many methods, however, and often the choice of a different method may result in improved efficiency, more even application or a savings in labor.

Resources

Free complementary PowerPoint:
http://www.tagmydoc.com/dl/2G4ZcE/gk6L

Parker, R. 2010. Plant and soil science: Fundamentals and applications. Clifton Park, NY: Delmar Cengage Learning. (Pgs. 207-210).

Irrigation
http://tinyurl.com/nx3kphx

Irrigation
http://www.epa.gov/agriculture/ag101/cropirrigation.html

Assessment

1. Type of irrigation used where the land is level.
    a.) border   b.) drip   c.) sprinkler   d.) furrow

2. Modern methods of irrigation were started as little as _____ years ago.
    a.) 100   b.) 150   c.) 175   d.) 200

3. T or F? Selection of the right watering system can save labor and water, and assure increased crop yields.

4. T or F? The four basic irrigation systems are drip, furrow, sprinkler and flood.

5. Which is the latest innovation in irrigation systems?
    a.) sprinkler irrigation   b.) drip irrigation   c.) furrow irrigation   d.) border irrigation

6. T or F? Scientific Irrigation Scheduling (SIS) saves water, energy, labor and fertilizer, but does not improve crop yields and crop quality.

Take assessment online here:

http://tinyurl.com/PlntSci-5

Hint: When the answer is incorrect, you will see: "Wrong answer! Go Back!"

Notes

10 Irrigation Terminology

Major Concept

Some unique terms describe water supply and availability for plants.

Objectives

- Define field capacity, saturation wilting point, permanent wilting point and available water
- Identify hygroscopic water
- Write the formula for available water

Link to Standards

PS.01. Develop and implement a crop management plan for a given production goal that accounts for environmental factors.

Key Terms

- Field Capacity (FC)
- Hygroscopic water
- Permanent Wilting Point (PWP)
- Solvent
- Saturation
- Tugor
- Water holding capacity
- Wilting Point (WP)

Water

- Water – the universal solvent

- Dissolves more substances than any other liquid

- One of our renewable natural resources

- World's supply constantly being recycled

- Exists on this earth as a solid, a liquid and in the gaseous state (vapor)

- Water held by and moved through the soil supplies the plant with water as well as mineral nutrients and oxygen (O_2).

Irrigation Terminology

- To understand water in the soil and its relationship to plants, these terms must be defined and explained: saturated, field capacity, wilting point, permanent wilting point and hygroscopic water.

- Saturated

    - When all of the pore (voids) spaces in the soil are full of water the soil is said to be **saturated**.

        - ✓ Unhealthy for the plant if it were to become a permanent situation, the oxygen (O_2) needed for respiration would be missing.

    - Number and size of soil pores varies with texture and structure.

    - Clays have more total voids (pores) than coarser soils and so have more total void (pores) space.

    - An equal volume of clay soil will hold more water than sandy soil when all of the voids are filled.

    - Ability of a soil to hold water is called its **water holding capacity**.

    - All of the water held in the soil against the pull of gravity.

- Field Capacity (FC)

    - When all of the excess water is drained by gravity the soil is said to be at **field capacity** (FC) – the ability to hold water.

- **Wilting Point** (WP) – Plant will not revive unless immediately irrigated.

    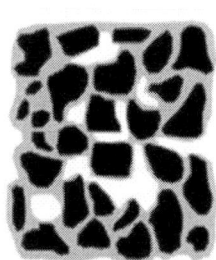

    - Soil moisture content at which a plant wilts.

        - ✓ Plants lose **turgor** (stiffness).

- **Permanent Wilting Point** (PWP)

  o Plant has not only lost turgor and wilted, but will not revive, even if watered immediately.

    ✓ Some water left in the soil at the point of wilt, perhaps even at the PWP but held by the soil particles is not available to the plants since it is held too tightly (electronically bonded) by the opposite charges of the soil and water.

- Available Water (AW)

  o Water available for plants use.

  o Water in the soil between field capacity and the wilting point.

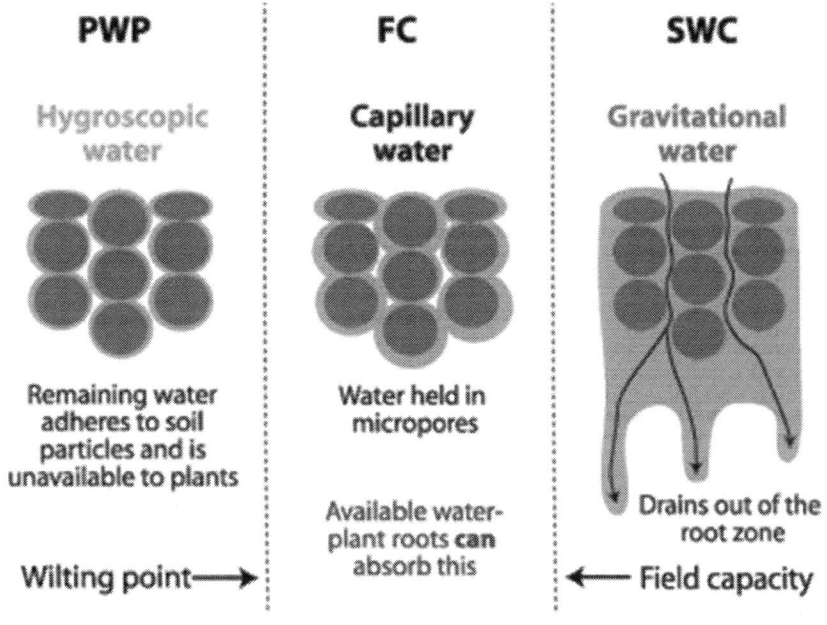

Available water for plant growth

  o Expressed as a formula: AW = FC-WP.

  o Water between field capacity and saturation is not available to the plants because it is lost through drainage (pulled out by gravity).

  o Plants vary in abilities to extract water from the soil near WP.

  o Not the same for all species of plants.

- Varies with the soil as well, because some soils are more charged than others (electrically), such as clay; water is held more tightly by the cation-anion bond.

  ✓ Water in the soil which exists at a microscopic level as a layer around particles of clay. **Hygroscopic water** is held by electrical attraction and unable to leave the soil.

- Plants with deep roots are able to use water from deeper in soil when the surface area of soil is already dry.

Summary

Water is the universal solvent; it dissolves more substances than any other liquid. It is one of our renewable natural resources; the world's supply is constantly being recycled. Water that is held by and moves through the soil supplies the plant with water as well as mineral nutrients and oxygen. Available water is used by the plant. Without water, plants wilt and die.

Resources

Free complementary PowerPoint:
http://www.tagmydoc.com/dl/1S954y/gk6R

Basic Irrigation Terminology
http://edis.ifas.ufl.edu/pdffiles/AE/AE11500.pdf

Irrigation in the Pacific Northwest
http://irrigation.wsu.edu/Content/Resources/Irrigation-Glossary.php

Irrigation Glossary
http://www.irrigation.org/Resources/Irrigation_Glossary_Pages/Irrigation_Glossary.aspx

Assessment

1. In which three forms does water exist on Earth?
   a.) Oceans, Streams, Lakes   b.) Ponds, Rivers, Canals   c.) Solid, Liquid, Gas

2. When all of the pore (voids) spaces in the soil are full of water the soil is said to be (at) _____.
   a.) maximum   b.) full potential   c.) saturated   d.) field capacity

3. T or F? An equal volume of clay soil will hold less water than sandy soil when all of the voids are filled.

4. All of the water held in the soil against the pull of gravity is called _____.
   a.) water holding capacity   b.) full potential   c.) saturated   d.) field capacity

5. Water held too tightly by the opposite charges of soil and water is called_____.
   a.) field capacity   b) permanent wilting point   c) hygroscopic water   d) saturated

Take assessment online here:

http://tinyurl.com/PlntSci-5b

Hint: When the answer is incorrect, you will see: "Wrong answer! Go Back!"

Notes

11 Irrigation Practices

Major Concept

Land, soil, water and drainage affect irrigation practices.

Objectives

- List three factors to consider when choosing land for irrigation
- Identify three sources of surface water used for irrigation
- List two benefits of providing proper drainage

Link to Standards

PS.01. Develop and implement a crop management plan for a given production goal that accounts for environmental factors.

Key Terms

- Distribution system

Irrigation Practices

- Irrigation diminishes one of the greatest risks in crop production, inadequate water supply.
  - Important considerations include: selecting land for irrigation, obtaining water, quality of water and drainage.

Selecting Land for Irrigation

- A careful examination must be made of the soil when choosing land for irrigation.

- Some of the factors to consider include:

  - Texture and depth of the soil.

    - Presence of gravel or impermeable layers within 6 feet of the surface.

  - Presence of soluble salts injurious (to crop) and the quantities of those salts.

- o Behavior of soil under irrigation.
- o Topography (slope, etc.) of the soil surface.

Obtaining Water

- Most irrigation water of the world is surface water.
  - o Usually obtained by building dams at higher elevations.
    - ✓ Runoff water from rainfall or melting snow provides the source.
  - o A **distribution system** of canals, ditches, and pipelines delivers the water to the individual farm.
    - ✓ Often this type of irrigation project is built by the government.
    - ✓ Payment for construction and maintenance is sometimes prorated to the landowners.
  - o Only about 20% of the irrigation water in the U.S. comes from well water.

Water Quality

- Careful attention needs to be given to the quality of the available water before an irrigation system is built.
  - o Presence of salts, especially sodium salts, in the water can cause soils to develop an undesirable structure.
    - ✓ This salinity can also be detrimental to plant growth if the concentration is high.
  - o Some waters contain boron in sufficient quantities to become toxic to crop plants.
  - o Effects of elements carried by the water on the crops grown will be determined by factors such as the salt content of the soil, soil texture, kind of clay minerals present and drainage.
  - o Presence of organic matter and other suspended solids must be removed when using drip irrigation; otherwise it will clog the irrigation equipment.

Drainage

- Providing proper drainage can produce several benefits.
    - Drainage can add additional volume of soil to the crops' root zone.
    - Can be used to flush out accumulated salts.
    - In some areas drainage can lower the water table, enabling roots to penetrate deeper.
    - Soil aeration, microbial action, and fertilizer efficiency are all improved by drainage.

Summary

Irrigation diminishes one of the greatest risks in crop production, inadequate water supply. A careful examination must be made of the soil when choosing land for irrigation. Providing proper drainage can produce several benefits.

Resources

Free complementary PowerPoint:
http://www.tagmydoc.com/irrigationpractices

Best Management Practice: Water-Efficient Irrigation
https://www1.eere.energy.gov/femp/program/waterefficiency_bmp5.html

Effective Irrigation Practices
http://tinyurl.com/lpdrn65

Irrigation Best Practices & Standards
http://www.irrigation.org/Resources/Best_Practices___Standards.aspx

Assessment

1. T or F? Careful examination of the behavior of soil under irrigation must be made of the soil when choosing land for irrigation.

2. Only about _____ % of the irrigation water in the U.S. comes from well water.
   a.) 15   b.) 10   c.) 17   d.) 20

3. What in the water can cause soils to develop an undesirable structure?
   a.) calcium   b.) nitrogen   c.) salt   d.) phosphorus

4. Some waters contain _____ in sufficient quantities to become toxic to crop plants.
   a.) copper   b.) sulfur   c.) boron   d.) potassium

5. T or F? Soil aeration, microbial action, and fertilizer efficiency are all improved by drainage.

Take assessment online here:

http://tinyurl.com/PlntSci-5a

Hint: When the answer is incorrect, you will see: "Wrong answer! Go Back!"

Notes

12 Knowing When to Irrigate

Major Concept

Knowing when and how to irrigate improves crop productivity and conserves water.

Objectives

- Identify three methods of determining when to irrigate
- List four reasons for the proper timing of irrigation
- Identify four signs in the plant and the soil indicating the need for irrigation
- List four factors that determine the time and frequency of irrigation

Link to Standards

PS.01. Develop and implement a crop management plan for a given production goal that accounts for environmental factors.

Key Terms

- Electrical conductivity
- Neutron moisture probe
- Remote sensing
- Tensiometer

Knowing When to Irrigate

- Irrigation general guidelines

    o Capable of giving enormous benefits.

    o Can be a wasteful and harmful practice if not applied correctly.

    o Principles of irrigation are simple.

    o Individual crops and individual areas vary greatly.

    o Roots "don't grow to water," they grow where water is already present.

    o To help decide when and how much water, the root zone of the plant(s) must be defined.

    o Watering efficiently is an important consideration.

- ✓ For example: Watering beyond the root zone wastes water.
  - o To have uniform plants in a crop; all those plants in the crop must be watered the same way and amount.
    - ✓ Ripening of the crop all at the same time improves ease of management, increases efficiency of harvest and saves money.
  - o Water not received by natural precipitation must be furnished by irrigation.
- Determining when to irrigate and how much water to apply are the main problems in irrigating.
  - o Time and frequency of irrigation is determined by:
    - ✓ Soil type
    - ✓ Area climate
    - ✓ Type of crop
    - ✓ Time of ripening and harvest (especially for fruit crops)
- Object of irrigation is to replace the water lost from the field soil by transpiration plus evaporation minus the annual rainfall (precipitation).
- Timing is critical.
  - o Plants under water stress during critical stages will not produce or reproduce optimally, even if adequate water is available later.
- Several methods are used to determine when to irrigate. Experience plays an important role.
  - o Most crops will indicate that the individual plants are under moisture stress by changing color - usually a duller, more ashen green-grey.
  - o Leaves will curl.
  - o Shoot tips will become harder and darker sometimes with a grey cast and sometimes lose turgor.
  - o Soil will feel and appear more crumbly and drier.

Degree of Moisture Feel Percent of Field Capacity

- One of the old reliable methods is the "feel method."

  - Growers place a small amount of soil in their hand to "feel" the moisture.

    - Dry - Powder dry = 0%

    - Low (critical) - Crumbly, will not form a ball = less than 25%

    - Fair (usual time) - Forms a ball, but will crumble upon being tossed several times = 25 - 50%

    - Good - Forms a ball that will remain intact after being tossed 5 times; will stick slightly with pressure = 50 - 75%

    - Excellent - Forms a durable ball and is pliable; sticks readily; a sizable chunk will stick to the thumb after soil is squeezed firmly = 75 - 100%

    - Too wet - With firm pressure, some water can be squeezed from the ball = In excess of field capacity

- The use of tensiometers proves useful in some crops such as orchards and vineyards.

  - A **tensiometer** consists of a porous cup filled with water that can be buried to a desired depth in the soil in the vicinity of roots.

  - Cup is connected by a water-filled tube to a vacuum gage.

    - As the soil dries, it sucks water out through the porous wall of the cup, creating a partial vacuum inside the tensiometer that can be read on the vacuum gauge.

    - As soil moisture is replaced, water re-enters the porous cup relieving the vacuum tension.

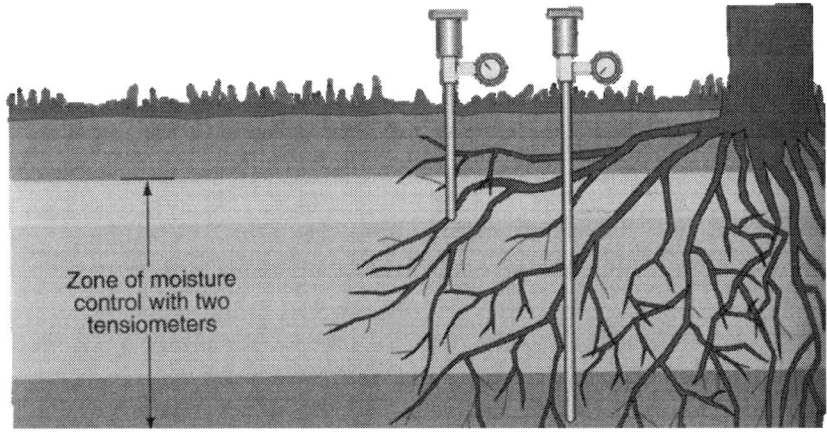

Zone of moisture control with two tensiometers

Other Methods for Determining When to Irrigate

- **Electrical Conductivity**

    o Electrical resistance blocks measure soil water more precisely than the feel method.

    ✓ Recommended for finer-textured soils.

- **Neutron Moisture Probe**

    o Measures soil water content using a radioactive source.

    ✓ Not recommended for small-scale irrigation scheduling.

- Evaporation Pans

    o Used to calculate the amount of water used by the crop.

- Computer Programs

    o Forecast the timing and amount of irrigation water necessary for optimum crop production.

    ✓ Computer irrigation scheduling is available from computer networks that provide scheduling programs for a service fee.

    ✓ Computer irrigation scheduling is available from computer networks that provide scheduling programs for a service fee.

- Water Budgeting using Evapotranspiration Data

    o Used to balance the available soil moisture.

    ✓ Rainfall and irrigation amounts represent credit entries.

    ✓ Evapotranspiration is a debit entry.

- **Remote Sensing**

    o Science of getting information about an object by acquiring data with a device not in contact with that object.

    o New uses for remotely sensed data include detection of crop stresses, pest management, fertility management, irrigation systems monitoring.

Crop Water Requirements

- Crop Water Use

Crop	Inches/year
Corn	23-28
Soybeans	20-25
Dry Beans	15-16
Sorghum	18-23
Winter Wheat	16-18
Alfalfa	31-36
Sugar Beets	24-26

Summary

Irrigation is capable of giving enormous benefits. Irrigation can also be a wasteful and harmful practice if not applied correctly. The principles of irrigation are simple. It is difficult to give hard and fast rules however, because individual crops and individual areas vary so greatly. Some tools are available to help growers irrigate more efficiently.

Resources

Free complementary PowerPoint:
http://www.tagmydoc.com/dl/1Me0Ct/gk93

Parker, R. 2010. Plant and soil science: Fundamentals and applications. Clifton Park, NY: Delmar Cengage Learning. (Pgs. 211-231).

Soil, Water, and Crop Characteristics Important To Irrigation Scheduling
http://www.bae.ncsu.edu/programs/extension/evans/ag452-1.html

Choosing an Irrigation Method
http://www.fao.org/docrep/s8684e/s8684e08.htm

Assessment

1. T or F? Ripening of a crop all at the same time improves ease of management, increases efficiency of harvest and saves money.

2. T or F? Experience plays an important role in determining when to irrigate.

3. T or F? Excellent soil moisture - Forms a durable ball and is pliable; sticks readily; a sizable chunk will stick to the thumb after some water can be squeezed from the ball.

4. Which method for determining when to irrigate measures soil water content using a radioactive source?
   a.) electrical conductivity   b.) neutron moisture probe c.) remote sensing
    d.) computer program

5. The tensiometer consists of a _____ cup filled with water that can be buried to a desired depth in the soil in the vicinity of roots.
   a.) clay b.) glass c.) porous d.) plastic

Take assessment online here:

http://tinyurl.com/PlntSci-5c

Hint: When the answer is incorrect, you will see: "Wrong answer! Go Back!"

Notes

13 Water Measurement and Soil Capacity

Major Concept

Water-holding capacity depends on soil type.

Objectives

- Identify the concept of water holding (or field) capacity of different soils
- Define acre inch, acre foot, water penetration and water holding capacity
- List four factors that determine water penetration and water-holding capacity of soil

Link to Standards

PS.01. Develop and implement a crop management plan for a given production goal that accounts for environmental factors.

Key Terms

- Acre Inch/Feet
- Water-holding Capacity

Water Measurements and Soil Capacity

- Cost of irrigation water varies widely throughout the U.S and the world.

  o Individual crops require a varying amount of water to reach marketable size, stage or maturity.

  o Crops will require 16 to 36 inches or more of useable (available) water.

  o Water is measured for agricultural uses.

- Rainfall report is given in inches of water precipitated.

  o One inch of water in the form of rainfall over an area means that the entire area received enough rain to cover it with a depth of one inch of water.

    ✓ If this were measured over a given area of one acre, it would be one "acre inch of water."

  o Typically water is measured in **acre feet**.

- Twelve inches of rain means water to cover each acre with one foot of water (one acre foot).

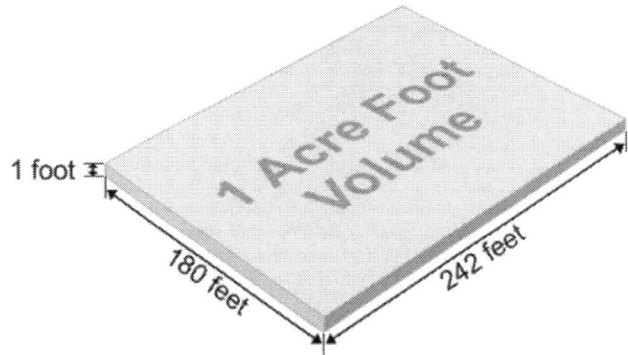

- In irrigation districts, the landowner is charged a given amount for each acre foot of water for example:
    - ✓ Grower uses 1.75 acre feet of water. Cost is $50.00 per acre foot.
    - ✓ Total cost per acre paid by the landowner is $87.50

- In irrigated areas growers supplement the natural precipitation (rain or snow) with irrigation water, for example:
    - If a crop requires 32 inches of water to reach maturity and rain supplied 12 inches, how much water would the grower have to add by irrigation?
    - 32 inches minus 12 inches = 20 inches of water needs to be added.
        - ✓ This would be the case for 100% efficiency of water use.
        - ✓ Seldom is the case, the best is 85-90% and common is 65-75%.
        - ✓ Therefore, water needs for the crop would be more than 20 inches of water and would be closer to 22 to 30 inches of water.
    - What would be the per acre cost of the irrigation water at $50.00 per acre foot?
        - ✓ 20 inches = 1.66 feet
        - ✓ So, 1.66 ft times $50.00 per acre foot = $83.00 per acre.

- Depth of water penetration for one inch of water is also a factor.
    - This will vary with the type of soil.
    - Typical ranges of penetration for each type of soil are:

- ✓ 10 to 12 inches penetration in sand
- ✓ 6 to 10 inches penetration in silt
- ✓ 4 to 6 inches penetration in clay
- Factors affecting water penetration include:
  - Soil texture
  - Organic matter content of the soil
  - Presence of impermeable layers
  - Amount of soil compaction
  - Amount of surface crusting
- Ability of a soil to retain (hold) water is called the **water-holding capacity**.
  - Water-holding capacity of soils will vary, especially with soil texture.
  - Typical water-holding capacities (water per foot of soil) by soil textures are:
    - ✓ 0.5 to 0.75 inches per foot of sandy soil
    - ✓ 0.75 to 1.25 inches per foot of loam soils
    - ✓ 1.25 to 2.0 inches per foot of clay soils

Summary

The cost of irrigation water varies widely throughout the U.S and the world. Individual crops require a varying amount of water to reach marketable size, stage or maturity. Crops will require 16-36 inches or more of useable water. In irrigated areas growers supplement the natural precipitation with irrigation water. Depth of water penetration for one inch of water is also a factor which varies with soil type.

Resources

Free complementary PowerPoint:
http://www.tagmydoc.com/dl/3k0hM/gk6T

Plant & Soil Science eLibrary: Soils - Part 2: Physical Properties of Soil and Soil Water:
http://passel.unl.edu/pages/informationmodule.php?idinformationmodule=1130447039&topicorder=10&maxto=10

Soil Moisture Measurement Technology
http://cecentralsierra.ucanr.edu/files/96233.pdf

Soil Properties Analysis
http://www.appstate.edu/~denbiggelaa/soilsampling.pdf

Assessment

1. Crops will require _____ inches or more of useable (available) water.
   a.) 12-24   b.) 36-48   c.) 16-36   d.) 18-30

2. T or F? One inch of water in the form of rainfall over an area means the entire area received enough rain to cover it with a depth of one inch of water.

3. T or F? Water is typically measured in centimeters.

4. T or F? The depth of water penetration for each soil type will always stay the same.

5. The ability of a soil to retain (hold) water is called _____.
   a.) water penetration   b.) holding-capacity   c.) water precipitation
   d.) impermeable layers

Take assessment online here:

http://tinyurl.com/PlntSci-e

Hint: When the answer is incorrect, you will see: "Wrong answer! Go Back!"

14 Transpiration

Major Concept

Transpiration cools the leaf and carries water and nutrients from the root throughout the plant.

Objectives

- Define a stomata and guard cell
- List two purposes of transpiration
- Identify three factors that affect transpiration

Link to Standards

PS.02. Apply principles of classification, plant anatomy, and plant physiology to plant production and management.

Key Terms

- Guard cell
- Stomata
- Transpiration

Transpiration

- Transpiration is the process in which a plant cools itself and releases water.

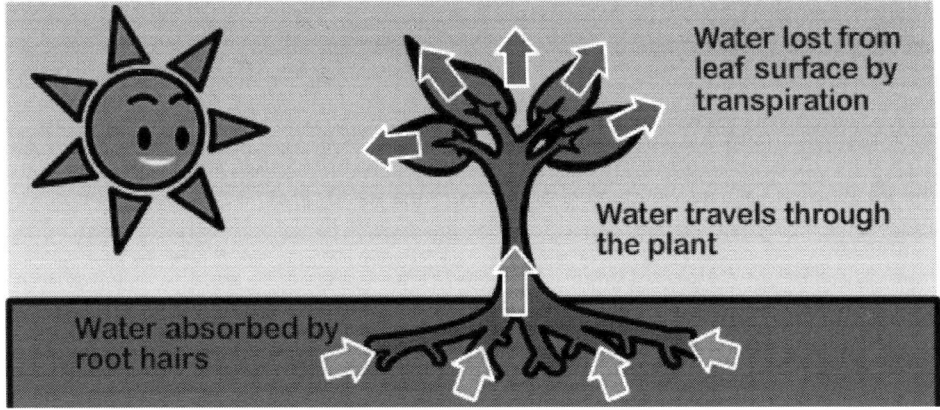

  o Respiration and photosynthesis produce water and heat.

- Transpiration "lifts" water from the roots, carrying nutrients to the plant.

- About 90% of all water that enters the plant is from the roots and is given off during transpiration. The remaining 10% becomes involved in chemical processes or is tied up in the plant's structure.

• The lower surface of the leaf is dotted with special pore-like structures called **stomata**.

- By the action of **guard cells** in the leaf, openings occur in the stomata during the daylight hours to permit the free exchange and release of water vapor, and the release of oxygen (O_2).

- The stomata close at night or when the plant is water stressed.

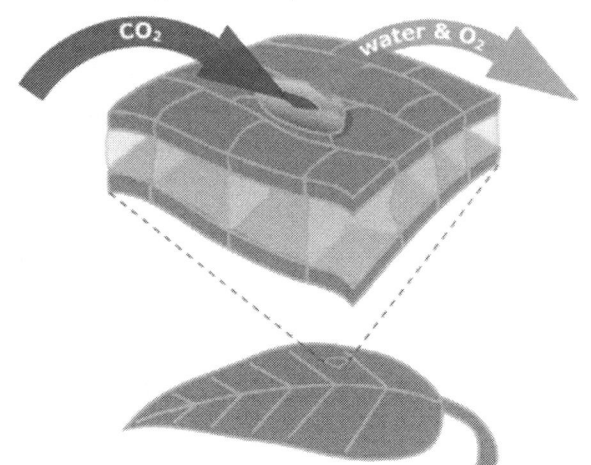

Environmental Factors Affecting Transpiration

- Light - plants transpire more stimulating the opening of the stomata.

- Temperature – transpiration is higher because water evaporates more quickly as temperature increases – leaf transpires three times greater at 86°F/30°C than 68°F/20°C.

- Humidity – diffusion of water out of leaf more rapid when surrounding air is drier.

Summary

Respiration and photosynthesis produce H_2O and heat. About 90% of all water that enters the plant from the roots is given off during transpiration while the other 10% becomes involved in chemical processes or is tied up in the plant's structure. This release of H_2O is called transpiration. The lower surface of the leaf is dotted with special pore-like structures called stomata, which permits the exchange of water vapor and oxygen. Light, temperature and humidity are factors which affect transpiration.

Resources

Free complementary PowerPoint:
http://www.tagmydoc.com/dl/PAqS5/gk6V

Parker, R. 2010. Plant and soil science: Fundamentals and applications. Clifton Park, NY: Delmar Cengage Learning. (Pg. 200).

The Water Cycle: Transpiration
http://ga.water.usgs.gov/edu/watercycletranspiration.html

Transpiration – Water Movement through Plants
http://passel.unl.edu/pages/informationmodule.php?idinformationmodule=1092853841&topicorder=6&maxto=8

Assessment

1. T or F? The process by which a plant cools itself and releases water is called transpiration.

2. By the action of _____, openings occur in the stomata during the daylight hours.
   a.) guard cells   b.) pores   c.) transpiration   d.) water vapor

3. T or F? Openings in the stomata prevent the free exchange and release of water vapor.

4. T or F? The stomata close at night or when the plant is water stressed.

Take the assessment online here:

http://tinyurl.com/PlntSci-5f

Hint: When the answer is incorrect, you will see: "Wrong answer! Go Back!"

15 Translocation

Major Concept

Translocation moves soluble, required nutrients within a plant.

Objectives

- Define translocation
- List three ways translocated water helps the plant

Link to Standards

PS.01. Develop and implement a crop management plan for a given production goal that accounts for environmental factors.

PS.02. Apply principles of classification, plant anatomy, and plant physiology to plant production and management.

Key Terms

- Phloem
- Turgor
- Xylem

Translocation

- Transport of soluble food material (minerals, sugars, etc.) within a plant via **phloem**, which distributes food and other materials made by photosynthesis throughout the plant, or **xylem**, which takes up water and nutrients through the roots of the plant.

- The process of translocation is made possible by the "solvent of life," plain water.

    - Plants produce carbohydrates (sugars) in their leaves by photosynthesis, but non-photosynthetic parts of the plant also require carbohydrates and other organic and nonorganic materials.

        - ✓ Water enters the plant through the root system transporting carbohydrates where needed.

- Functions of translocated water:

  o Transportation: Water is moved up through the sieve tubes from the roots though the xylem carrying nutrients and metabolites (products of the chemical reactions of the plant) to the rest of the plant.

  o Transportation of photosynthetic products: Water moves through the phloem sieve tubes to transport sugar produced by the leaves during photosynthesis to all parts of the plant, including the roots.

  o Translocated water adds physical support or **turgor** (stiffness) to the cells supporting leaves and new tissue.

Other Functions of Translocation

- Enables transpiration

- Buffers temperature changes

- Stabilizes the pH

- Maintains the volume of the cytoplasm

- Enables all chemical reactions by supplying water

Summary

Translocation is the transport of soluble food material, minerals, sugars, etc. within a plant via phloem or xylem. The process of translocation is made possible by plain water. Water enters the plant through the root system and is transported throughout the plant. Water's ability to be translocated serves many functions such as transportation of nutrients, transportation of photosynthetic products and physical support. Translocation serves several other functions. Among these are stabilizing pH and buffering temperature changes.

Resources

Free complementary PowerPoint:
http://www.tagmydoc.com/dl/UsgZE/gk6X

Parker, R. 2010. Plant and soil science: Fundamentals and applications. Clifton Park, NY: Delmar Cengage Learning. (Pgs. 198-200).

Translocation Animations
http://tinyurl.com/translocation

The Pressure Flow Model
http://bcs.whfreeman.com/thelifewire/content/chp36/36020.html

Assessment

1. During transportation of nutrients, water is moved up through the _____ from the roots.
   a.) sieve tubes   b.) roots   c.) leaves   d.) soil

2. During translocation, the water carries nutrients and important _____.
   a.) vitamins   b.) metabolites   c.) photosynthesis   d.) minerals

3. _____ takes up water and nutrients through the roots of the plant.
   a.) Metabolism   b.) Phloem   c.) Xylem   d.) Soil

4. T or F? Sugar is produced by the leaves during photosynthesis.

5. T or F? Translocated water adds turgor to the cells supporting leaves and new tissue.

Take the assessment online here:

http://tinyurl.com/PlntSci-5d

Hint: When the answer is incorrect, you will see: "Wrong answer! Go Back!"

16 Nutrients Essential to Plant Growth

Major Concept

Optimal plant growth requires essential nutrients.

Objectives

- List the primary, secondary and micro-nutrients
- Identify signs of a nitrogen, phosphorus or potassium deficiency
- Define chlorosis

Link to Standards

PS.02. Apply principles of classification, plant anatomy, and plant physiology to plant production and management.

Key Terms

- Chlorosis
- Chlorotic
- Elements
- Macronutrients
- Micronutrients
- Mottled
- Necrotic
- Rosetting

Introduction

- Plants require **elements** (chemical substances) which are absolutely necessary for their (normal) growth.

- Many of these elements are the same as those required by livestock and humans.

Sixteen Essential Elements

- In addition to carbon, hydrogen, and oxygen, which the plant gets from the air and water, 13 elements are required by plants.

    o These are obtain from the soil and are divided into four classes:

- Essential Elements

    o Non-mineral
        - Carbon (C)
        - Hydrogen (H)
        - Oxygen (O)

    o Primary
        - Nitrogen (N)
        - Phosphorus (P)
        - Potassium (K)

    o Secondary
        - Sulfur (S)
        - Calcium (Ca)
        - Iron (Fe)
        - Magnesium (Mg)

    o Use this mnemonic to remember these essential elements –
        "C HOPKNS CaFe Mg"

- Micronutrients
  - Boron (B)
  - Chlorine (Cl)
  - Copper (Cu)
  - Manganese (Mn)
  - Molybdenum (Mo)
  - Zinc (Zn)

Functions of Plant Elements Metabolism and Their Deficiencies

- **Macronutrients** are required in large quantities.

- Nitrogen (N)
  - Function: Promotes rapid vegetative growth and gives plants healthy green color.
  - Deficiency signs: Stunted growth, pale yellowish color, burning of tips and margins of leaves starting at bottom of plant.

- Phosphorus (P)
  - Function: Stimulates early growth and root formation, hastens maturity, promotes seed production, makes plants hardy.
  - Deficiency signs: Small growth especially in roots, spindly stalk, delayed maturity, purplish discoloration of leaves on certain plants, dying of tips of older leaves, poor fruit and seed development.

- Potassium (K)
  - Function: Improves plant's ability to resist disease and cold, aids in the production of carbohydrates.
  - Deficiency signs: Slow growth, margins on leaves develop a scorched effect starting on older leaves, weak stalk, shriveled seed or fruit.

- Calcium (Ca)

- - Function: Aids in the movement of carbohydrates in plants, essential to healthy cell walls and root structure.

  - Deficiency signs: Terminal bud dies under severe deficiency, margins of younger leaves scalloped, blossoms shed prematurely, weak stalk or stem structure.

- Magnesium (Mg)

  - Function: An ingredient of chlorophyll. Aids in the translocation of starch within a plant, essential for formation of oils and fats.

  - Deficiency signs: Yellowing of leaves between veins starting with lower leaves, leaves abnormally thin, tissues may dry and die, leaves have a tendency to curve upward.

- Sulfur (S)

  - Function: Aids in the formation of oils and parts of the protein molecules.

  - Deficiency signs: Young leaves light green to yellowish in color. In some plants, older tissue may be affected also. Small and spindly plants. Retarded growth rate and delayed maturity. Interveinal **chlorosis** (insufficient chlorophyll) on corn leaves.

Micronutrients

- **Micronutrients** are required in small amounts.

- Boron (B)

  - Function: Aids in the assimilation of calcium; amount required is extremely small.

  - Deficiency signs: Death of terminal growth, causing lateral buds to develop and produce a "witches-broom" effect. Thickened, curled, wilted and **chlorotic** (bleached) leaves. Soft or **necrotic** (dead) spots in fruit or tubers. Reduced flowering or improper pollination.

- Copper (Cu)

  - Function: Promotes formation of Vitamin A, excess is very toxic.

  - Deficiency signs: Stunted growth. Dieback of terminal shoots in trees. Poor pigmentation. Wilting and eventual death of leaf tips. Formation of gum pockets around central pith in oranges.

- Manganese (Mn)

  - Function: Serves as an activator for enzymes in growth processes. Assists iron in chlorophyll formation. Generally required with zinc in foliar spraying of citrus.

  - Deficiency signs: Interveinal (between veins) chlorosis of young leaves. Gradation of pale green coloration with darker color next to veins. No sharp distinction between veins and interveinal areas as with iron deficiency. Development of gray specks (oats) interveinal white streaks (wheat) or interveinal brown spots and streaks (barley).

- Zinc (Zn)

  - Function: An essential constituent of several important enzyme systems in plants. It controls the synthesis of indoleacetic acid, an important plant growth regulator. The micronutrient most often needed by western crops. Many tree crops, grapes, beans, onions, tomatoes, cotton, rice, and corn require zinc fertilization.

- o Deficiency signs: Decrease in stem length and a **rosetting** (circular arrangement of leaves) of terminal leaves. Reduced fruit bud formation. **Mottled** (spotted or blotched) leaves (interveinal chlorosis). Dieback of twigs after first year. Striping or banding on corn leaves.

- Molybdenum (Mo)

    - o Function: Required by plants for use of nitrogen. Plants cannot transform nitrate nitrogen into amino acids without molybdenum. Legumes cannot fix atmospheric nitrogen symbiotically unless molybdenum is present.

    - o Deficiency signs: Stunting and lack of vigor. This is similar to nitrogen deficiency due to the key role of molybdenum in nitrogen use by plants. Marginal scorching and cupping or rolling of leaves. "Whip-tail" of cauliflower. Yellow spotting in citrus.

- Chlorine (Cl)

    - o Function: Required in photosynthetic reactions of plants. Deficiency is not seen in the field due to its universal presence in nature.

    - o Deficiency signs: Wilting, followed by chlorosis. Excessive branching of lateral roots. Bronzing of leaves. Chlorosis and necrosis in tomatoes and barley.

- Iron (Fe)

    - o Function: Essential for formation of chlorophyll, releases energy from sugars and starches.

    - o Deficiency signs: Leaves yellowish or whitish (young leaves first), veins green, affected leaves curl up.

Summary

In addition to carbon, hydrogen, and oxygen, which the plant gets from the air and water, there are thirteen elements required by plants which are obtained from the soil. There are several functions of elements in plant metabolism and symptoms related to their deficiencies. Micronutrients are required in small amounts, while macronutrients are required in large amounts.

Resources

Free complementary PowerPoint:
http://www.tagmydoc.com/dl/1wlAab/gk6f

Parker, R. 2010. Plant and soil science: Fundamentals and applications. Clifton Park, NY: Delmar Cengage Learning. (Pgs. 133-143).

Plant Nutrients
http://www.ncagr.gov/cyber/kidswrld/plant/nutrient.htm

Roles of the 16 Essential Nutrients In Crop Development
http://www.eldoradochemical.com/fertiliz1.htm

Assessment

1. T or F? The three essential elements a plant gets from the air are carbon, hydrogen and carbon dioxide.

2. T or F? Macronutrients are only required in small quantities.

3. Magnesium is an ingredient of _____.
   a.) protein molecules   b.) chlorophyll   c.) fat molecules   d.) starch

4. T or F? Micronutrients are required in large amounts.

5. _____ promotes formation of Vitamin A, which excess is very toxic.
   a.) Iron   b.) Chlorine   c.) Copper   d.) Molybdenum

Take assessment online here:

http://tinyurl.com/PlntSci-6b

Hint: When the answer is incorrect, you will see: "Wrong answer! Go Back!"

Notes

17 Primary Plant Nutrients

Major Concept

Primary elements for plant growth come from several sources and are available in several forms.

Objectives

- List two sources for each of the primary elements (N, P, K)
- Identify quickly available and slowly available sources of N
- Identify forms of N, P, K used for plant nutrition

Link to Standards

PS.03. Propagate, culture and harvest plants and plant products based on current industry standards.

Key Terms

- Compost
- Greensand
- Langbeinite
- Legumes
- Slag
- Slow-release
- Soluble

Sources of Plant Nutrients

- Two categories of nitrogen sources based on availability in the soil:

    1. Quickly available: Inorganic salts that are readily **soluble** in water. These are industrially produced from raw materials such as natural gas and minerals.

        ✓ Examples: Ammonium Sulfate, Ammonium Nitrate, Ammonium Phosphate, and Potassium Nitrate, Urea.

    2. Slowly available: Do not go readily into solution in water but will release slowly with time. These are referred to as **slow-release** such as SCU (Sulfur-coated urea).

- ✓ Examples: Slowly soluble forms: UF (Urea Formaldehyde) and IBDU (Isobutylidene diurea)
    - o Natural organic types: Emphasizes rotation with leguminous cover crops and application of compost or manure.
        - ✓ Activated sewage sludge manures – Treated residuals from wastewater treatment used beneficially.
        - ✓ **Compost** – Decomposed organic matter
        - ✓ **Legumes** – Plants grown for seed value and nitrogen-fixing ability such as alfalfa and peanuts

- Phosphorus Sources
    - o Rock phosphate (PO_4^{3-}), mined, ground and treated with acid to form the two principal phosphorus sources.
        - ✓ Super phosphate ($CaH_4P_2O_8$), formed by treating rock phosphate with sulfuric acid.
        - ✓ Treble super phosphate Ca $(H_2PO_4)_2H_2O$, formed by treating rock phosphate with phosphoric acid.

- Other Sources
    - o Ammonium phosphate - produced by reacting phosphoric acid (H_3PO_4) with anhydrous ammonia (NH_3).
    - o Organic phosphorus sources - rock phosphate (PO43-), bone meal (animal bones ground into powder) and colloidal phosphate (a soft-rock phosphate).
        - ✓ **Slag** - a byproduct of steel manufacturing.

- Potassium Sources
    - o Potassium Chloride or Muriate of Potash (KCl); processed from mined potassium salts.
    - o Sulfate of Potash (K_2SO_4) and Potassium chloride treated with sulfuric acid.
    - o Potassium Nitrate (KNO_3) - Potassium chloride treated with Nitric Acid.

- Organic Sources of Potassium

- **Greensand** - Sandy rock or sediment containing a high percentage of the green mineral glauconite and has a very slow K release rate.

- **Langbeinite** (Potassium-magnesium sulfate) - this material ($K_2SO_4 \cdot MgSO_4$) is allowed as a nutrient source if it is used in the raw, crushed form without any further refinement or purification.

- Sylvinite (Potassium Chloride) KCl is restricted in the USDA standards unless it is from a mined source (such as sylvinite) and undergoes no further processing.

Summary

Availability of nitrogen in the soil is based on two categories – quick or slow. Natural organic types include activated sewage sludge manures, compost and legumes. Other plant nutrient sources include various forms of phosphorus and potassium.

Resources

Free complementary PowerPoint:
http://www.tagmydoc.com/dl/1YnkIA/gk6l

Parker, R. 2010. Plant and soil science: Fundamentals and applications. Clifton Park, NY: Delmar Cengage Learning.

Guide to Symptoms of Plant Nutrient Deficiencies
http://ag.arizona.edu/pubs/garden/az1106.pdf

Plant Nutrients
http://extension.psu.edu/agronomy-guide/cm/sec2/sec23

Assessment

1. T or F? Super phosphate ($CaH_4P_2O_8$) is formed by treating rock phosphate with sulfuric acid.

2. T or F? Potassium nitrate is not an inorganic salt.

3. T or F? Greensand - a sandy rock or sediment containing a high percentage of the green mineral glauconite and has a very slow K release rate and is an inorganic source of potassium.

4. Activated sewage sludge manures are natural _____ type nitrogen sources.
    a.) organic   b.) slowly available   c.) quickly available   d.) inorganic

5. T or F? Potassium Chloride or Muriate of Potash (KCl) are processed from mined potassium salts.

Take assessment online here:

http://tinyurl.com/PlntSci-6d

Hint: When the answer is incorrect, you will see: "Wrong answer! Go Back!"

Notes

18 Signs of Nutrient Deficiencies

Major Concept

Plants show signs of nutrient deficiencies in their leaves.

Objectives

- Identify three signs of a nutrient deficiency in older leaves and younger leaves

Key Terms

- Chlorosis
- Necrotic

Link to Standards

PS.02. Apply principles of classification, plant anatomy, and plant physiology to plant production and management.

A Key to Nutrient Deficiency Signs

- Older Leaves: Effects are mostly generalized over entire plant; lower leaves dry up and die.

  - Nitrogen (N)

    ✓ Plants light green, lower leaves yellow, drying to brown, stalks become short and slender.

  - Phosphorus (P)

    ✓ Plants dark green, often red or purple colors appear, lower leaves yellow, drying to dark green, stalks become short or slender.

    ✓ Effects are mostly localized, mottling or **chlorosis** (loss of normal green coloration of plant leaves); lower leaves do not dry up but lose the normal green coloration of leaves; leaf margins cupped or tucked.

- Magnesium (Mg)
  - Leaves mottled or chlorotic, sometimes reddened, **necrotic** spots (the death of most or all of the cells or tissue due to disease), stalks slender.
- Potassium (K)
  - Mottled or chlorotic leaves, necrotic spots small and between veins or near leaf tips and margins, stalks slender.
- Zinc (Zn)
  - Necrotic spots large and general, eventually involving veins, leaves thick, stalks short.

- Young Leaves. Terminal buds die; distortion and necrosis of leaves occur.
  - Calcium (Ca)
    - Young leaves hooked, then die back at tips and margins.
  - Boron (B)
    - Young leaves light green at bases, die back from base, leaves twisted.

- Terminal buds remain alive but chlorotic or wilted, without necrotic spots.
  - Copper (Cu)
    - Young leaves wilted, without chlorosis, stem tip weak.
    - Young leaves not wilted, chlorosis occurs.
  - Manganese (Mn)
    - Small necrotic spots, veins remain green.
    - No necrotic spots.
  - Iron (Fe)
    - Veins remain green.
  - Sulfur (S)
    - Veins become chlorotic.

Summary

Nutrient deficiency effects on older leaves are mostly generalized over entire plant, lower leaves dry up and die. Whereas, with young leaves, the terminal buds die, distortion and necrosis of young leaves occur.

Resources

Free complementary PowerPoint:
http://www.tagmydoc.com/dl/Ld0qx/gk6n

Parker, R. 2010. Plant and soil science: Fundamentals and applications. Clifton Park, NY: Delmar Cengage Learning. (Pg. 134).

Guide to Symptoms of Plant Nutrient Deficiencies
http://ag.arizona.edu/pubs/garden/az1106.pdf

Recognizing Plant Nutrient Deficiencies
http://www.unce.unr.edu/publications/files/ho/2002/fs0265.pdf

Symptoms of Deficiency in Essential Minerals
http://5e.plantphys.net/article.php?ch=t&id=289

Assessment

1. T or F? In older leaves, nutrient deficiency effects are mostly generalized over a whole plant.

2. Young leaves that are hooked, then die back at tips and margins are showing signs of _____ deficiency.
   a.) boron   b.) calcium   c.) sulfur   d.) magnesium

3. T or F? In young leaves, terminal buds die and distortion and necrosis of leaves occur.

4. Death of most or all of the cells or tissue due to disease is called _____.
   a.) chlorosis   b.) mottlosis   c.) necrosis   d.) wilt

Take the assessment online here:

http://tinyurl.com/PlntSci-6e

Hint: When the answer is incorrect, you will see: "Wrong answer! Go Back!"

Notes

19 Plant Growth Requirements

Major Concept

Plant growth requires optimal temperature, light, moisture, carbon dioxide (CO_2) and nutrients.

Objectives

- Identify the importance of each of these items to plant growth: temperature, light, moisture, CO_2, and nutrients
- Define phototropism and photoperiodism
- Classify nutrients in broad categories

Link to Standards

PS.01. Develop and implement a crop management plan for a given production goal that accounts for environmental factors.

PS.02. Apply principles of classification, plant anatomy, and plant physiology to plant production and management.

Key Terms

- Capillary water
- Gravity water
- Hygroscopic water
- Photoperiodism
- Phototropism

Plant Growth Requirements

- Basics requirements for optimal plant growth are temperature, light, moisture (water), carbon dioxide and nutrients.

    o Higher or lower temperatures increase or decrease the rate of reactions, such as absorption of minerals and water.

        ✓ Sunscald of plant's leaves occurs at high temperatures and may also cause desiccation or kill protoplasm of cells.

- ✓ Plants also have a minimum temperature tolerance below which the plant may be injured or in some cases killed.

- ✓ Greenhouses are set for optimal growth conditions according to the plant type.

- ✓ Photosynthesis is slower at lower temperatures and rising to a certain point as the temperature increases.

- Light affects plants based on intensity, quality and duration.

  - Light Intensity

    - ✓ Provides energy for photosynthesis which is also affected by availability of water, CO_2 and sunlight.

    - ✓ Plants will grow until their food reserves are exhausted and they may appear elongated and abnormal.

    - ✓ **Phototropism** in plants is the tendency to "lean" in the direction of the greatest light intensity.

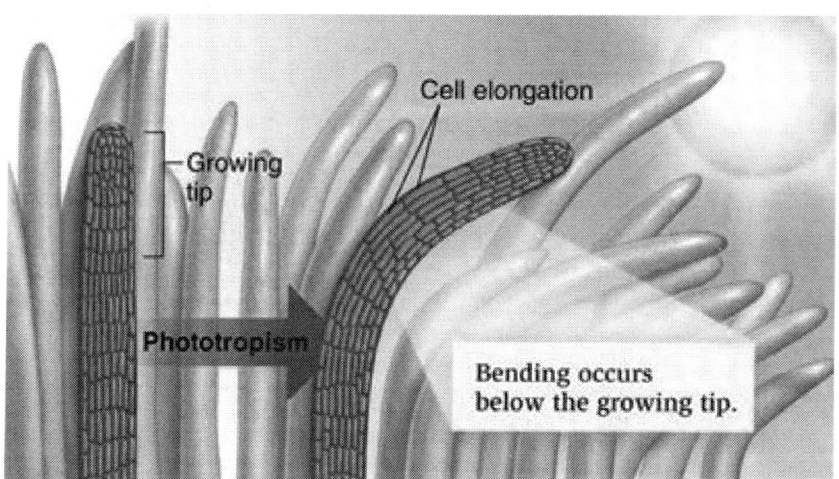

  - Light Quality

    - ✓ Major source is the sun.

    - ✓ Normal plant growth requires white light or sunlight.

    - ✓ Chlorophyll absorbs the red and blue portions of the light spectrum and appears to be green, since the leaf reflects green light.

- Light Duration
  - ✓ Plants are classified as short-day, long-day or day-neutral.
  - ✓ **Photoperiodism** is the growth response to the length of dark period and affects whether a plant is growing vegetatively or is in the flowering stage.

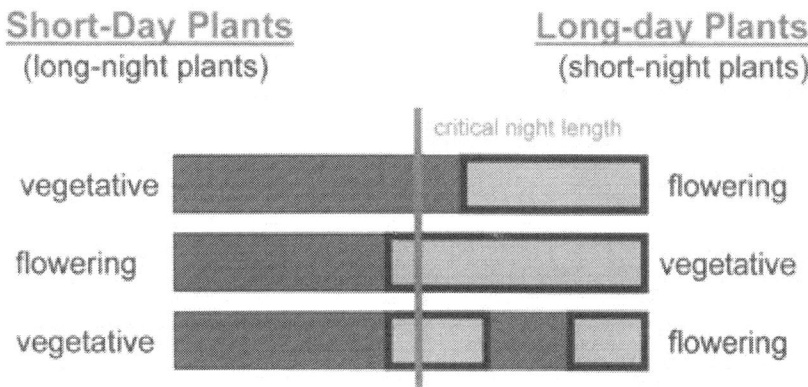

  - ✓ Short-day – require long periods of darkness. Some examples include: Upland cotton, winter rice, soybeans and strawberries.
  - ✓ Long-day requires only a short night to flower and bloom only when they receive more than 12 hours of light (upland cotton, winter rice, soybeans and strawberries).
  - ✓ Day-neutral plants – form flowers regardless of day length (winter barley, oats, winter wheat, spinach and timothy hay).

Note: Black cloth and artificial light are ways to shorten or lengthen the light requirements of plants.

- Moisture (water)
  - Water carries essential nutrients from the roots and acts as a solvent for essential salts and minerals.
  - Water translocates photosynthetic products from the leaves via the phloem.
  - Water is a chemical reactant in many plant processes including photosynthesis.
  - Water provides turgidity by supporting the structure of plants and adding cell turgor to all plant cells.
  - Water cools the plant during transpiration.

- - **Capillary water** used by plants and moves freely in the soil.
- Forms of soil water not available to plants include:
  - **Hygroscopic water** bonds to the soil particles due to an electrical bonding related to the size of the soil particle and its electrical charge. The charge is opposite that of water and will attract or hold the water in the soil which makes it unavailable to the plant.

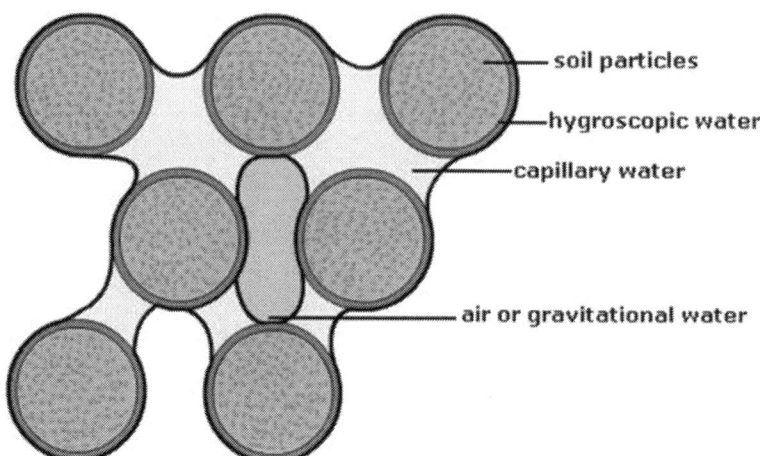

  - **Gravity water** is lost to drainage.

- Carbon dioxide (CO_2)
  - Required for photosynthesis.
  - CO_2 is taken in through the stomata.
  - Air normally contains 0.03% carbon dioxide. In greenhouse conditions, CO_2 can be added during bright winter days and in some instances a better crop can be grown.

- Nutrients
  - Sixteen essential nutrients are used by plants.
  - Normally available in the soil and classified by use.
  - Primary nutrients include N, P, K (nitrogen, phosphorus, potassium).
  - Secondary nutrients: Ca, S, Mg (calcium, sulfur, magnesium).
    - ✓ Trace or micronutrients Mn, Fe, Zn, Cu, Cl, B, Mo (manganese, iron, zinc, copper, chloride, boron and molybdenum).

- Carbon, hydrogen, and oxygen are usually not limited since they are freely available in the air and water.

Summary

Temperature affects many essential plant growth processes including most biochemical reactions in the plant. Light affects plants based on its intensity, duration and quality. Moisture is another essential for plant growth. CO_2 is required for photosynthesis. There are 16 essential nutrients which plants use. They are normally available in the soil and are classified by their use.

Resources

Free complementary PowerPoint:
http://www.tagmydoc.com/dl/1v43Gl/gk6j

Parker, R. 2010. Plant and soil science: Fundamentals and applications. Clifton Park, NY: Delmar Cengage Learning.

Plant Biology
http://www.bbc.co.uk/bitesize/higher/biology/cell_biology/photosynthesis/revision/5/

Assessment

1. T or F? Reaction rates decrease with higher temperatures.

2. T or F? Gravity water will attract or hold the water in the soil which makes it unavailable to the plant.

3. T or F? The major source of light is from the sun.

4. Photoperiodism is the growth response to the length of _____ period.
    a.) light   b) dark   c) dusk   d) time

5. CO_2 is taken in through the _____.
    a.) gravity   b.) petals   c.) stomata   d.) roots

Take the assessment online here:

http://tinyurl.com/PlntSci-6c

Hint: When the answer is incorrect, you will see: "Wrong answer! Go Back!"

Notes

20 Fertilizer Labels and Calculations

Major Concept

Understanding fertilizer labels and calculations are required to correctly apply fertilizers to crops.

Objectives

- Identify the information that must be stamped on fertilizer bags according to law
- Calculate the content of N-P-K in a fertilizer container
- Determine the fertilizer application needed to meet a crop's requirement for N, P or K

Link to Standards

PS.02. Apply principles of classification, plant anatomy, and plant physiology to plant production and management.

Key Terms

- Guaranteed analysis
- Fertilizer number
- Fertilizer grade
- WIN

Fertilizer Labels

- Information always included on the label:
  - Net weight
  - Brand and grade under which the commercial fertilizer is distributed.
  - Guaranteed analysis giving the minimum percentage of each nutrient claimed to be contained in the fertilizer.
  - Name and address of manufacturer.
- Other valuable information that may be found on the label:
  - Percentage (%) of water insoluble nitrogen (**WIN**)

- Potential Acidity
- Salt index
- Source or carrier
- Percentage of minor elements
  - ✓ The label also provides the consumer with the necessary information to make cost comparisons, calculate rates, and calibrate spreaders to deliver the recommended nutrient amounts.

Nutrient Content of Commercial Fertilizers

- The nutrient content of commercially available fertilizer is expressed as a percent called the **guaranteed analysis** or **fertilizer grade**.
  - This always appears as percentage total nitrogen (N), percentage available phosphate (P), or phosphoric acid and percentage soluble potash (K).
    - ✓ Nutrient content always appears in this order:
      1. Nitrogen (N)
      2. Phosphorus (P) [phosphate (P_2O_5), or phosphoric acid]
      3. Potassium (K) [potash (K_2O)]
- **Fertilizer number** refers to a ratio of nitrogen (N) to phosphorus (P) to potassium (K) and reflects the percentage of nutrients in the material.
  - 5-10-5 fertilizer has a total of 20% nutrients, with the other 80% of the material being inert or carrier material.
    - ✓ This is typically some inert material
- Using the analysis (grade) of the fertilizer and the total weight of the bag, the actual amount of the plant nutrients in the bag can be easily calculated.
  - For example, a 50 lb. bag of 5-10-15 contains 5% nitrogen, 10% phosphate and 15% potash.
  - By multiplying the nutrient percentages times the total weight in the bag, shows that the bag contains 2.5 lbs. of nitrogen, 5 lbs. of phosphate and 7.5 lbs. of potash (K).

✓ Also, the bag contains 15 lbs. of plant nutrients and 35 lbs. of inert ingredients.

Calculating the Best Buy

- Fertilizer A is a 16-8-8 complete fertilizer and sells for $19.95 per 50 lb bag;

- Whereas, fertilizer B is a 10-5-5 and costs $9.50 per 20 lb bag.

- Which is the best buy on the basis of nitrogen?

    1. Compile the necessary information:

	A	B
Analysis:	16-8-8	10-5-5
Cost:	$19.95/50 lbs	$9.50/20 lbs

    2. Calculate amount of N per bag = bag wt. x % N

A	B
50 lbs x 0.16 = 8 lbs N	20 lbs x 0.10 = 2 lbs N

    3. Calculate cost per lb N

    cost per bag/amount of N = x / 1 lb N per bag

    A $19.95 / 8 lbs N = x / 1 lb N   x = $2.50

    B $9.50 / 2 lbs N = x / 1 lb N   x = $4.75

    <u>Fertilizer A is the best buy</u>

Determining How Much Fertilizer to Apply to get Recommended Nutrient Amounts

- Assume: 16-8-8 fertilizer is being used; N recommendation is 1 lb/1,000 sq. ft.; the area is 16,725 sq. ft.

    o Total fertilizer = Recommended N rate

    1 lb N per 1,000 sq. ft. / % N in fertilizer = lbs of 16-8-8 needed for each 1000 sq. ft.

    1 / .16 = 6.25 (number of lbs of 16-8-8 to fertilize 1000 sq. ft.)

Find how many 1000 sq. ft. areas are in the area to be fertilized
16,725 / 1,000 = 16.725

6.25 x 16.725 = 105 lbs 16-8-8 fertilizer will be needed to treat 16,725 sq. ft. of turf.

- Amount of phosphorus (P) applied when recommended N rate is applied:
  Lbs of 16-8-8 x % P in fertilizer/number of 1000 sq ft areas to be fertilized.

  105 x .08 / 16.725 = 0.5 lb P_2O_5 per 1,000 sq. ft will be applied if fertilizer is applied at the recommended N rate.

- Amount of potassium (K) applied when recommended N rate is applied:
  Lbs of 16-8-8 x % P in fertilizer/number of 1000 sq ft areas to be fertilized.

  105 x .08 /16.725 = 0.5 lb. K_2O per 1,000 sq. ft. will be applied if fertilizer is applied at the recommended N rate.

Fertilizing Crops for Production

- Factors to consider before determining fertilizer application

  1. Production goal
  2. Yield goal
  3. Soil reserve
  4. Crop residue

- Commercial Fertilizer Quantity Calculation

  1. Record recommended quantity of nutrient: 60 lbs/acre

  2. Record the percentage of nutrient in the preferred product, muriate of potash.
     60%

  3. Convert the percentage of nutrient to a decimal fraction by multiplying the % by .01

     $\rightarrow$ 60 x 0.01

  4. Calculate the quantity of muriate of potash required in lbs/acre: divide the recommended quantity of nutrient by the nutrient content expressed as a decimal or a fraction.

     $$\frac{60 \text{ lbs/acre}}{0.60} = 100 \text{ lbs/acre}$$

Determining Fertilizer Need

- Production Goal: Total lbs/acre   N - P - K

    - ✓ Soil reserve   N - P - K
    - ✓ Crop residue   N
    - ✓ Manure   N - P - K
    - ✓ Commercial fertilizer + lb/A   N - P - K

- An Example

    - Calculating quantity of commercial fertilizer required to meet a nutrient recommendation.

    Pace Bean Farm:

    - Needs 60 lbs./A of potash (K_2O) on his soybean crop
    - Broadcasts muriate of potash (0-0-60) pre-plant

        60 x 0 =   0 lbs N
        60 x 0 =   0 lbs P_2O_5
        60 x .60 = 36 lbs K_2O

Determining Crop Production Goal

- A most important factor in developing accurate nutrient management plans is determining realistic production goals.

    - Producers often strive for crop yield goals they would like to obtain, but cannot achieve due to factors beyond their control. This wastes resources.

    - Realistic crop yields can be determined by:

        1. Looking at the crop production history of the field.

        2. Reviewing the Soil Survey Map and Soil Capability Chart (these provide soil engineer's assessments at the potential production ability of the soil in the field).

        3. Investigating how the crop species and varieties grown in an area and in research and demonstration plots.

4. Checking with the Farm Service Agency (FSA) records on the yields of some crops that are reported to them by producers.

5. Experimenting with a small, limited planting of a new crop before committing to a large planting provides valuable experience on how to grow the crop and what kind of yield to expect.

Determining Yield Goal

- Actual crop yields from the farm are best for setting yield estimates.

    o Taking the average yield for typical crop production years grown in a certain field can provide a good estimate of yield.

    o Taking an average of three of the top five growing seasons can make another yield estimate.

Soil Reserve

- Keeping an eye on the nutrients in the soil reserve is essential to maintaining good soil fertility.

    o Soil testing for these nutrients is simple, economical and can be obtained through private industry and university labs.

    o Soil tests should be done annually for high production crops like alfalfa and annual crops.

    o Permanent pastures, grass and mixed hay fields can be soil tested every three to five years once the fertility level for best plant growth has been met.

Crop Residue

- Plant fertility benefits left in the soil by a previous crop is often overlooked and not taken advantage of by producers.

    o Leguminous crops provide the most benefit to following crops since they "fix" nitrogen (N) and leave it in the soil for following crops to utilize.

        ✓ The amount of N left depends on the species of legume and the stand density and maturity.

        ✓ Leguminous crops can be used as crops grown for either cash, or animal feed, or as a cover crop.

Common Commercial Fertilizers

- Urea   46 - 0 - 0
- Ammonium nitrate   34 - 0 - 0
- UAN   30 - 0 - 0
- Ammonium sulfate   21 - 0 - 0
- Diammonium phosphate   18 - 46 - 0
- Triple superphosphate   0 - 46 - 0
- Muriate of potash   0 - 0 - 60

How Much (N) to Feed Plants

- For many plants the N recommendations can be found in tables on the label.

- For example the table below provides N recommendations for various plants (based on products with 13-17% N).

Nitrogen Fertilizer Recommendations

Crop/Plant	Amount per	Ammonium nitrate or ammonium phosphate	Ammonium sulfate	Calcium nitrate	Urea	When to apply
Annual Vegetables	60-foot row during each growing season	3 cups plus 3 tbsp.	2 ¾ cups	2 ¼ cups plus 2 tbsp.	4 ¼ cups	Half early in the season; repeat in 4-6 weeks
Bulbs	Plant during each growing	2 tbsp.	1½ tsp.	1 tbsp. plus 1 tsp.	2½ tbsp.	When bulb leaves emerge, fertilize as you water season or scatter on soil around plant
Citrus	100 sq ft under leaf	3 cups	2½ cups plus 2 tbsp.	2¼ cups	4 cups	Half in May, half in June

Crop/Plant	Amount per	Ammonium nitrate or ammonium phosphate	Ammonium sulfate	Calcium nitrate	Urea	When to apply
	canopy per year					
Deciduous Fruit & Nut Trees	100 sq ft under leaf canopy per year	3 cups	2½ cups plus 2 tbsp.	2¼ cups	4 cups	Half in April, half in June
Roses	Plant during each growing season	6½ tbsp.	5½ tbsp.	4½ tbsp.	½ cup	One-third when new growth starts; repeat after each bloom cycle
Others	100 sq ft under leaf canopy per year	¾ cup plus 1 tbsp.	½ cup plus 3 tbsp.	½ cup plus 1 tbsp.	1 cup	Half in April, half in June
Evergreen Shrubs/trees, Rhododendrons	10 sq ft under leaf canopy per year	¼ cup	3½ tbsp.	3 tbsp.	1/3 cup	Half as flower buds start to swell (March/April); repeat after deadheading flowers (May)
Others, including Conifers	10 sq ft under leaf canopy per year	¼ cup	3½ tbsp.		1/3 cup	Half in mid-spring; repeat after bloom or, with conifers, 2 months later
Flowering Annuals	100 sq ft during each growing season	2 cups	1¾ cups	1½ cups	2 – 2/3 cups	Half immediately after planting; repeat 6 weeks later
Flowering Perennials	Plant per growing	2 cups, 3 tbsp.	1 cup	¾ cup plus 2½	1½ cups	Half when new growth has

Crop/Plant	Amount per	Ammonium nitrate or ammonium phosphate	Ammonium sulfate	Calcium nitrate	Urea	When to apply
	season			tbsp.	plus 1½ tbsp.	started; repeat 6 weeks later
Lawns	1,000 sq ft per year	19 lbs	19 lbs	19 lbs	19 lbs	One-third of it at three equal intervals spanning the growing season

Summary

The fertilizer label provides the consumer with the necessary information to make cost comparisons, calculate rates, and calibrate spreaders to deliver the recommended nutrient amounts. For many plants, the N recommendations can be found in tables on the label.

Resources

Free complementary PowerPoint:
http://www.tagmydoc.com/dl/18d4QK/gk6b

Parker, R. 2010. Plant and soil science: Fundamentals and applications. Clifton Park, NY: Delmar Cengage Learning. (Pgs. 149-153).

Fertilizer Reckoning for the Mathematically Challenged
http://www.agry.purdue.edu/ext/corn/news/articles.02/fert_math-0326.html

Soil and Fertility
http://www.lsuagcenter.com/en/lawn_garden/commercial_horticulture/turfgrass/soil_fertility/Calculating+Fertilizer+Application+Rates.htm

Assessment

1. T or F? Fertilizer labels do not always include the name and address of manufacturer.

2. T or F? How much to feed plants can be found by referring to the fertilizer label.

3. T or F? Fertilizer net weight will always be found on the label.

4. T or F? Guaranteed analysis giving the minimum percentage of each nutrient claimed to be contained in the fertilizer will always be on the label.

5. If 60 lbs of starter (6-10-8) were applied per acre, how many pounds of phosphorus are applied to an acre?
   a.) 4.8   b.) 3.0   c.) 6.0   d.) 3.6

Take the assessment online here:

http://tinyurl.com/PlntSci-6a

Hint: When the answer is incorrect, you will see: "Wrong answer! Go Back!"

Notes

21 Fertilizer Applications

Major Concept

Fertilizer application method depends on factors such as timing, type of crop, type of fertilizer, soil, water source.

Objectives

- Name three common times of fertilizer application
- List four ways to apply pre-plant fertilizers
- Define foliar applications, top dressing and band placement
- Describe calibration of a fertilizer spreader

Link to Standards

PS.02. Apply principles of classification, plant anatomy, and plant physiology to plant production and management.

Key Terms

- Adjuvant
- Broadcast
- Calibrate
- Drop spreader
- Pesticide
- Post-emergence
- Pull-type spreader
- Side dressing
- Top dressing

Methods of Fertilizer Application

- Fertilizers are used to supply nutrients that are not present in the soil in amounts necessary to meet the needs of the growing crop. When choosing the methods of application, growers should consider:

    o Rooting characteristics of the crop to be planted.

    o Crop's demand for various nutrients at different stages of growth.

- Physical and chemical characteristics of the soil.
- Physical and chemical characteristics of the fertilizer materials to be applied.
- Availability of moisture.
- Kind of irrigation systems used if irrigation is the only, or major, source of water.

Pre-plant Applications: Broadcast or Injection

- **Broadcast**
  - Consists of uniformly distributing dry or liquid materials over the soil surface with one of these methods: drop spreader, pull-type spreader, self-propelled spreader and liquid spreader.

- **Drop Spreader**
  - An inverted triangle-shaped hopper is mounted between two wheels and usually pulled by a tractor or pickup truck.

- **Pull-type Spreader**
  - Consists of a bin mounted on a two- or four-wheeled trailer frame and pulled by a tractor or truck.
    - ✓ Can be pulled across the field at speeds up to 20 mph.
    - ✓ Fertilizer is usually spread by a horizontal spinning disc in a 20- to 40-foot swath.

- Self-propelled Spreader
  - Consists of a large bin mounted on a large truck or a special three- or four-wheeled vehicle equipped with flotation tires.
    - ✓ Can hold from 7-10 tons of dry fertilizer material.
    - ✓ The fertilizer is spread in a swath 30 to 60 feet wide by means of one or two spinning horizontal discs at the rear of the bin at speeds up to 35 mph.

- Liquid Spreader
  - The basic requirements for a liquid fertilizer broadcast applicator consist of a tank, pressure gauge and regulator, pump, pipes, hoses, fittings, nozzles, and a boom.

- ✓ The applicator can be mounted on a truck, flotation vehicle or trailer, or directly on a tractor.

- ✓ The speed of application is determined by the rate of flow.

- Injection

    o Refers to placing fertilizers below the soil surface.

    - ✓ Accomplished by using tool bar-mounted knives or shank openers, drop pipes for liquid fertilizers, or flexible tubes or dry fertilizers, deliver fertilizers into the channels made by the opening tools.

    o All fertilizers that can be broadcast on the soil surface can also be injected.

    o An excellent method of putting immobile nutrients into the crop root zone, where they may be more efficiently used.

At-Planting Applications

- Placement with Seed

    o Fertilizer placed directly with the seed is frequently called "pop-up."

    - ✓ Purpose is to get the crop off to a fast start.

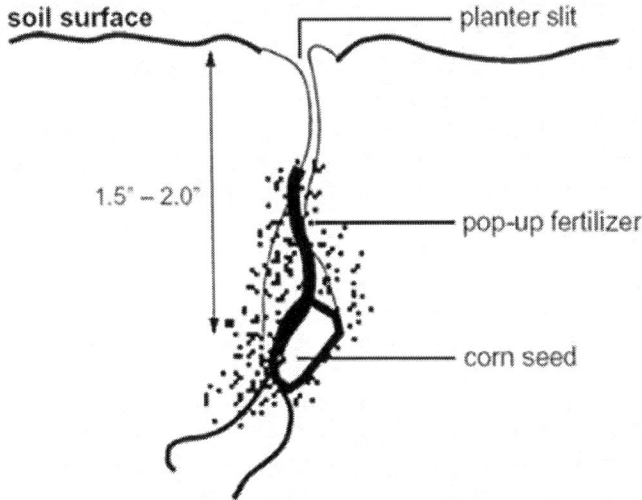

    o Fertilizer hopper attached to the planter, and the fertilizer is metered out according to predetermined rates.

- Only low rates of pop-up fertilizer should be used, particularly with respect to nitrogen (N) and potash (K), since germination can be reduced.

- Band Placement

    o Consists of placing fertilizer to the side of and/or below the seed.

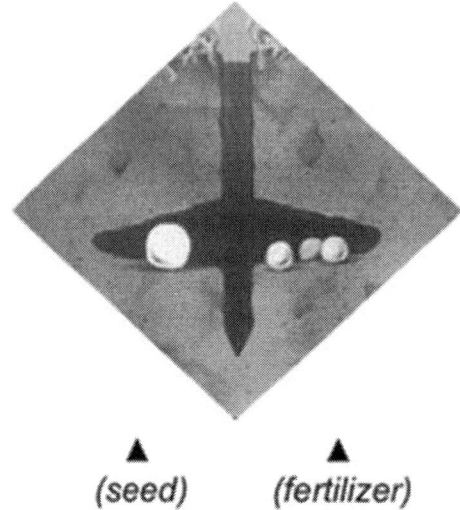

▲ ▲
(seed)   (fertilizer)

    o Applicators usually mounted on the same tool bar or bed sled as the seeder/planter and are powered by the same drive that powers the seeder/planter.

    o A tube connected to the fertilizer hopper delivers the fertilizer to a furrow opened by a shoe or disc.

        ✓ Depending on the crop and soil type, the band may be placed to the side and below the seed, or it may be placed directly below the seed.

Post-Emergence Applications: Side or Top Dressing

- **Post-emergence** – application of an herbicide after weed or plant has emerged (and is usually visible) from the soil.

- **Side Dressing**

    o Refers to the placement of fertilizers beside the crop rows.

    o Applications may be made at the same time the rows are cultivated.

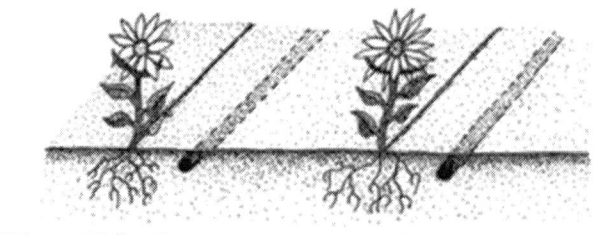

FERTILIZER PLACED IN BANDS BESIDE ROWS

- Both liquid and dry fertilizers usually consists of two large hoppers mounted on tool bars on either side of a tractor, ahead of the operator, or one or more hoppers mounted on a three-point hitch tool bar behind the operator.

- Flexible tubing connects the hopper to spouts mounted ahead of, between, or behind discs or shovels.

    ✓ Desired amount of fertilizer is metered into a small furrow and is covered by the cultivating unit.

- **Top Dressing**

    - Consists of spreading fertilizers on the soil surface after crop emergence.

    - Same equipment used for pre-plant broadcast applications of dry and liquid fertilizer may be used for top dressing.

    - Equipment should be equipped with flotation tires to minimize crop damage and soil compaction.

        ✓ Aerial applications may be used to eliminate damage from equipment.

        ✓ Aerial top-dressed applications are commonly made on rice.

Water-Run Applications: Open or Closed Systems

- Savings in time, labor, equipment, and fuel costs are advantages of water-run fertilizer applications.

- Applications may be pre-plant or post emergence, using either liquid or dry fertilizer materials.

    - Open Systems – These systems include lined and unlined open ditches and gated pipes that are used for furrow and flood irrigation methods.

    - Closed Systems – These systems include sprinkler, spitter, trickle, drip, and dual-wall tubing systems.

Foliar Applications

- Nutrients applied to plant foliage as sprays or through over-head sprinkler systems.

    - Used in situations in which a quick response is required, such as when an unexpected deficiency develops during the growing season or where soil-applied nutrients were ineffective.

- Micronutrient deficiencies can frequently be corrected by foliar application.

- Concentration is generally less than 1 to 2% to prevent injury to foliage.

  - Addition of an **adjuvant** (herbicide performance enhancer) to the spray recommended for better coverage.

- Most crops respond better to foliar feeding when the nutrients are applied during the morning hours.

Fertilizer-Pesticide Mixtures

- Used to fertilize crops and control soil-borne insects, diseases, nematodes, and weeds.

  - When making a dry fertilizer-pesticide mix, the fertilizer should be impregnated with the **pesticide** (substance used to destroy harmful organisms) to avoid segregation.

  - Mixture must be applied within a short time or the pesticide may deteriorate.

- Pesticides can be successfully mixed and applied with both liquid mix fertilizers and liquid nitrogen (N) solutions.

Calibration of Fertilizer Spreaders

- Drop Spreaders: The following procedure should be followed to **calibrate** (mark with a gauge or instrument with a standard scale of readings) a drop spreader:

  - Measure width of the spreader.

  - Measure off 100 ft and mark starting and ending points.

  - Attach the catch pan to the spreader.

  - Be sure the holes are closed in the hopper and fill the hopper 1/2 full with materials to be applied.

  - Starting 10 ft before the starting line, push the spreader and open the hopper holes as you go over the starting point.

  - Continue over the 100 ft distance at normal walking speed, and close the hopper holes as you go over the finish line.

  - Carefully remove the hopper pan and weigh the collected material.

- Solve the following equation:

  Weight of material dispensed = x
  Spreader width x 100 ft.   1,000 sq. ft.

- Compare the material applied per 1,000 sq. ft. with the target application rate, and adjust hopper openings to deliver more or less material if necessary.

- Repeat steps 3 through 9 until target rate is achieved.

• Rotary Spreaders (The following procedure should be followed to calibrate a rotary spreader)

  - Fill spreader with material.

  - Measure the width of application.

    ✓ This can be done by a second person watching and marking the distance which material is broadcast to the left and right of the spreader.

  - Empty the hopper.

  - Measure a distance of 100 feet, and mark the starting and ending points.

  - Fill the hopper with a known amount of material (5 lb.).

  - Giving a 10 ft. head start, open the hopper holes as the starting line is passed and continue to the finish line at normal speed.

  - Close the hopper holes as the finish line is crossed.

  - Empty the remaining material onto the plastic sheet.

  - Transfer material to the bucket and weigh.

  - Solve the following equation:

    Weight of material dispensed = x
    100 ft. x width of application (ft.)   1,000 sq. ft.

  - Compare the material applied per 1,000 sq. ft. with the target application rate and adjust the hopper openings to deliver more or less material if necessary.

  - Repeat steps 5 through 11 until the desired rate is achieved.

Summary

Fertilizers are used to supply nutrients that are not present in the soil in amounts necessary to meet the needs of the growing crop. When choosing the methods of applications there are several things to consider: Pre-plant applications, at-planting applications, post-emergence applications, water-run applications, foliar applications, fertilizer-pesticide mixtures and calibration of fertilizer spreaders.

Resources

Free complementary PowerPoint:
http://www.tagmydoc.com/dl/1Gq9ef/gk6Z

Parker, R. 2010. Plant and soil science: Fundamentals and applications. Clifton Park, NY: Delmar Cengage Learning. (Pgs. 149-154).

Nutrient Management and Fertilizer
http://www.epa.gov/agriculture/tfer.html

Managing Agricultural Fertilizer Application to Prevent Contamination of Drinking Water
http://www.epa.gov/safewater/sourcewater/pubs/fs_swpp_fertilizer.pdf

Assessment

1. When choosing the methods of application, one important thing to consider is the availability of _____.
   a.) moisture   b.) equipment   c.) applicants   d.) fertilizers

2. Fertilizer placed directly with the seed is frequently called _____.
   a.) pop up   b.) drop spreader   c.) injection   d.) pre-fertilization

3. T or F? Band placement consists of placing fertilizer to the side of and/or below the seed.

4. T or F? Basic requirements for a drop spreader consist of a tank, pressure gauge and regulator, pump, pipes, hoses, fittings, nozzles and a boom.

5. Most crops respond better to foliar feeding when the nutrients are applied during the _____.
   a.) night time hours   b.) early spring   c.) summer months   d.) morning hours

Take assessment online here:

http://tinyurl.com/PlntSci-6

Hint: When the answer is incorrect, you will see: "Wrong answer! Go Back!"

Notes

22 Photosynthesis

Major Concept

Photosynthesis captures and converts light energy and carbon dioxide into chemical energy for plants and animals providing oxygen as a by-product.

Objectives

- Describe the photosynthesis reaction in chemical terms
- Define autotrophic and heterotrophic
- Give one example of a photosynthate
- Identify the light reaction and the dark reaction

Link to Standards

PS.02. Apply principles of classification, plant anatomy, and plant physiology to plant production and management.

Key Terms

- Autotrophic
- Chlorophyll
- Chloroplast
- Dark reaction
- Heterotrophic
- Light reaction
- Photosynthates
- Photosynthesis

Importance of Photosynthesis

- Photosynthesis is the "reaction of life."

- Conversion of the sun's energy into a form humans and other living creatures can use is done almost entirely by plants through **photosynthesis**.

    o Root meanings of the words "photo" (light) and "synthesis" (to put together).

    o During photosynthesis, a plant converts the energy of light to chemical energy.

    o Occurs in green plant possessing chlorophyll.

    o Original source of all important fuels including oil, coal, wood and natural gas.

- Source of all foods, since all animals are dependent on plants at some point in the food chain.

$$6CO_2 + 6H_2O \xrightarrow[\text{Enzymes}]{\text{Energy}} C_6H_{12}O_6 + 6O_2$$

6 carbon dioxide   6 water   glucose   12 oxygen

- Photosynthesis accomplishes three important processes in plants:

    1. Transforms light energy from the sun into chemical energy which can be transported and stored in plants.

    2. "Fixes" carbon from carbon dioxide (CO_2) in the atmosphere to a solid form.

    3. Produces oxygen as an important by-product.

- Energy Transformation

    - Earth receives vast quantities of energy from the sun each day in the form of solar radiation or light.

    - Through photosynthesis, radiation energy is changed to chemical energy.

    - Principal product of photosynthesis is sugar, one energy-yielding chemical.

- Carbon Fixation

    - Photosynthesis "fixes" vast quantities of carbon from atmospheric carbon dioxide and converts into carbohydrates.

    - Energy is used by plants themselves in conducting their life processes, and by other creatures using plants as a food source.

- Oxygen Production

    - While oxygen is considered a by-product of the photosynthetic process, plants produce enough to be considered the primary source, worldwide.

    - Rain-forests of the tropics, and the vast populations of phytoplankton in the oceans, produce the oxygen necessary to sustain respiration processes and animal life.

- Photosynthesis makes plants unique:
    - Because of their ability to "produce" their own energy directly, they are self-sufficient or **autotrophic**.
    - All other forms of life, including animals, fungi, bacteria, and even viruses derive their sustenance from other living creatures are **heterotrophic.**

Process of Photosynthesis

- Requirements of photosynthesis are:
    - A living plant, in good health
    - An ample supply of carbon dioxide (CO_2) from the atmosphere
    - Water (H_2O), from the soil or atmosphere
    - Light, usually from the sun
- Factors affecting photosynthesis are:
    - Light quality
    - Light intensity and duration
    - Carbon dioxide concentration
    - Temperature
    - Water quality
- Products of photosynthesis are:
    - Carbohydrates (CHO's) such as sugars, starches and other complex compounds refer to these products collectively as "**photosynthates**"
    - Water (H_2O)
    - Oxygen (O_2)

- Photosynthesis is a collection of many complex reactions involving many pathways and enzymes.

    o These reactions can be summarized into one basic reaction expressed as follows:

    ✓ In a green plant:

    $$6CO_2 + 12H_2O \longrightarrow C_6H_{12}O_6 + 6H_2O + 6O_2$$
    (Carbon Dioxide + Water → Sugar + Water + Oxygen)

- Reaction reads as follows:

    o "Six molecules of carbon dioxide plus twelve molecules of water combine, in the presence of a green plant and light energy, to form one molecule of sugar plus six molecules of water and six molecules of oxygen."

    o Water appears on both sides of the equation so the reaction for photosynthesis is expressed as:

    ✓ Green Plant

    $$6CO_2 + 6H_2O \xrightarrow{\text{Light Energy}} C_6H_{12}O_6 + 6O_2$$

    ✓ Six waters subtracted from each side of the equation, leaves an expression of the "net" photosynthesis reaction.

- Light and Dark Reactions

    o The overall process described above is the result of two primary reactions in the plant cells - the "light" reaction and the "dark" reaction.

    o **Light reaction** occurs only during the daylight, and is driven by the energy of sunlight. In the light reaction. Light received by the plant is used to create energy-holding chemicals, used in the later stages of photosynthesis for other metabolic process.

    o Dark reaction takes place at any time (it is not dependent on light for energy).

    ✓ In the **dark reaction**, the energy-holding chemicals created in the light reaction are used to change carbon dioxide (CO_2) to carbohydrates (sugar) and water.

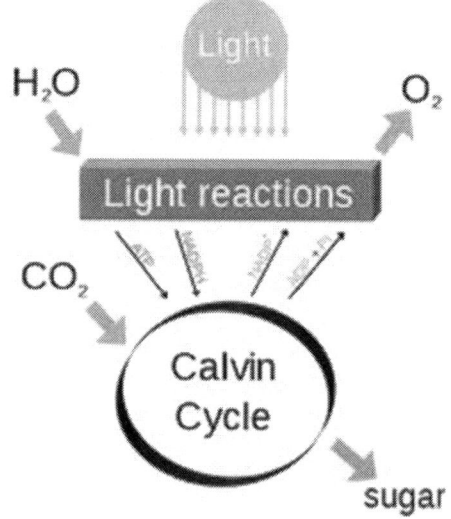

✓ Process is varied and involves many different steps in different types of plants.

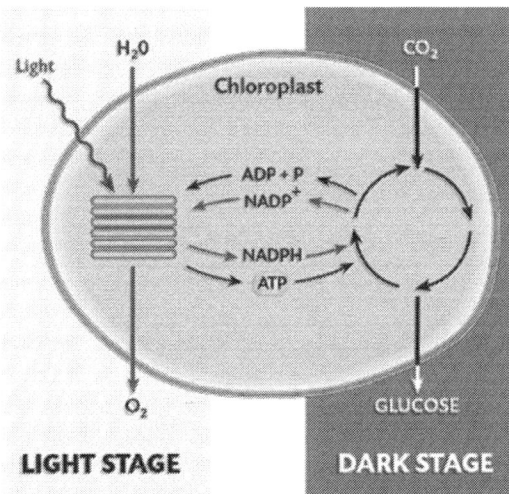

- Photosynthetic chemical activity takes place within plant cell organelles, called **chloroplasts**.

  o Chloroplasts are present mostly in leaves, but are also present in green stems and unripe fruit.

  o Photosynthesis is dependent on the presence of the chemical **chlorophyll**, which is green, within the chloroplasts.

- Efficiency of Photosynthesis

  o Light energy is not converted very efficiently to chemical energy during photosynthesis (usually between 0.1% and 3.0%).

  o Photosynthesis is going on constantly when the precursors are present.

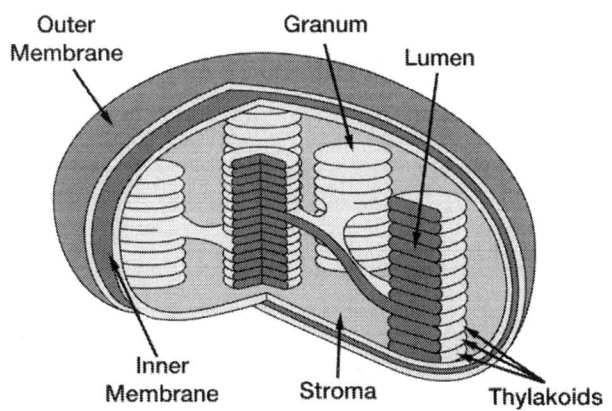

Summary

Conversion of the sun's energy into a form man and other living creatures can use is done almost entirely by plants through photosynthesis. Photosynthesis makes plants unique because of their ability to directly produce their own energy. The overall process of photosynthesis is the result of the light and dark reactions in the plant cells or plant organelles called chloroplasts. Factors affecting photosynthesis are light quality, light intensity, light duration, carbon dioxide concentration, and temperature and water availability.

Resources

Free complementary PowerPoint:
http://www.tagmydoc.com/dl/G8VKW/gk6q

Parker, R. 2010. Plant and soil science: Fundamentals and applications. Clifton Park, NY: Delmar Cengage Learning. (Pgs. 280-288).

Photosynthesis
http://faculty.clintoncc.suny.edu/faculty/michael.gregory/files/bio%20101/bio%20101%20lectures/photosynthesis/photosyn.htm

Photosynthesis Introduction
http://www.phschool.com/science/biology_place/biocoach/photosynth/intro.html

Assessment

1. T or F? All animals are dependent on plants at some point in the food chain.

2. Photosynthesis transforms light energy from the _____ into chemical energy.
   a.) heat   b.) wind   c.) plants   d.) sun

3. T or F? Photosynthesis is a collection of many complex reactions involving many pathways and enzymes.

4. Earth receives vast quantities of _____ from the sun each day in the form of solar radiation or light.
   a.) plants   b.) carbon dioxide   c.) water   d.) energy

5. T or F? The dark reaction takes place only at night.

Take the assessment online here:

http://tinyurl.com/PlantSci-9

Hint: When the answer is incorrect, you will see: "Wrong answer! Go Back!"

Notes

23 Respiration

Major Concept

The process of respiration requires an energy source and occurs in all living things.

Objectives

- Compare respiration to photosynthesis
- List three factors affecting respiration
- Provide two examples of how respiration affects agricultural production

Link to Standards

PS.01. Develop and implement a crop management plan for a given production goal that accounts for environmental factors.

PS.02. Apply principles of classification, plant anatomy, and plant physiology to plant production and management.

Key Terms

- Adenosine diphosphate (ADP)
- Adenosine triphosphate (ATP)
- Byproducts
- Citric acid cycle
- Combustion
- Glycolysis
- Oxidative phosphorylation
- Respiration

Respiration Process

- **Respiration** is the controlled expenditure of an organism's energy reserves to sustain the life processes and is necessary in all living cells.

    o A plant respires 24 hours a day in all of it cells, while photosynthesis occurs only during daylight hours in tissues containing chlorophyll.

- Respiration uses up stored energy and gives off heat.

    o Respiration is the "opposite" of photosynthesis because it releases energy, evolves carbon dioxide (CO_2) and uses up oxygen (O_2). Actual biochemical pathways are not closely related, so the net result of respiration is opposite the net result of photosynthesis.

- Respiration and combustion are similar processes.

  - When a carbohydrate such as sugar is burned, the resulting **byproducts** are carbon dioxide (CO_2), water (H_2O) and heat. These same byproducts result from respiration.

- The difference is the rate of the reactions. Respiration is a controlled, "stepwise" release of energy put to useful purposes by the plant, as it occurs.

  - In contrast, **combustion** releases energy all at one time, like a fire or an explosion.

- Like photosynthesis, respiration is a total of many reactions, some of which are complex. These reactions can be summarized as follows:

$$C_6H_{12}O_6 + 6O_2 \rightarrow 6CO_2 + 6H_2O + ENERGY$$
$$\text{Sugar + Oxygen} \rightarrow \text{Carbon Dioxide + Water + ENERGY}$$

- Sugar is the main "fuel" for respiration.

  - Many other chemicals such as starches, fats, proteins and organic acids are consumed in respiration as it occurs in gradual steps through glycolysis, the citric acid cycle, and the electron transport chain that result in conversion of the energy stored in glucose to usable chemical energy in the form of adenosine triphosphate (ATP).

  - ATP is constantly used or converted to adenosine diphosphate (ADP) and regenerated into ATP Waste products of cellular respiration (carbon dioxide [CO_2] and water [H_2O]) are released through exhaled air, sweat and urine.

- **Glycolysis** is a metabolic pathway that is found in the cytoplasm of cells in all living organisms.

  - The process converts one molecule of glucose into two molecules of pyruvate (pyruvic acid), and makes energy in the form of two net molecules of ATP.

  - **Citric acid cycle**, also called Krebs cycle or the tricarboxylic acid cycle, produces acetyl-CoA from the pyruvate when oxygen is present. Once acetyl-CoA is formed, two processes can occur, aerobic or anaerobic respiration.

  - When oxygen is present, the mitochondria will undergo aerobic respiration, which leads to the Krebs cycle. However, if oxygen is not present, fermentation of the pyruvate molecule will occur.

- ✓ In the presence of oxygen, when acetyl-CoA is produced, the molecule then enters the citric acid cycle (Krebs cycle) inside the mitochondrial matrix, and gets oxidized to CO_2.

- ✓ **Oxidative phosphorylation** occurs in the mitochondrial cristae. It comprises the electron transport chain that establishes a proton gradient (chemiosmotic potential) across the inner membrane by oxidizing the NADH produced from the Krebs cycle.

- ✓ ATP is synthesized by the ATP synthase enzyme when the chemiosmotic gradient is used to drive the phosphorylation of ADP.

- ✓ The electrons are finally transferred to exogenous oxygen and, with the addition of two protons, water (H_2O) is formed.

- ✓ The complete oxidation of each glucose molecule to CO_2 and H_2O produces 38 ATPs.

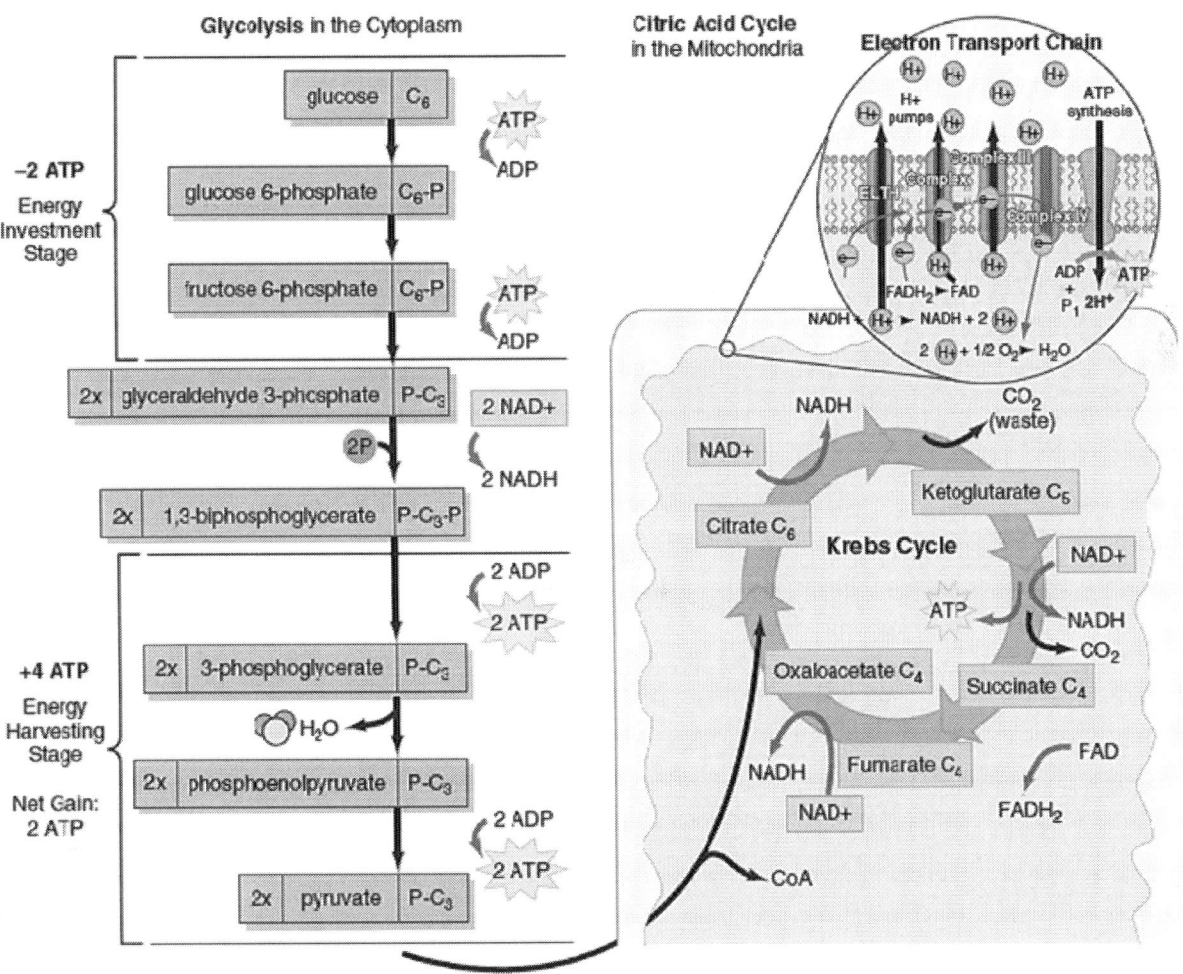

Factors Affecting Respiration

- Temperature, oxygen concentration, soil conditions and light affect the rate of respiration.

  - Temperature: Respiration increases as the temperature increases. At normal temperatures, respiration increases two to four times for each 18°(F) rise in temperature.

  - Oxygen Concentration: Low concentrations of oxygen will result in a lower rate of respiration.

  - Soil Conditions: Compacted or water-logged soils exclude air, and therefore oxygen so respiration in a plant's root system is inhibited.

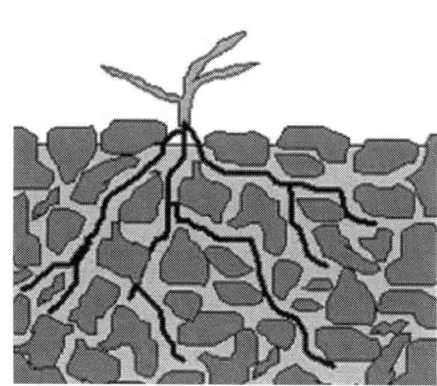

  - Light: Since plants grown in low light photosynthesize at a reduced rate, the level of available carbohydrates, sugars among others, and rate of respiration, is also reduced.

Importance of Respiration to Agriculture

- Crop Management: Since respiration is taking place 24 hours a day, plants must be able to photosynthesize enough during the day to provide for respiration during the day and night.

  - Most plants grow best when night temperatures are about 9°(F) lower than daytime temperatures.

  - Night-time temperatures in a greenhouse kept too warm will cause respiration rates to be high and stall a crop's growth. Temperatures too cool lower respiration rates causing stagnation of the crop, and slowing the growth process.

- Post-Harvest Handling of Crops: Respiration is closely tied to the degradation or breakdown of the tissues (rotting), of harvested crops. Slowing respiration rates after harvest improves the quality of goods reaching the consumer.

  - Two strategies to slow respiration are:

    1. Refrigeration: Cooling a fruit, vegetable or floral crop helps to slow the rate of respiration and the associated deterioration processes.

2. Increasing atmospheric concentration of nitrogen (N): This pushes oxygen out of the air surrounding the crop bringing the rate of respiration to a very low level. This process is used to store a variety of fruit crops over a long period of time, for example, apples.

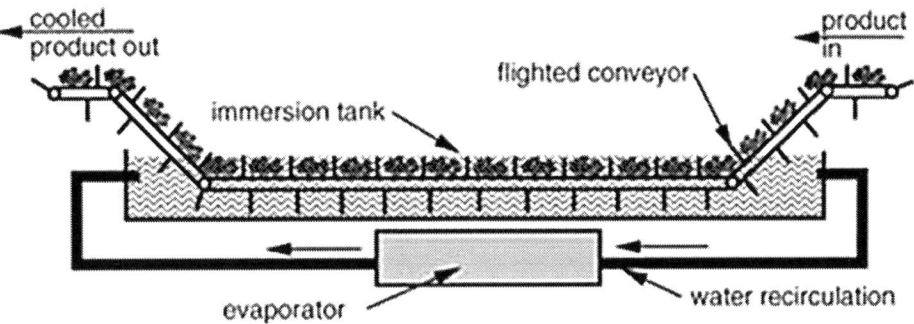

Vegetable Processing Hydrocooler

Summary

Respiration occurs in all living cells. It is the controlled expenditure of an organism's energy reserves to sustain its life processes. Respiration uses up stored energy, and gives off heat and CO_2. Respiration is a total of many reactions, some of which are complex. Factors affecting respiration include: temperature, oxygen concentration, soil conditions and light. Understanding respiration is important to crop management and post-harvest handling of crops.

Resources

Free complementary PowerPoint:
http://www.tagmydoc.com/dl/1QBPX7/gk71

Parker, R. 2010. Plant and soil science: Fundamentals and applications. Clifton Park, NY: Delmar Cengage Learning. (Pgs. 299-303).

Aboveground Respiration
http://biology.duke.edu/bio265/zhangmin/Aboveground.htm

Cycle of Photosynthesis & Respiration
http://www.vtaide.com/png/photosynthesis.htm

Assessment

1. T or F? A plant only respires while the sun is shining.
2. T or F? Respiration is the opposite of photosynthesis.

3. Identify one of the byproducts of respiration?
    a.) oxygen   b.) water   c.) cool temperature   d.) sugar

4. The main "fuel" for respiration is _____.
    a.) oxygen   b.) soil   c.) water   d.) sugar

5. T or F? Most plants grow best when night temperatures are about 19° (F) lower than daytime temperatures.

Take the assessment online here:

http://tinyurl.com/PlntSci-10

Hint: When the answer is incorrect, you will see: "Wrong answer! Go Back!"

Notes

24 Mitosis

Major Concept

Plant propagation and growth require mitosis.

Objectives

- Define mitosis
- Name five steps in mitosis

Link to Standards

PS.02. Apply principles of classification, plant anatomy, and plant physiology to plant production and management.

PS.03. Propagate, culture and harvest plants and plant products based on current industry standards.

Key Terms

- Anaphase
- Cell plate
- Daughter cells
- Furrowing
- Interphase
- Metaphase
- Mitosis
- Parent cells
- Prophase
- Telophase

Mitosis

- **Mitosis** is the division of cells in which the genetic material of the cell is duplicated exactly.

    o Cells simply divide and produce new cells like themselves.

    o Daughter cells have the same genetic makeup as **parent cells**.

    ✓ Process involves six basic steps.

Steps of Mitosis

- Step 1: The Resting Stage - called **Interphase**.

    o   This is the period between one division and the next. Individual chromosomes are not visible but the nuclear membrane is visible.

    o   Although chromosomes cannot be seen, they are present inside the nucleus. Chromosomes are the parts in the nucleus that control inherited traits.

    o   During this period, a most important event takes place; each chromosome makes an exact copy of itself. For example, if there are four chromosomes (or "two pair") in a resting cell, there are eight after copying.

- Step 2 Preparing to Divide - called **Prophase.**

    o   Identical chromosomes are joined together. There are now two complete sets of chromosomes in the nucleus.

    o   Chromosomes are now coiled tightly. The coiled chromosomes can be seen through a microscope.

    o   Nuclear membrane begins to disappear at this time.

- Step 3: Mitosis Starting - called **Metaphase**.

    o   There is no longer a division between the nucleus and the cytoplasm.

    o   Chromosomes become thicker and shorter and are now easier to see.

    o   The nuclear membrane has faded away. If the cell in Step 1 had four chromosomes, there are now four double chromosomes.

    o   After making a copy, each chromosome appears as a doubled chromosome.

        ✓ The original and copies appear side by side and are attached to each other.

    o   Pairs of identical chromosomes line up in the center of the cell. Thin fibers called spindle fibers attach to the chromosomes.

        ✓ These fibers define the direction in which the chromosomes will later move into the two "daughter cells".

- Step 4: Mitosis Continuing - called **Anaphase**.

  o Pairs of identical chromosomes separate from each other.

  o Chromosomes move toward the center of each new cell.

  o As one member of each pair moves to the end of the cell, the other member of the pair moves to the other end of the cell.

  o There are now two groups of identical chromosomes at opposite ends of the cell.

  ✓ These two groups are composed of four identical chromosomes.

  o Chromosomes are once again single stranded and identical to originals.

- Step 5: Mitosis - called **Telophase**.

  o A nuclear membrane begins to form around both sets of chromosomes.

  o Chromosomes "uncoil" and no longer appear as distinct structures.

  o Cytoplasm separates as a new cell membrane (or membrane-like material) forming in the middle of the old parent cell.

  ✓ This is called **furrowing** in animal cells, in which the cell pinches in on all sides until two daughter cells are formed.

  ✓ Because of the structure of plant cells, they do not furrow; instead a **cell plate** is formed between the two daughter cells.

  o Original **parent cell** has become two new "**daughter**" cells with identical chromosomes and is smaller than the original cell from which they came.

  o Each cell can grow and divide again.

  ✓ There are now two cells and each again has four chromosomes, the same number as the original "parent" cell.

- Step 6: The new cells return to the Interphase.

Summary

Mitosis is the division of cells in which the genetic material of the cell is duplicated exactly. The cells simply divide and produce new cells like themselves. Daughter cells have the same genetic makeup as parent cells. The steps of mitosis are as follows: Step 1: Resting Stage – called Interphase. Step 2: Preparing to Divide – called Prophase. Step 3: Mitosis starting – called Metaphase. Step 4: Mitosis continuing – called Anaphase. Step 5: Mitosis – called Telophase. The new cells return to the Interphase.

Resources

Free complementary PowerPoint:
http://www.tagmydoc.com/dl/1yvzgK/gk75

Parker, R. 2010. Plant and soil science: Fundamentals and applications. Clifton Park, NY: Delmar Cengage Learning. (Pgs. 78-80).

Glass M. and R. Parker. 2009. Fundamentals of plant science. Clifton Park, NY: Delmar Cengage Learning. (Pgs. 168-172).

Free app for an iPad: Mitosis Interactive Learning Experience
http://www.mitosisapp.com/index.html

Plant Cell Mitosis
http://www.youtube.com/watch?v=4govZdjEBrs

Assessment

1. During mitosis, the cells simply _____ and produce new cells like themselves.
a.) dissolve   b.) uncoil   c.) divide   d.) furrow

2. T or F? Chromosomes control inherited traits.

3. During metaphase, thin fibers called _____ attach themselves to the chromosomes.
   a.) spindle fibers   b.) chromosomes   c.) daughter cells   d.) strands

4. During which phase are two groups of identical chromosomes at opposite ends of the cell?
   a.) Prophase   b.) Telophase   c.) Interphase   d.) Anaphase

5. T or F? During metaphase, chromosomes move toward the center of each new cell.

Take the assessment online here:

http://tinyurl.com/PlntSci-11

Hint: When the answer is incorrect, you will see: "Wrong answer! Go Back!"

Notes

25 Vegetative Growth

Major Concept

Plants are classified according to their life/growing cycles as annuals, biennials or perennials.

Objectives

- Identify three annuals, three biennials and three perennials
- Define the major difference among annals, biennials and perennials

Link to Standards

PS.02. Apply principles of classification, plant anatomy, and plant physiology to plant production and management.

Key Terms

- Annuals
- Biennials
- Perennials

Annuals

- **Annuals** complete their life/growing cycle in less than one year and must be planted again.

    o Shoot growth starts after germination and continues in a fairly uniform pattern until stopped by frost or some senescence-inducing factor.

    o Flowering followed by fruit and seed production occurs during the summer.

    ✓ Examples include: corn, wheat, rice, lettuce, peas, watermelon, beans, zinnia and annual flowers such as petunias and marigolds.

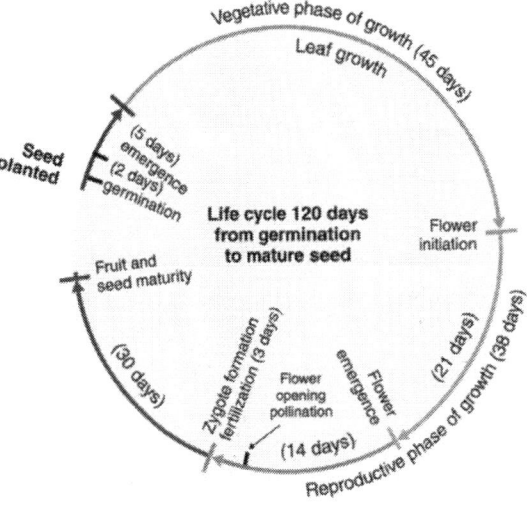

Biennials

- **Biennials** complete their growing cycle in two growing seasons, not necessarily two years but more than one year.

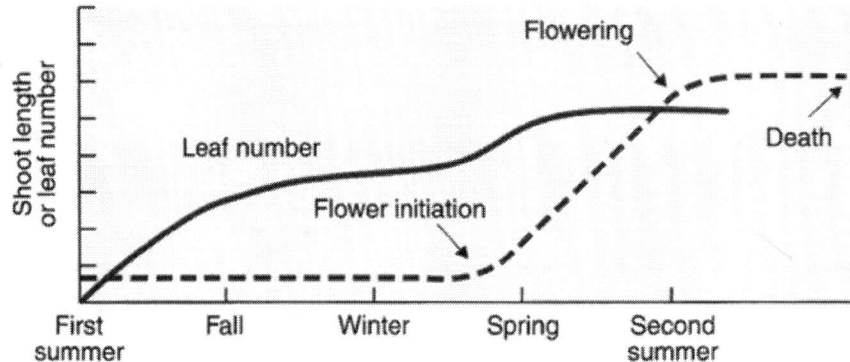

  - Energy stored by the plant during its first year is used in the reproductive phase during the second year.

  - Stem growth is limited during the first growing season and the plant remains alive but dormant through the winter.

  - Exposure to cold temperatures triggers hormonal changes, causing stem elongation.

  - Flowering, fruit formation and seed set occur during the second growing season with senescence and death of the plant following shortly after.

    - ✓ Examples include: carrots, celery, onions, parsley, parsnips, sugar beets and asparagus.

Perennials

- **Perennials** continue to grow for more than two years.

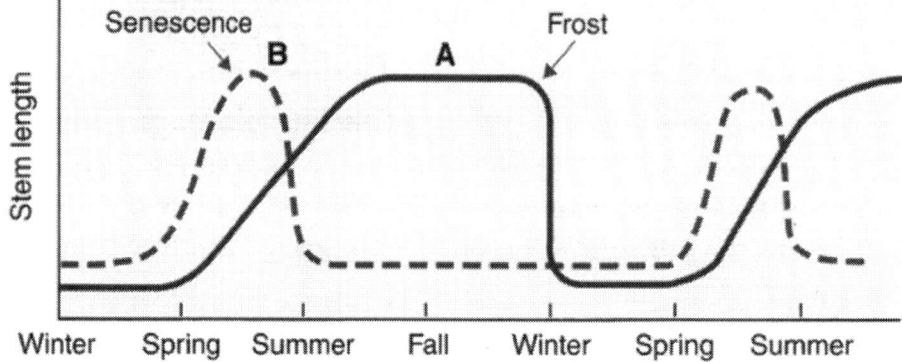

- Plant continues to develop vegetatively during and after the reproductive phase.
- Shoot growth continues each spring from latent or adventitious buds at the crown of the plant.
    - ✓ Perennial fruit examples include: apple, apricot, avocado, grape, pear, raspberry and tomato.
    - ✓ Perennial herb examples include: alfalfa, chives, dill, garlic, hyssop, horseradish, mint, oregano, rosemary, sage, thyme and yarrow.
    - ✓ Perennial vegetable examples include: asparagus, broccoli, eggplant, leek, okra, potato, rhubarb, shallot, sweet potato, taro and watercress.
    - ✓ Bermuda grass and all shrubs and trees are perennial.

Summary

Annual plants complete a life cycle in less than one year and must be planted again. Biennial plants complete a life cycle in less than two years but more than one year and perennial plants continue to grow for more than two years.

Resources

Free complementary PowerPoint:
http://www.tagmydoc.com/dl/1OwRnE/gk77

Parker, R. 2010. Plant and soil science: Fundamentals and applications. Clifton Park, NY: Delmar Cengage Learning. (Pgs. 338-339).

Classification of Horticultural Crop Based on Life Span of Plants
http://www.agriinfo.in/?page=topic&superid=2&topicid=1015

Plant Life Cycles
http://pubs.cas.psu.edu/FreePubs/pdfs/xj0023.pdf

Plant Classification
http://www.ndsu.edu/pubweb/chiwonlee/plsc210/topics/chap2-classification/classification.html

Assessment

1. Which one is an example of an annual?
    a.) parsnips   b.) carrots   c.) tomato   d.) rice

2. T or F? Biennials complete their life cycle in less than one year.

3. Which one is an example of a biennial?
    a.) rice   b.) parsnips   c.) rosemary   d.) apple

4. T or F? Perennial plants stop developing after the reproductive phase.

5. Which one is an example of a perennial?
    a.) Bermuda grass   b.) tomato   c.) rice   d.) carrot

Take the assessment online here:

http://tinyurl.com/PlntSci-12

Hint: When the answer is incorrect, you will see: "Wrong answer! Go Back!"

Notes

26 Plant Propagation by Seed

Major Concept

Sexual reproduction in plants produces seeds.

Objectives

- Outline the process of pollination and fertilization
- Describe a seed
- Name five important seed crops

Link to Standards

PS.03. Propagate, culture and harvest plants and plant products based on current industry standards.

Key Terms

- Dormant
- Fertilization
- Pollination
- Zygote

Plant Propagation by Seed

- Plants reproduced by seed are created by the sexual method of plant propagation.

- **Pollination** is the transfer of pollen from the anther to the stigma.

  o After pollination, a small tube grows from the pollen grain down through the style into the ovary.

- A seed is produced through the process of **fertilization** resulting in a zygote which becomes the plant embryo. The **zygote** divides to form new cells creating a new plant.

  o Most common, efficient and economical method for reproducing annual crops such as corn, wheat, beans, annual bedding plants, etc.

- Sexual reproduction differs from vegetative reproduction in that it involves the combination of two different sets of genes to create offspring with a new genetic makeup.

- Sexual reproduction is commonly used for annuals and on plants which grow quickly from seed and produce a plant *similar* to the parents.

- Completes the process of reproduction in plants that started with the development of flowers and pollination.

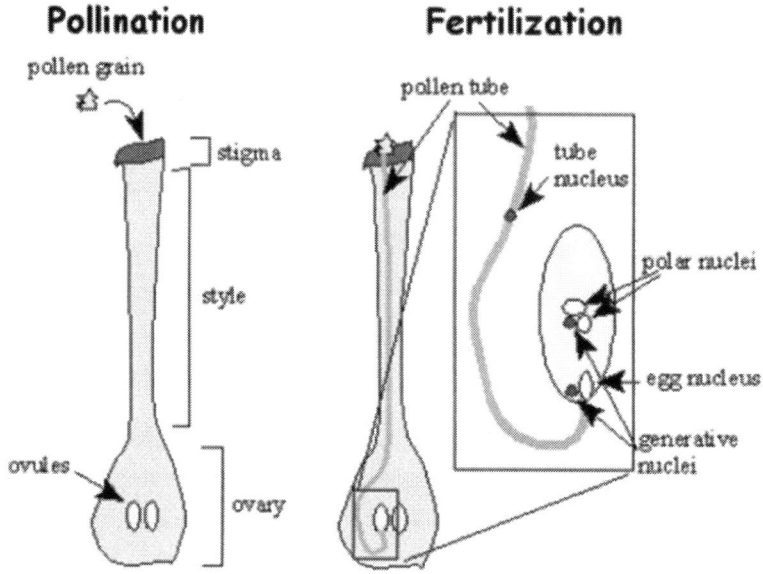

Seeds

- As the fertilized egg within the ovule develops into an embryo, the ovule walls develop into a seed coat, forming the ovule into a seed.

  - The seed serves as the unit of dispersal for the new plant.

  - Most seeds contain a built-in food supply called endosperm which is made of proteins, carbohydrates and fats.

  - Seeds are used for planting and are also harvested – a double purpose.

  - Crop status largely depends on the quality of seed materials used for sowing. Good quality seeds contribute to increased yields.

  - Modern plant breeding methods and biotechnological advances in the seed industry play a significant role in the development of high yielding varieties and hybrids.

More about Seeds

- Seeds are living organisms in a **dormant** or inactive state.

  o Most important food/feed crops are harvested as seeds.

    ✓ Most of the annual crops harvested in agriculture are the seeds of wheat, dry beans, soybeans, corn, barley and oats.

  o Cotyledons or endosperm, feed the embryo until the young plant can make its own food.

  o Embryo made up of young shoot (plumule), the stem (hypocotyl) and the root (radicle).

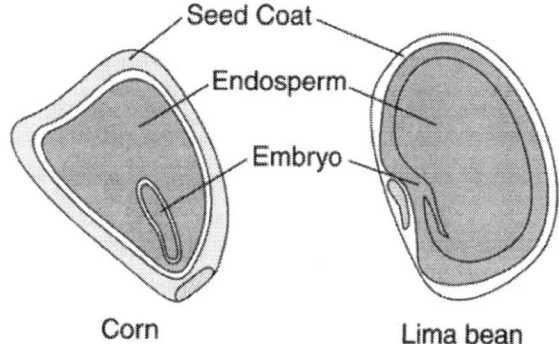

Corn   Lima bean

  o Germination critical factors include: moisture, temperature, oxygen and light.

    ✓ Many different sizes, shapes and colors.

    ✓ Good quality seeds to improved varieties can contribute to an increase in yield.

Summary

Plants reproduced by seed are created by the sexual method of plant propagation while pollination is the transfer of pollen from the anther to the stigma. A seed is produced through the process of fertilization resulting in a zygote which becomes the plant embryo. The zygote divides to form new cells creating a new plant. As the fertilized egg within the ovule develops into an embryo, the ovule walls develop into a seed coat, forming the ovule into a seed. Seeds are living organisms in a dormant or inactive state.

Resources

Free complementary PowerPoint:
http://www.tagmydoc.com/dl/21dNnl/gk79

Parker, R. 2010. Plant and soil science: Fundamentals and applications. Clifton Park, NY: Delmar Cengage Learning. (Pg.352).

Plant Propagation from Seed
http://pubs.ext.vt.edu/426/426-001/426-001.html

Propagating Plants from Seed
http://cru.cahe.wsu.edu/CEPublications/pnw0170/pnw0170.pdf

Assessment

1. T or F? A seed is produced through the process of fertilization.

2. A small tube grows from the pollen grain down through the style into the ovary after _____.
   a.) sexual reproduction   b.) pollination   c.) division   d.) dispersion

3. Most seeds contain a built-in food supply called _____ which is made of proteins, carbohydrates and fats.
   a.) zygote   b.) ovule   c.) endosperm   d.) hypocotyl

4. T or F? Plants not producing offspring similar to the parents must be propagated by vegetative means.

5. The embryo is made up of a young shoot, the stem and the _____.
   a.) root   b.) pistil   c.) stamen   d.) cotyledon

Take the assessment online here:

http://tinyurl.com/PlntSci-13

Hint: When the answer is incorrect, you will see: "Wrong answer! Go Back!"

Notes

27 Starting Plants from Seed

Major Concept
Propagating plants from seeds involves special requirements, skills and knowledge.

Objective
- List factors that cause poor seed germination
- Identify four aspects of seedbed preparation
- Name three important things that must be considered when planting in flats

Link to Standards
PS.01. Develop and implement a crop management plan for a given production goal that accounts for environmental factors.

PS.02. Apply principles of classification, plant anatomy, and plant physiology to plant production and management.

PS.03. Propagate, culture and harvest plants and plant products based on current industry standards.

Key Terms
- Damping-off
- Firming
- Seedbed

Propagation from Seed
- Why we use seeds to propagate plants:
    - Properly managed, planted seeds can be extremely reliable, resulting in very uniform crops.
    - Seeds provide convenience and low cost.

- Convenience

    - Planting: Whether planting in small or large quantities, seed is very easy to handle and manage. Particularly important in large field plantings, where seeds are planted mechanically.

    - Transportation and storage: Not only is the seed nature's device for reproduction of plants, but it is a natural "package" for the transportation and storage of living plant material.

        - ✓ Over-wintering, storage and transportation of seed are convenient.

        - ✓ Seed should always be stored at cool temperatures and at low humidity.

        - ✓ Relatively low cost due to low amount of labor required to transport, store and handle seed.

Seedbed Preparation and Planting

- Field Planting: Most of our food and fiber crops are planted directly into the field.

- Moisture: Soil of the seedbed should be moist.

- **Seedbed**: Should be of smooth, fine, crumbly soil and free of clods.

- Planting Depth: Depends mainly on the size of the seed: the larger the seed, the deeper it should be planted.

    Note: For complete details refer to "Planting Field Crops" outline.

Planting in Flats

- Many ornamental crops and plants with fine seed are started in flats inside the greenhouse.

    - Controlled conditions and warm temperatures allow seeds to germinate quickly.

- Germinating medium: The most important requirement is a sterile medium which will hold moisture but drain readily.

- Sowing: Seed can be broadcasted evenly over the flat or planted in rows.

    - Seed planted too densely will result in spindly seedlings.

- **Firming**: Once sown, seeds should be pressed into firm contact with the medium (soil) using a tamp.

    o This insures the seed will receive adequate moisture as it germinates.

- Covering: Most seed should be covered with a thin layer of growing medium.

    o Certain seeds will not germinate well without light and should not be covered.

- Fungicide: Germinating seedlings are very susceptible to attack by fungus, (**damping-off** disease) and may require protection by the use of a fungicide.

    o The best strategy to avoid damping-off is to work only with clean tools and equipment, sterile growing medium, sterile container and clean seed.

    o If problems with damping-off persist, use a fungicide drench when first watering in the seed.

- Watering: After watering the seed initially, cover the flat with glass or plastic to retain moisture and increase humidity.

    o The flat will probably need only occasional watering until germination.

    o Should the medium covering the seeds dry out, water lightly until the flat drains.

- Temperature: As a general rule, seed germinates best at temperatures between 70° and 80°F.

    o This temperature can be maintained by the use of a thermostatic heating pad.

        ✓ Old seed causes poor seed germination.

Factors Causing Poor Seed Germination

- Old seed: Seed should be fresh, and should have been stored under cool, dry conditions. Seed loses viability as it gets older.

- Uneven moisture: Seed must have a constant supply of moisture as it swells and germinates.

    o Geminating seedlings are very susceptible to drying out as they have no root system to supply moisture.

- Temperatures too low or too high: Temperature requirements vary by species, but 70°- 80°F is generally a good range for germinating seed.

- o In the field, seed will not germinate if planted too early in the season when night temperatures are too low.

- o In the greenhouse, seedlings should be grown at temperatures 5° to 10°F lower than germination. Also helps prevent too-tall, spindly growth.

- Fungus: Damping-off organisms such as Rhizoctonia directly attack germinating seedlings.

  - o Plants are at the most susceptible stage of their life cycle when germinating, and must be provided a clean and protected environment.

- Improper Planting Depth

  - o Seed planted too deep will not have enough stored energy to emerge.

  - o Seed planted too shallow will dry out.

  - o These are concerns mainly when germinating seed in the field.

- Seedling care: After germination, seedlings require watchful care, as they are very tender and susceptible to damage, drying and disease.

- Watering: Seedlings must have a constant supply of moisture until roots have a chance to develop.

- Fertility: Fertilization should be at low levels until plants are well established.

- Light: Bright light will keep seedlings from becoming spindly.

- Temperature: Correct temperature necessary for seed germination.

Transplanting

- Maturity: Seedlings can generally be transplanted after their first true leaves have fully developed.

  - o Seedlings to be planted directly in the field should be considerably more mature.

- Hardening off: Seedlings require a "hardening" process before transplanting.

  - o Hardening involves gradually reducing day and night-time growing temperatures and reducing the frequency of watering.

- Handling: When transplanting, handle seedlings only by their leaves, preferably the seed leaves.

    o Do not hold seedlings by the stem, which is susceptible to damage, particularly in small or tender seedlings.

        ✓ Most seedlings can be planted deep.

        ✓ Tall or spindly seedlings, especially, should be planted deeply so they can stand upright.

        ✓ Throw away seedlings which are damaged or exhibit poor root development.

        ✓ Group larger, more vigorous seedlings together in the same flat

- Watering transplants: This is the most critical point in the transplanting process.

    o Watering should be done immediately after transplanting.

    o Plants should be double watered after transplanting to insure solid contact of the roots with moist growing media.

- Soil fertility

    o Withhold high levels of fertilizer from transplants until they are solidly reestablished.

Care of Young Plants

- Light: Young plants must be protected from light intensities high enough to cause sunburn.

- Water: Adequate moisture should be provided without overwatering.

    o Overwatering and waterlogging are common causes of root rot and slow growth in young stock.

- Soil fertility: Fertilizer levels can be increased as plants grow, moving from higher levels of phosphorous and potassium to a higher nitrogen level as transplants becomes established.

- Temperature: Young transplants are generally tender, and require protection against extreme temperatures, especially cold.

- Protection: Young transplants usually need a protective environment in which to become established.

    o A lath house or shade structure of some kind will provide protection against drying winds, excessive sun and cold temperatures.

- Pests and diseases: As previously mentioned, young plants are quite susceptible to pest and disease problems.

    o While pesticides can be used to combat such problems, it is a better strategy to prevent pest and disease problems to begin with by careful cultural practices.

    o If a disease does take hold, it is often better to cull the diseased material and cut losses at an early stage, rather than devoting excessive resources of time and money to get rid of the disease.

Summary

Properly managed, the results we get from planting seed can be extremely reliable, resulting in very uniform crops. Most of our food and fiber crops are planted directly in the field. Many ornamental crops and plants with fine seed are started in flats inside the greenhouse. Seed loses viability as it gets older. Young plants must be protected from light intensities high enough to cause sunburn. Young transplants usually need a protective environment in which to become established.

Resources

Free complementary PowerPoint:
http://www.tagmydoc.com/dl/2EVIYe/gk7E

Parker, R. 2010. Plant and soil science: Fundamentals and applications. Clifton Park, NY: Delmar Cengage Learning. (Pgs. 349-354).

NC State University - Starting Plants from Seeds
http://www.ces.ncsu.edu/hil/hil-8703.html

Colorado State University Extension - Growing Plants from Seed
http://www.ext.colostate.edu/pubs/garden/07409.html

Assessment

1. T or F? Seed should always be stored at cool temperatures and at low humidity.

2. The inability for a plant to break through the soil surface and sprout is called
   _____.
   a.) crusting   b.) hardening   c.) damping-off   d.) improper planting

3. Seed planted too densely will result in _____ seedlings.
   a.) weak   b.) hard   c.) spindly   d.) dry

4. Germinating seedlings are very susceptible to attack by _____.
   a.) mold   b.) fungus   c.) bacteria   d.) insects

5. T or F? Watering should be done immediately after transplanting.

Take the assessment online here:

http://tinyurl.com/PlntSci-13b

Hint: When the answer is incorrect, you will see: "Wrong answer! Go Back!"

Notes

28 Plant Propagation by Vegetative Means

Major Concept

Many plants are propagated by vegetative or asexual methods.

Objectives

- List six vegetative methods for propagating plants
- Compare sexual propagation to asexual propagation

Link to Standards

PS.03. Propagate, culture and harvest plants and plant products based on current industry standards.

Key Terms

- Asexual
- Budding
- Cuttings
- Divisions
- Grafting
- Layering
- Rhizomes
- Stolons
- Tillers

Vegetative Reproduction

- **Asexual** (without sexual means)

    o Uses plant parts such as leaves, roots and stems to start new plants.

    o Because no new genetic material is introduced through pollination, the products of vegetative reproduction will be "identical" to the parent plants.

Eight Common Types

1. **Cuttings**

    o A portion of a plant is removed and made to form roots. Several types of cuttings are stem, tip, leaf and root.

✓ Commonly used to propagate shrubs and house plants.

Single-eye cutting

Double-eye cutting

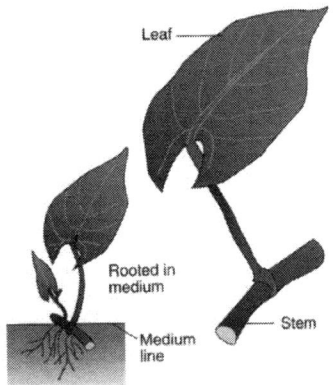
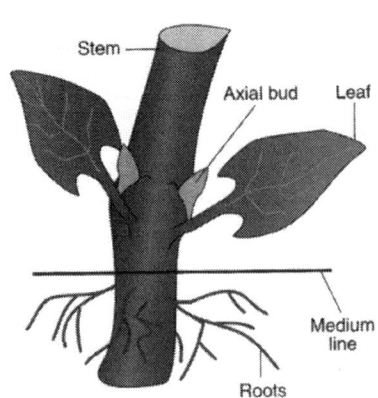

2. **Grafting**

   o A shoot or scion is removed from the desired plant and grafted onto the cambium layers of the scion.

   ✓ Used with some fruit and nut trees.

(A) The scion before any cuts are made.
(B) The first cut is made in the scion.
(C) The second cut is made in the scion.
(D) The root, before any cuts are made.
(E) The first cut is made in the root.

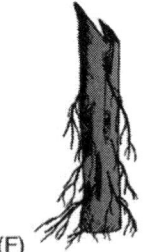

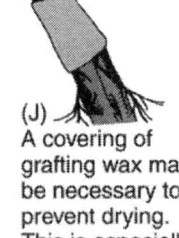

(F) The second cut is made in the root.
(G) The scion and root are positioned for joining.
(H) The scion and root are pushed together. (Cambrium must match on at least one side.)
(I) The two pieces are tied together.
(J) A covering of grafting wax may be necessary to prevent drying. This is especially important if the scion and the rootstock are not the same.

4. **Budding**

    o A bud with bark is removed from the desired plant and placed on the rootstock.

    ✓ Used with some fruit trees and ornamentals such as roses.

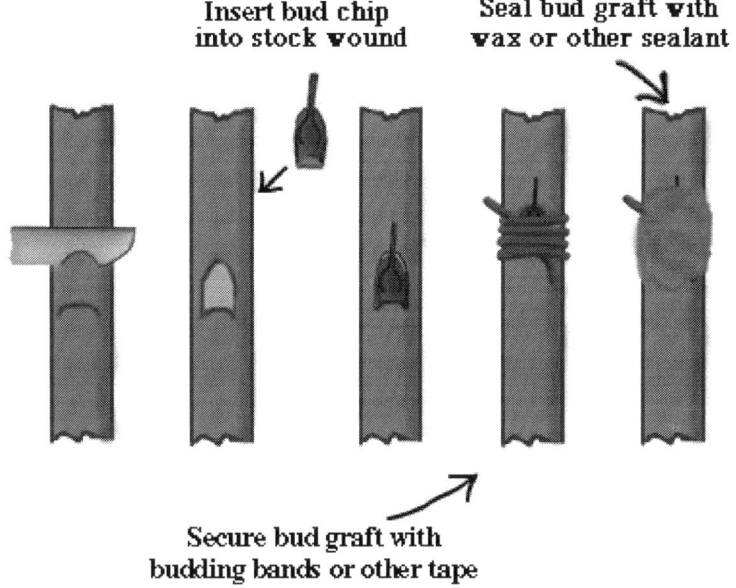

5. **Layering**

    o A portion of an attached root is partially buried underground where roots develop. When the new plant is formed it can then be separated from the parent plant.

    ✓ Figs, raspberries, blackberries and many ornamentals can be propagated by layering.

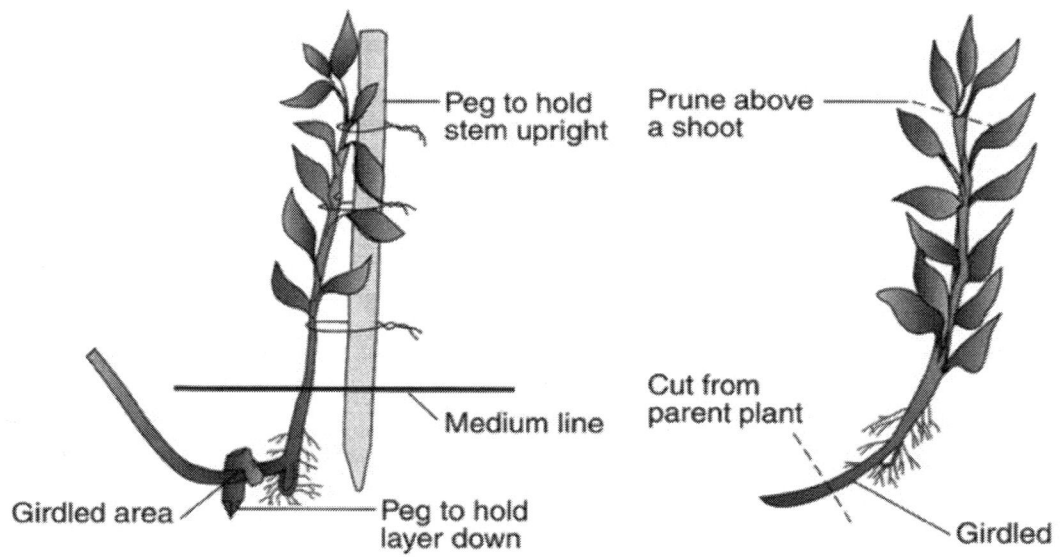

6. **Division**

    o   Plants like daylilies, mums and daffodils form clumps of plants through division. These may be dug and cut apart and planted to form new plants.

Hosta root clump before division   Hosta root divisions

7. **Rhizomes**

    o   Rhizomes can be dug, cut into sections and the sections planted. Iris, Bermuda grass, Johnsongrass and other plants produce underground stems called rhizomes.

    ✓ New plants and roots grow from joints on the rhizomes.

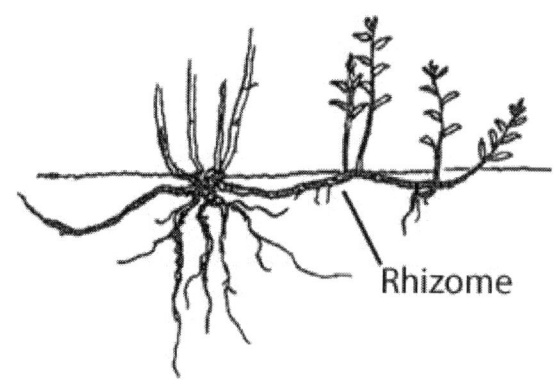

Stolons

    o   New plants that produce horizontal stems which root. When rooted, new stems are formed at the joints along the stolons.

    ✓ Strawberries produce stems that grow horizontally along the soil surface.

8. **Tillers** or Suckers

    o Forms at the base of some trees like mimosa, sassafras and some plums when the trees are cut. They can be cut free from the main plant to form new plants.

    ✓ Blackberries, rabbit eye blueberries, raspberries and many grasses produce tillers.

Summary

Vegetative reproduction is asexual. There are eight common types of vegetative propagation. Some of these include cuttings, grafting, budding and layering. New plants are also formed by division, rhizomes and stolons. Tillers or suckers grow at the base of some trees and can be used to form new plants.

Resources

Free complementary PowerPoint:
http://www.tagmydoc.com/dl/1PxhnY/gk7B

Parker, R. 2010. Plant and soil science: Fundamentals and applications. Clifton Park, NY: Delmar Cengage Learning.

Glass M. and R. Parker. 2009. Fundamentals of plant science. Clifton Park, NY: Delmar Cengage Learning.

Assessment

1. Which method is commonly used to propagate shrubs and house plants?
   a.) rhizomes   b.) cuttings   c.) tillers   d.) division

2. T or F? The products of vegetative reproduction will not be identical to the parent plants.

3. _____ form at the base of trees and can be cut free to form new plants.
   a.) Pistils   b.) Rhizomes   c.) Stolons   d.) Tillers

4. T or F? New plants and roots grow from joints on the rhizomes.

5. Grafting involves matching up a plants _____ layer with another plant.
   a.) leaf   b.) division   c.) cambium   d.) shoots

Take the assessment online here:

http://tinyurl.com/PlntSci-13a

Hint: When the answer is incorrect, you will see: "Wrong answer! Go Back!"

Notes

29 Introduction to Plant Pests

Major Concept

Proper identification of plant pests is of major importance in controlling them.

Objectives

- List the four types of plant pests
- Define weed
- List two examples of invertebrate and vertebrate pests
- Name three general classes of disease agents
- List two challenges growers have when competing with pests

Link to Standards

PS.03. Propagate, culture and harvest plants and plant products based on current industry standards.

PS.03. Propagate, culture and harvest plants and plant products based on current industry standards.

Key Terms

- Invertebrate
- Mollusks
- Nematodes
- Pathogen
- Vertebrate
- Weeds

Introduction to Plants Pests

- Plant pests include all life forms destructive to plants.

    o The whole biological spectrum is represented.

- Pests are organisms that compete with people for food or fiber, interfere with raising our crops and livestock and damage our belongings.

- Proper identification is important - without proper identification of the pest, control is not possible.

- Four main groups of pests include:

    1. Weeds

    2. Invertebrates

    3. Vertebrates

    4. Disease agents

Weeds

- **Weeds** are undesirable plants, sometimes defined as "any plant growing out of place."

- A "cultivated weed" might be a landscape plant of importance, but when it grows in a lawn, it is a pest!

- Adapt well to local climates and soils and can compete successfully with cultivated plants for available resources.

- Most weeds produce a large number of seeds.

- Some weed seeds can remain dormant in the soil for 20 years before germinating.

- Can be persistent and difficult to eradicate, because some have vegetative means of reproduction in addition to seeds.

- Compete with agricultural crops for water, nutrients, light and space.

- Interfere with farming operations, and can harbor insects and plant diseases.

- Some weeds are toxic to livestock.

- A simple way to identify weeds is to compare them to colored photographs and drawings.

- Growers need to become familiar with plant classification system and the weeds' physical features, developmental stages and life cycles.

Invertebrates

- Invertebrate pests include insects and their relatives, nematodes, snails and slugs.

- Term "**invertebrate**" signifies animals without backbones (no vertebrae).

- Insects have three body parts: head, thorax, abdomen and six legs.

- Ticks, mites and spiders have only two body parts and eight legs.

- **Nematodes** are a large group of unsegmented worms that can be plant parasites.

- Snails and slugs are **mollusks** that prefer cool, moist surroundings.

Vertebrates

- **Vertebrates** are animals with backbones.

- Included fish, amphibians, reptiles, birds and mammals.

- Growers most concerned with birds and mammals.

- Pest birds harbor **pathogens** (disease causing organisms, eat or damage crops, cause damage to buildings or make too much noise.)

- Rodents are mammals that interfere with people, or cause harm to crops and livestock.

- Rats, mice, and squirrels cause most of our vertebrate problems.

- Animal pests are similar to weeds, i.e., any animal out of place, such as a deer in a hay field, stray dogs in with sheep, livestock that break through a fence, etc. are pests.

Disease Agents

- Cause diseases in plants and animals.

- Many of these organisms are submicroscopic, making identification difficult.

- Pests may be identified by the type of symptoms caused or damage done to their host animals or plants.

- Included in this group of pests are bacteria, fungi and viruses.

Challenges of Pests

- Growers throughout the world must compete with weeds, insects, plant parasites, birds and rodents.

  - Energy, time and expense used to combat these problems are economically significant.

- Loss of food to our world food supply, because of these competitors, is a continuing problem and can become disastrous.

  - New methods and concepts for their control important to feeding a hungry world.

- One major challenge, for agriculturalists today, is controlling pests without causing other related problems such as environmental pollution.

  - Pollutants resulting from pest control may indirectly or directly damage or kill beneficial plants and animals and/or man.

  - Toxic residues may be left in plant and animal products destined for human (or even animal) consumption.

Summary

Plant pests include all life forms destructive to plants. Pests are organisms that compete with people for food or fiber, interfere with raising our crops and livestock and damage our belongings. Proper identification is important – without proper identification of the pest, control is not possible. Four main groups of pests include weeds, invertebrates, vertebrates, and disease agents. One of the major challenges for agriculturalists today is to control pests without causing other related problems such as environmental pollution.

Resources

Free complementary PowerPoint:
http://www.tagmydoc.com/dl/Bk5Vg/gk7S

Parker, R. 2010. Plant and soil science: Fundamentals and applications. (pgs. 386-404) Clifton Park, NY: Delmar Cengage Learning.

Plant Pest Handbook
http://www.ct.gov/caes/cwp/view.asp?a=2823&q=377510

Introduction of plant pests, noxious weeds, or organisms affecting plant life
http://apps.leg.wa.gov/rcw/default.aspx?cite=17.24.051

Assessment

1. T or F? Weeds adapt well to local climates and soils and can compete successfully with cultivated plants for available resources.

2. Most weeds produce a large number of _____.
    a.) flowers   b.) roots   c.) seeds   d.) pollutants

3. T or F? Weeds compete with agricultural crops for water, nutrients, light and space.

4. The term _____ signifies animals without backbones.
    a.) invertebrate   b.) vertebrates   c.) nematodes   d.) organisms

5. Pest birds harbor _____.
    a.) disease   b.) pathogens   c.) toxic residues   d.) pollutants

Take assessment online here:

http://tinyurl.com/PlntSci-14pest

Hint: When the answer is incorrect, you will see: "Wrong answer! Go Back!"

Notes

Introduction of plant pests, noxious weeds, or organisms affecting plant life
http://apps.leg.wa.gov/rcw/default.aspx?cite=17.24.051

Assessment

1. T or F? Weeds adapt well to local climates and soils and can compete successfully with cultivated plants for available resources.

2. Most weeds produce a large number of _____.
   a.) flowers   b.) roots   c.) seeds   d.) pollutants

3. T or F? Weeds compete with agricultural crops for water, nutrients, light and space.

4. The term _____ signifies animals without backbones.
   a.) invertebrate   b.) vertebrates   c.) nematodes   d.) organisms

5. Pest birds harbor _____.
   a.) disease   b.) pathogens   c.) toxic residues   d.) pollutants

Take assessment online here:

http://tinyurl.com/PlntSci-14pest

Hint: When the answer is incorrect, you will see: "Wrong answer! Go Back!"

Notes

30 Damage Caused by Plant Diseases

Major Concept

Plant diseases can be identified by their symptoms.

Objectives

- List four general types of pathogens that cause plant disease
- Identify six possible symptoms of plant diseases
- Define bacteria, fungus, nematode and virus

Link to Standards

PS.03. Propagate, culture and harvest plants and plant products based on current industry standards.

Key Terms

- Bacteria
- Chlorotic
- Fungi
- Nematodes
- Stuntiny
- Viruses

Damage Caused by Plant Diseases

- Causes of plant diseases include fungi, bacteria and nematodes.

- Plant **pathogens** (disease producing organisms) can cause various symptoms to appear on affected plants:

    o Dwarfing of growth

    o Yellowing of foliage

    o Leaf spotting

    o Blasting of grain heads

    o Stem cankers

- Fruit rot
- Seed decay
- Damping off (destruction of seedlings near the soil line)
- Wilt
- Defoliation
- Root rot
- Galls

Disease-Causing Organisms

- Includes: fungi, bacteria, nematodes and viruses.
- **Fungi** are microscopic plants that lack chlorophyll and conductive tissues.
  - Produce diseases like stem rust, corn smut, powdery mildews, brown rot and damping off.

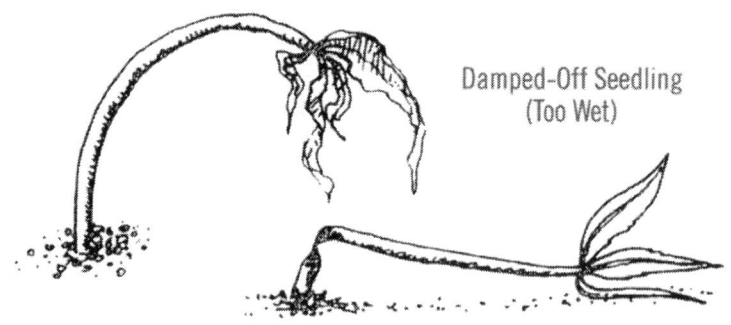

  - Reproduce mainly by means of spores.
  - Particularly damaging to plant propagation operations.
- **Bacteria** are microscopic, single-celled organisms.
  - Cause diseases such as galls, leaf spots, soft rots, scabs and systemic disorders.

- o A significant cause of plant disease, because they can multiply very rapidly when proper environmental conditions are present.

- o As damaging to plant propagation operations as are fungi.

- **Nematodes** are very small round worms, usually invisible to the naked eye.

  - o Cause galls on roots, root lesions, injure root tips and sometimes cause excessive root branching.

  - o Reproduce by eggs.

- **Viruses** are pathogenic particles that infect cells of plants and animals.

  - o In plants they cause such symptoms as **stuntiny** (leaves with yellow mosaic patterns), flower break and vein clearing; veins are **chlorotic**, (lack green color; without chlorophyll).

  - o A virus can multiply only in living cells.

Summary

Plant diseases are caused by fungi, bacteria and nematodes. Agriculturalists are concerned with these organisms because of the damage they do to our crops and ornamental plants. The organisms that cause these symptoms include fungi, bacteria, nematodes and viruses. Viruses are pathogenic particles that infect higher plants and animals.

Resources

Free complementary PowerPoint:
http://www.tagmydoc.com/dl/mYRER/gk7M

Parker, R. 2010. Plant and soil science: Fundamentals and applications. Clifton Park, NY: Delmar Cengage Learning.

Guidelines to Identification and Management of Plant Disease
http://edis.ifas.ufl.edu/mg441

Plant Pathology
http://www.ext.colostate.edu/mg/gardennotes/331.html

Assessment

1. Fungi are microscopic plants that lack _____ and conductive tissues.
   a.) sun   b.) chlorophyll   c.) chlorosis   d.) pathogens

2. Which is a disease produced by fungi?
   a.) leaf spots   b.) scabs   c.) root lesions   d.) corn smut

3. Fungi reproduce mainly by means of _____.
   a.) living cells   b.) eggs   c.) spores   d.) bacteria

4. T or F? Bacteria are microscopic, multi-celled organisms.

5. _____ are very small round worms that produce eggs.
   a.) Viruses   b.) Nematodes   c.) Bacteria   d.) Fungi

Take assessment online here:

http://tinyurl.com/PlntSci-14damage

Hint: When the answer is incorrect, you will see: "Wrong answer! Go Back!"

Notes

31 Cultural Methods of Plant Disease Control

Major Concept

Crop cultural practices can help control plant disease.

Objectives

- Define the term cultural control as applied to plant diseases
- List two or more methods of cultural control of plant diseases

Link to Standards

PS.03. Propagate, culture and harvest plants and plant products based on current industry standards.

Key Terms

- Epidemic
- Pathogen
- Saprophytes

VectorCultural Methods of Plant Disease Control

- Include activities aimed at controlling disease through cultivation methods/techniques.

- Some methods are aimed at eliminating the **pathogen** (disease-producing organism) from the plant or the area in which the plants are growing.

- Other methods are aimed at increasing resistance of the host to the pathogen.

- Still other methods work at obtaining pathogen-free propagative material.

- Finally, methods may control the disease **vector** (carriers of disease) such as insects and nematodes.

Cultural Disease Control

- Host eradication

- - When, in spite of quarantine, a pathogen is introduced into a new area, a plant **epidemic** (any increase of disease in a population) usually follows.
    - ✓ All plants infected or suspected to be infected must be removed and burned.
    - ✓ This results in elimination of the pathogen and prevents greater losses from its spread.
  - Bacterial canker of citrus in Florida and other southern states have been controlled in this way.
  - Some pathogens of annual crops can be controlled by eradicating the wild host plants of that area.
    - ✓ Ecological impact of this method may be at best impractical, and at worst illegal.

- Crop Rotation
  - Some pathogens can be controlled by planting a non-host crop for 3 or 4 years.

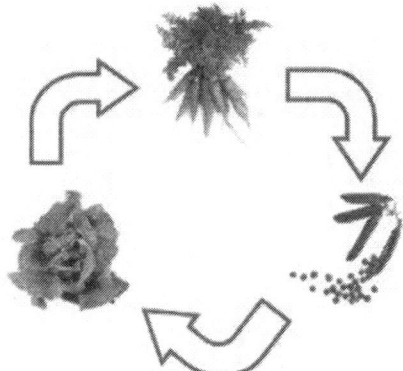

  - ✓ This method is ineffective when dealing with pathogens that survive as **saprophytes** (live on dead or decaying matter) or produce long lived spores.
  - ✓ This method can be useful by making it possible to grow an economically successful crop in a rotation every third or fourth year.

- Sanitation
  - Includes all activities aimed at reducing or eliminating pathogens present in a plant, field or warehouse.
  - Also includes methods used to prevent the spread of pathogens to healthy plants or plant products.

- o Washing soil off farm equipment before moving to another field is another good sanitation measure.

- Improving plants growing conditions

    - o Cultural practices that improve the vigor of plants often helps increase resistance to the attack of pathogens.

    - o Proper fertilization, drainage, irrigation, plant spacing and weed control will help achieve plant vigor.

- Creating conditions unfavorable to the pathogen

    - o Some cultural practices can reduce the number of pathogens by starvation, lack of oxygen or by desiccation.

    - o Proper aeration of stored products hastens drying and thus reduces bacterial and fungal infection.

- Control of Insect Vectors

    - o Many examples of losses by bacteria, viruses, and mycoplasma-like disease-causing agents.

    - o Can be reduced by controlling aphids, leafhoppers, thrips, beetles, and other carriers of these disease-causing agents.

- Use of genetic engineering in developing disease-resistant plants

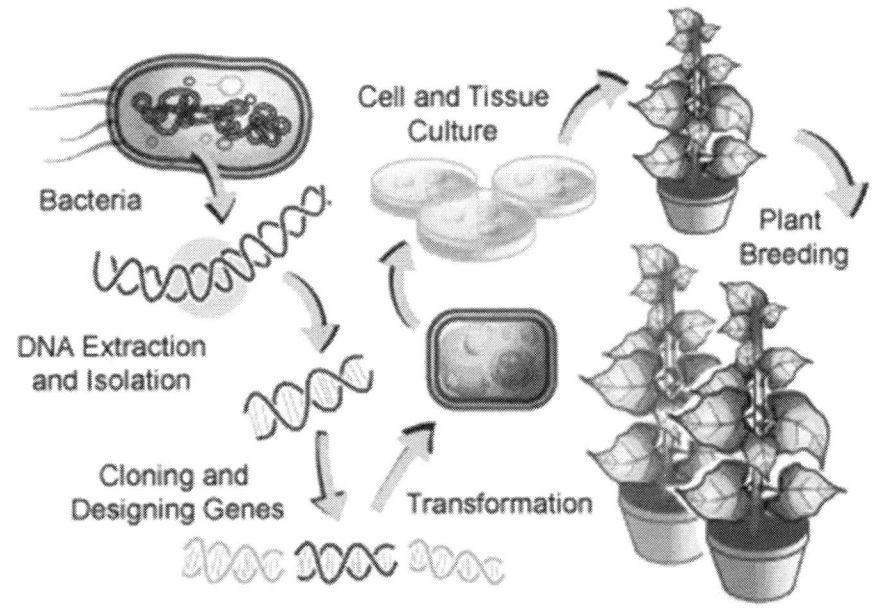

- o Techniques of genetic engineering can be used to manipulate the genetic material of a cell in order to produce a new characteristic in an organism.

- o Organisms that have had genes from other species inserted into their genome (the full complement of an organism's genes) are called transgenic.

- o Production of pathogen-resistant transgenic plants has been achieved by this method.

- o Specific genes inserted into the plant's genome that confer resistance to such pathogens as viruses, fungi, and insects.

- o Transgenic plants that are tolerant to herbicides and that show improvements in other qualities also have been developed.

- o Most successful genetically modified (GM) crops include: corn (maize), soybeans and cotton.

- o All GM crops valuable to farmers with respect to producing increased yields and having economic advantages.

Summary

Cultural methods of plant disease control include activities aimed at controlling disease through cultivation methods/techniques. Some of these methods are aimed at eliminating the pathogen from the plant or from the area in which the plants are growing. Other methods are aimed at increasing resistance of the host to the pathogen. Still other methods work at obtaining pathogen-free propagative material or eliminating the disease vector such as insects or nematodes. Insect vectors can be reduced by controlling aphids, leafhoppers, thrips, beetles and other carriers of these disease-causing agents. The use of genetic engineering in developing disease-resistant plants is another method of control.

Resources

Free complementary PowerPoint:
http://www.tagmydoc.com/dl/23D5cf/gk7K

Parker, R. 2010. Plant and soil science: Fundamentals and applications. Clifton Park, NY: Delmar Cengage Learning.

Nonchemical Disease Control
http://www.ext.colostate.edu/pubs/garden/02903.html

Cultural Management Practices
http://bugs.bio.usyd.edu.au/learning/resources/PlantPathology/disease_mgmt/cultural_mgmt.html

Assessment

1. T or F? When a pathogen is introduced into a new area, a plant epidemic usually follows.

2. All plants infected or suspected to be infected must be removed and _____.
    a.) burned   b.) trashed   c.) treated   d.) replanted

3. Some pathogens of annual crops can be controlled by _____ the wild host plants of that area.
    a.) replacing   b.) eradicating   c.) destroying   d.) burning

4. T or F? Cultural practices that improve the vigor of plants often helps increase resistance to the attack of pathogens.

5. T or F? Proper aeration of stored products slows drying and thus increases bacterial and fungal infection.

Take assessment online here:

http://tinyurl.com/PlntSci-14cult

Hint: When the answer is incorrect, you will see: "Wrong answer! Go Back!"

Notes

32 Chemical Methods of Disease Control

Major Concept

Chemical control measures for plant diseases are important to agriculture.

Objectives

- List two general types of chemical control measures for diseases
- Identify why seeds are chemically treated
- Demonstrate knowledge of the problems with controlling post- harvest disease
- Define fumigant, fungicide, adjuvant and volatile
- Identify the challenge in controlling insect vectors

Link to Standards

PS.03. Propagate, culture and harvest plants and plant products based on current industry standards.

Key Terms

- Adjuvant
- Bactericides
- Fungicides
- Vector
- Volatile

Disease Control Chemicals

- Most common method of controlling plant diseases in the field and greenhouse is by the use of chemical compounds that are toxic to the pathogens.

  o Some chemicals are toxic to all or most pathogens while others affect only one kind of pathogen.

  o Most chemicals applied to plants can only protect them from subsequent infection, but cannot stop or cure disease once started.

Foliage Sprays and Dusts

- Most commonly used to control fungi and less often used to control bacterial diseases.

- Most fungicides and bactericides are protectants, so they must be present on the plant surface before the pathogen is present in order to prevent infection.

    - **Fungicides** usually will not allow fungus spores to germinate or will kill spores upon germination.

    - **Bactericides** may inhibit bacterial multiplication, or cause their death.

    - Fungicides and bactericides appear to be more efficient when used as sprays rather than dusts.

- **Adjuvants** (defined as a "helper") are added to these sprays to increase their spreading (detergents) or sticking (starch and oils) ability which increases overall coverage and efficiency.

    - Sprays with these materials usually certain 0.5 to 2 lbs of chemical to 100 gallons of water (0.5% to 2% of the total).

- Many control measures present potential health hazard to humans, so regulations for use are very strict.

Seed Treatment

- Seeds, bulbs, roots, and tubers are usually treated with chemicals to prevent their decay by pathogens carried on the seed, bulb, etc. or present in the soil.

    - All can be treated with dusts, thick water suspensions, or soaked in a water solution containing the chemicals.

- Care must be taken so enough chemical is present for protection without affecting the germination of these organs.

- Chemicals used for treating seeds, bulbs, roots, and tubers include inorganic coppers and zinc compounds and organic compounds such as maneb, zineb, thiram and streptomycin (an antibiotic).

Controlling Postharvest Diseases

- Prevents several problems harmful to marketing products to consumers (i.e., the stuff looks bad and no one will buy it, or it doesn't pass standards, etc.).

- Most products effective against storage diseases are harmful to the consumers' health and are very thoroughly regulated.

- Many materials used cause injury to the products in storage.

- Some chemicals give off undesirable odors.

    - Most chemical are used as dilute solutions on fruits or vegetables.

    - Some are used as dusts (e.g. sulfur) or gases (e.g. SO_2).

    - Other materials commonly used include borax, biphenyl, thiabendazole, capstan, and benzoic acid.

        - ✓ Most of these materials are used for the control of storage rots.

Soil Treatment

- Soils to be planted in trees, ornamentals or vegetables are often treated with **volatile** (evaporates rapidly) chemical fumigants for control of bacteria, fungi and nematodes.

- Treatment is done days, weeks or months before planting.

- Some chemicals are so volatile that plastic or other coverings are used to hold the fumes in the soil longer.

- Most common soil fumigants are chloropicrin (tear gas), methyl bromide, ethylene dibromide (EDB), Vapam, Vorlex and Zinophos.

Disinfestation of Warehouses

- To prevent infection of stored product by pathogens, warehouses are cleaned of debris and maybe treated with a copper sulfate of formaldehyde solution between crops, depending on the crop.

- Fumigants typically require least 24 hours before opening the building for aeration.

Controlling Insect Vectors

- When pathogens are transmitted by insect **vectors** (carriers of disease), controlling the vectors is easier than the pathogen itself.

- o Control of insects that carry bacterial or fungus diseases have been quite successful.

- o Recommended practice for control of several insect-carried pathogens.

- o Challenge is to kill or control the vector without harming beneficial insects or animals.

- o In the case of virus or virus-like diseases, control has generally been successful when the insect vectors are controlled on plants on which they overwinter or feed, prior to entering the crop.

Treating Tree Wounds

- Pruning cuts and other wounds to perennial plants need to be protected from drying and the entry of damaging pathogens through wounds.

- Exposed areas of wood are traditionally first treated with a 10 to 20% Clorox solution or with a 70% ethyl alcohol solution.

- Then the entire wound is painted with a permanent type of wound dressing such as a 10:2:2 mixture of lanolin, rosin and gum or Bordeaux paint.

- One cup copper sulfate mixed with 1 quart raw linseed oil is helpful

- Treatment is most likely needed for large wounds/cuts

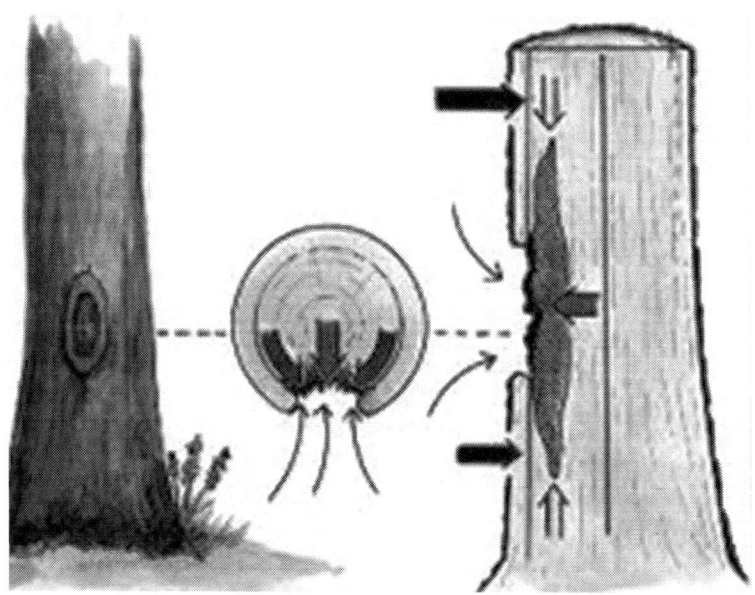

Resistance and Hazards

- Continuous use of some pesticides leads to resistance development in pathogens and other pests.

  o Examples include the development of resistant strains of fireblight by the continuous use of streptomycin (an antibiotic) and the resistance of brown rot in peaches to the fungicide, Benlate.

  o Development of resistance can be slowed by using a mixture of wide spectrum fungicides and by altering sprays with various alternate materials.

- Dealing with substances that control for pests is a challenge for the agriculturalist.

- In many cases, substances that will kill pests will also kill or injure humans.

- Safety measures must be used and regulations followed when using such substances.

- Often a problem in a localized area with misuse can affect the marketing of other untainted product simply by association in the consumer's mind.

Summary

The most common method of controlling plant diseases in the field and greenhouse is by the use of chemical compounds that are toxic to the pathogens. Most of the chemicals applied to plants can only protect them from subsequent infection, but cannot stop or cure a disease once it has started. Most products effective against storage diseases are harmful to human health and are very thoroughly regulated. Many of the materials used may cause injury to the products in storage. Continuous use of some pesticides leads to resistance developed in pathogens and other pests. Dealing with substances that control for pests is a true challenge for the agriculturalist.

Resources

Free complementary PowerPoint:
http://www.tagmydoc.com/dl/gboki/gk7l

Parker, R. 2010. Plant and soil science: Fundamentals and applications. Clifton Park, NY: Delmar Cengage Learning.

Chemical Control
http://tinyurl.com/chemcontrol

Fungal Root Rots and Chemical Fungicide Use
http://tinyurl.com/luslkok

Assessment

1. T or F? Sprays and dusts are most commonly used to control fungi and less often used to control bacterial diseases.

2. Most fungicides and bactericides are _____ so they must be present on the plant surface before the pathogen is present in order to prevent infection.
   a.) substances   b.) toxic   c.) protectants   d.) resistant

3. T or F? Most products effective against storage diseases are harmful to the consumers' health and are very thoroughly regulated.

4. T or F? Continuous use of some pesticides leads to resistance developed in pathogens and other pests.

5. T or F? Treatment is most likely not needed for trees with large wounds.

Take assessment online here:

http://tinyurl.com/PlntSci-14chem

Hint: When the answer is incorrect, you will see: "Wrong answer! Go Back!"

Notes

33 Biology of Insects

Major Concept

Many different body parts and life cycles make up an insect.

Objectives

- List three unique characteristics of insects Identify the four variations of metamorphosis

Link to Standards

PS.03. Propagate, culture and harvest plants and plant products based on current industry standards.

Key Terms

- Larvae
- Metamorphosis
- Molt
- Pupa
- Segmentation

Biology of Insects

- Body of an insect is broken into three main segments: the head, thorax and abdomen.

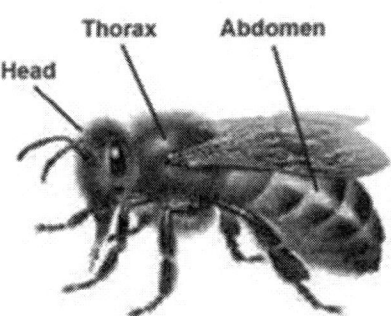

- Word insect comes from the Latin, insectum which means "cut into."

    o Thus the insect body is separated by constrictions or divided into three distinct sections.

- Segmented characteristic of insects gives them the advantage of movement and activity.

- **Segmentation** (parts of body) also provides efficiency.

    - Each body segment is specialized into functions such as securing food, locomotion and reproduction.

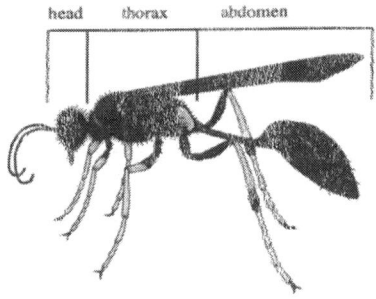

Insect Body

- Head contains the antennae and mouthparts.

    - Eyes - simple or compound.

    - Antennae - used for smelling and feeling.

    - Mouthparts - used for sucking or chewing.

        ✓ Mouthparts are the most variable of all insect characteristics.

        ✓ Often used to determine the type of control measures that will be the most effective for a particular insect.

- The thorax is the locomotion segment of an insect.

    - Contains the wings and legs.

    - An insect may have no wings, one pair of wings or two pair of wings.

    - Thorax also has three pairs of legs.

- Abdomen contains the digestive, reproductive, respiratory and excretory organs of the insect.

    - Abdomen shrinks or swells according to the state of these organs.

- Variations in size of the abdomen occur as the insect eats, produces eggs or fills with excrement.

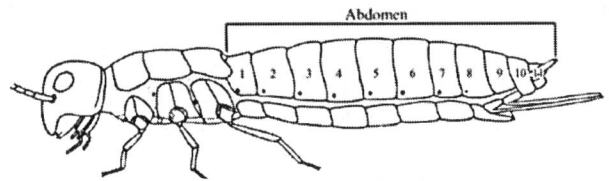

Life Cycle

- Many insects go through a life cycle of several stages before they reach maturity.

    - These changes in form and structure are called **metamorphosis**.

- Four variations of metamorphosis in insects include.

    1. No metamorphosis
    2. Gradual metamorphosis
    3. Incomplete
    4. Complete

- No metamorphosis

    - Insects emerge from eggs looking exactly like adults, except smaller.
        - ✓ An example is silverfish.

- Gradual metamorphosis

    - Insect changes shape gradually.
        - ✓ Examples are grasshoppers and crickets.

- Incomplete metamorphosis

    - Change is gradual until the last stage is reached.
    - They change quickly into the adult stage after the last **molt** or shedding of their exterior shell.
        - ✓ Dragonflies are an example.

- Complete metamorphosis

  o Insect goes through four distinct stages: the egg, **larvae** (active immature form of an insect), **pupa** (inactive immature form) and adult.

  o None of the young stages look like the adult.

    ✓ Moths and butterflies are the most common examples.

- Understanding metamorphosis of insects helps the grower understand techniques of insect control, for example:

  o Egg and pupa stages are most resistant to chemical sprays.

  o Larval stages are the most destructive, but are most vulnerable to sprays.

  o Adult stage is also sometimes destructive, yet is controllable.

Summary

The word insect comes from the Latin, insectum which means "cut into." Thus the insect body is separated by constrictions or divided into three distinct sections. The segmented characteristics of insects give them the advantage of movement and activity. Segmentation also provides efficiency. Each body segment is specialized into functions such as securing food, locomotion and reproduction. Most insects go through a life cycle of several stages called metamorphosis before they reach maturity.

Resources

Free complementary PowerPoint:
http://www.tagmydoc.com/dl/26EpJi/gk7G

Parker, R. 2010. Plant and soil science: Fundamentals and applications. Clifton Park, NY: Delmar Cengage Learning.

Insect Biology and Ecology: A Primer
http://www.biocontrol.entomology.cornell.edu/bio.html

Assessment

1. T or F? The body of an insect is broken into three main segments.

2. The head contains the _____ and mouthparts.
    a.) antennae   b.) reproduction   c.) body   d.) thorax

3. T or F? The abdomen is the locomotion segment of an insect.

4. How many variations of metamorphosis are there in insects?
    a.) three   b.) six   c.) five   d.) four

5. T or F? All insects go through metamorphosis.

Take assessment online here:

http://tinyurl.com/PlntSci-14

Hint: When the answer is incorrect, you will see: "Wrong answer! Go Back!"

Notes

34 Insect Control

Major Concept
Insects cause injury to plants.

Objectives
- List five ways insects cause losses in plants
- Identify four control practices used for insects and give an example of each

Link to Standards
PS.03. Propagate, culture and harvest plants and plant products based on current industry standards.

Key Terms
- Beneficial insects
- Harmful insects
- Pathogens

Damage Caused by Insects
- Insects injure plants directly or indirectly from their attempts to secure food.

- Human's chief rival for the available food supply of the world.

- Some insects prefer living tissue, some prefer dead tissue, others raw, sweet, sour, hard or soft foods.

- Insects that help man by pollinating, providing food and other helpful materials are called beneficial; some insects are both **beneficial** (pollination) and **harmful** (competing with man for food).
    - Some harmful effects of insects include:
        - ✓ Chewing of plant parts - leaves, roots, stems, bark, flowers, or fruit.
        - ✓ Sucking sap from plant parts.
        - ✓ Boring holes between the surfaces of leaves (leaf miners) or other plant parts.

- ✓ Laying eggs in some parts of the plant.
- ✓ Using parts of plants for their shelter or nests.
- ✓ Carrying other insects to the plant and establishing them there.
- ✓ Disseminating organisms of plant disease and making wounds through which other harmful organisms may enter.

Insect Control

- Insect control is divided into four types:
    1. Physical
    2. Cultural
    3. Biological
    4. Chemical

- Physical control includes direct removal of insects, by interrupting their physiological processes, prevention of their entry into an area, or physically destroying them with machinery. Examples include:
    - Light at night interrupts insect behavior.
    - High temperatures can kill insects in stored grain.
    - Low temperatures prevent insect attack on furs and fabric.
    - Aluminum foil, screens, trenches, sticky bands and traps are used as barriers to keep insects out.

- Cultural control can prevent pest damage. Some examples include:
    - Use of crop rotation interrupts an insect's food supply.
    - Soil tillage and removal of crop residues to reduce insects' food supply.
    - Early or delayed planting can lessen amount of food available when the insect is in its larval stages.
    - Use of resistant (to insect pests) varieties and strains of plants.
    - Destruction of weeds that may act as a host plant or shelter for the insect.

- Biological control is the use of other insects or pathogens to control economic pests.
  - Parasites deposit eggs on their victim. The larvae then consume the pest. The adult parasite then emerges from the insect "mummy." Examples:
    - Spotted alfalfa controlled by a parasitic wasp.
    - Purple scale of oranges controlled by wasps.
  - Predators kill and consume pests. Examples:
    - Assassin bugs suck life fluids from pink boll worms.
    - Lady bird beetles and their larvae eat aphids. Insect control is divided into four types,
    - Vedalia beetles have been imported from Australia to control cottony-cushion scale in California and Florida citrus.
  - **Pathogens** (disease-producing organisms) are used to control insect pests. Examples:
    - Bacteria, *Bacillus thurengensis*, kill butterfly and moth larvae.
    - Use of water suspensions of spores of brown, red and yellow fungi for whitefly and scale control on Florida citrus has been successful.
    - 250 viruses are known to be pathogenic to insects.
    - Investigation continues on new and innovative applications.
- Chemical control implies the use of liquids, gases, powders or granules to control insects.
  - Stomach poisons are used to control chewing insects.
    - Poison can be put on the leaves of the plants or in the soil (or water) and taken into the plant system.
  - Contact poisons are used on both chewing and sucking insects.
    - Implies contacting the insect directly with the chemical.
  - Fumigants are actually poison gasses which enter the insects' respiratory system.

✓ Nervous system is most affected by these control measures.

Summary

Most injuries to plants by insects results directly or indirectly from their attempts to secure food. They are human's chief rival for the available food supply of the world. When insects desire food that man also desires, they become our enemy and we call them harmful. Because of their diversity there are insects that desire apparently every kind of organic material found on earth. Insects that help man by pollinating, providing food and other helpful materials are called beneficial; some insects are both beneficial and harmful. Insect control is divided into four types, physical, cultural, biological and chemical.

Resources

Free complementary PowerPoint:
http://www.tagmydoc.com/dl/mhz6e/gk7Q

Parker, R. 2010. Plant and soil science: Fundamentals and applications. (pgs. 402-405) Clifton Park, NY: Delmar Cengage Learning.

Controlling Pests in Agriculture
http://www.epa.gov/pesticides/controlling/agriculture.htm

2013 Insect Control Recommendations for Field Crops
https://utextension.tennessee.edu/publications/documents/PB1768.pdf

The General Approaches to Insect Control: An Overview
http://www.entomology.wisc.edu/mbcn/fea102.html

Assessment

1. How many types of insect control?
   a.) six   b.) four   c.) five   d.) three

2. T or F? Biological control implies the use of liquids, gases, powders or granules to control insects.

3. The nervous system of insects is most affected by these control measures.
   a.) poisons   b.) fumigants   c.) bacteria   d.) pathogens

4. Stomach poisons are used to control _____ insects.
   a.) large   b.) poisonous   c.) chewing   d.) flying

5. T or F? Chemical control is the use of other insects or pathogens to control economic pests.

Take assessment online here:

http://tinyurl.com/PlntSci-14control

Hint: When the answer is incorrect, you will see: "Wrong answer! Go Back!"

Notes

35 Pesticide Safety: High Toxicity

Major Concept
Protective clothing and equipment are needed for pesticide application.

Objectives
- List all items of protective equipment and appropriate times to use them

Link to Standards

CRP.08. Utilize critical thinking to make sense of problems and persevere in solving them.

CRP.07. Employ valid and reliable research strategies.

CRP.05. Consider the environmental, social and economic impacts of decisions.

Key Terms
- Protective equipment
- Toxic

Pesticide Safety - High Toxicity

- Poisonous (**toxic**) pesticides require the use of personal safety equipment necessary to prevent accidental exposure to pesticides through clothing, body openings or skin.

    - Specific equipment will protect your eyes and prevent inhalation of toxic chemicals.

    - Personal safety equipment is effective only if it fits correctly, is cleaned and maintained and used properly.

    - Always select equipment that gives maximum protection.

- Pesticides contacting the skin are the greatest cause of pesticide poisoning.

- Not all parts of your body will absorb pesticides at the same rate.

- Adequate equipment in one situation may not be satisfactory for another.
    - Precautionary statements on the label will describe hazards associated with a pesticide and type of protective equipment that must be worn when handling, mixing or applying the pesticide.

Protective Equipment

- Recommended protective clothing and equipment will include some or all of the following:
    - Waterproof apron made from rubber or synthetic material.
    - Waterproof boots or foot covering made of rubber or synthetic materials.
    - Daily change of coveralls or clean outer clothing.
        - ✓ Wear waterproof pants and jackets if there is any chance of becoming wet with spray.
        - ✓ Never wear cotton fabric without additional protective clothing when there is a chance of getting wet.
    - Face-shield, goggles or full face respirator
    - Waterproof gloves
        - ✓ Must not have any type of absorptive lining.
        - ✓ Should be made from rubber or synthetic material.
    - Waterproof, wide brimmed hat with a non-absorptive headband.
    - Cartridge-type respirator
        - ✓ Includes a fitted rubber face-piece and replaceable filters.
        - ✓ Need to fit properly to be safe and effective.
        - ✓ Must have filters and cartridges on hand in case one needs to be replaced during use.
- Particular types of pesticide handling jobs such as in packaging them at the manufacturing plants require very special types of safety clothing and equipment be used.

- These include powered air cartridge respirators and supplied air respirators.
- Some resemble the full body suits worn by scuba divers.

Summary

Poisonous pesticides require the use of personal safety equipment necessary to prevent accidental exposure to pesticides through clothing, body openings or skin. Particular types of pesticide handling jobs such as in packaging them at the manufacturing plants require very special types of safety clothing and equipment be used. The precautionary statement of the label will describe the hazards associated with a pesticide and the type of protective equipment that must be worn when handling, mixing or applying the pesticide.

Resources

Free complementary PowerPoint:
http://www.tagmydoc.com/dl/2CTNZC/gk8s

National Pesticide Information Center
http://npic.orst.edu/index.html

Human Health Issues
http://www.epa.gov/pesticides/health/human.htm

Signs and Symptoms of Pesticide Poisoning
http://www.rst2.edu/ties/DDTS/university/docs/toxic.pdf

Toxicity of Pesticides
http://edis.ifas.ufl.edu/pi008

Assessment

1. Pesticides contacting the _____ are the greatest cause of pesticide poisoning.
    a.) eyes   b.) clothing   c.) skin   d.) hair

2. T or F? All parts of your body absorb pesticides at the same rate.

3. T or F? Adequate equipment in one situation will always be satisfactory for another.

4. Never wear _____ fabric without additional protective clothing when there is a chance of getting wet.
    a.) black   b.) wool   c.) red   d.) cotton

5. T or F? Water proof gloves should be made from rubber or synthetic material.

Take assessment online here:

http://tinyurl.com/PlntSci-14high

Hint: When the answer is incorrect, you will see: "Wrong answer! Go Back!"

Notes

36 Pesticide Safety: Low Toxicity

Major Concept
Knowledge of pesticide labels and proper procedures are imperative in case of poisoning.

Objectives
- Identify information that must be contained on a pesticide label
- List three potential human health hazards of pesticide use
- Identify the general rules when using pesticides
- Compare steps to follow in case of pesticide poisoning on the skin or clothing, in the eyes or swallowed

Link to Standards

CRP.05. Consider the environmental, social and economic impacts of decisions.

CRP.08. Utilize critical thinking to make sense of problems and persevere in solving them.

Key Terms
- Cholinesterase
- Dose
- Enzyme
- First aid
- LD50
- Regulations
- Signal word

Pesticide Label Information and Low Toxicity Pesticides

- Problems associated with the misuse of pesticides and agricultural chemicals could be eliminated by adherence to safe, approved methods of handling and application.

    o Read and follow label instructions explicitly; they are for information and protection.

    o Labels include the type of protective clothing and gear that must be used while working with a particular pesticide.

    o Labels tell what to do in case anyone has been exposed to the pesticide through an accident.

- Potential human health hazards of pesticide use are:
    - Ingestion of contaminated food.
    - Inhalation of vapors.
    - Absorption through the skin.
- **Regulations** establish the format for pesticide labels and prescribe what information they must contain.
- Labels must contain the following information:
    - Brand name
    - Chemical name
    - Common name
    - Formulation
    - Ingredients
    - Contents (by weight or liquid volume)
    - Manufacturer
    - Registration and establishment numbers
    - **Signal word** (WARNING, DANGER, CAUTION, etc.)
    - Precaution statement
    - Statement of practical treatment
    - Statement of use classification
    - Directions for use
    - Misuse statement
    - Re-Entry statement
    - Storage and disposal directions
    - Warranty

General Rules

- Pesticide applicators are the key to preventing pesticide accidents.
- General rules for using pesticides:
    - Avoid mixing, loading and spraying during the heat of the day.
    - Handle undiluted formulations with extreme care.
    - Stand up-wind when loading.
    - Pour slowly to avoid spill, splash or drift.
    - Close lid on spray system when agitating.
    - Avoid touching other parts of body unless hands are washed.
    - Avoid prolonged exposure.
    - Don't spray if it is windy or blustery.
    - Avoid spray drift.
    - Avoid inhalation of chemical drift or fumes.
    - Don't eat or smoke while mixing or spraying chemicals.
    - Bathe and change to clean clothing at the end of each day.
    - Applicators handling pesticides on a regular basis should have a periodic "cholinesterase test."
        - ✓ Many pesticides are cholinesterase inhibitors - which means they block or stop the body from using cholinesterase. (The "ase" indicates that this compound is an **enzyme** – something that helps or starts biochemical reactions.)
        - ✓ **Cholinesterase** is the enzyme in the body that breaks down acetylcholine, which makes nerves fire, which makes the rest of the body work.
        - ✓ If the enzyme cholinesterase is not available to breakdown acetylcholine, the nerves fire out of control across the nerve to muscle junction and the individual dies.
        - ✓ Too much pesticide exposure too often, the amount of cholinesterase in the body decreases and it poses a severe health hazard.

- **LD50**
    - Refers to the **dose** (amount) in "milligrams per kilogram" that will kill 50% of a test group of animals.
        - ✓ 28,571.5 milligrams = 1 ounce
        - ✓ 1 kilogram = 2.2 pounds
- Used to assess the relative toxicity of a substance.
    - A lower number of milligrams per kilogram means greater toxicity and the more lethal the compound.

First Aid

- **First aid** is the assistance given to a person exposed to pesticides before professional help is available.
- First aid is not a substitute for professional medical care.
- Poisoning can occur if pesticides are splashed onto skin, into eyes, swallowed, or if vapors, dusts or fumes are inhaled.
- Type of exposure determines what first aid measures are used and what further medical treatment is required.
- Pesticides on the skin or clothing
    - Remove victim from contaminated area
    - Restore breathing
    - Prevent further exposure
    - Get medical care
- Pesticides in the eye(s), immediate action is required
    - Wash the eyes using only clean, running water
    - Hold eyelids open to assure thorough washing
    - Continue flushing for at least 15 minutes

- o Obtain medical care as soon as possible
- Inhaled pesticides
  - o Remove victim from contaminated area
  - o Loosen clothing
  - o Restore breathing
  - o Treat for shock
  - o Watch for convulsions
  - o Get immediate medical care
- Swallowed pesticides
  - o Dilute the swallowed pesticide (Use water or milk give 1 quart to an adult, one large glass to a child under age 7).
  - o Possibly induce vomiting but read the label. Never induce vomiting if the swallowed pesticide is corrosive or petroleum-based because it can cause more damage on the way out of the stomach.
  - o Obtain *IMMEDIATE* medical care.

Summary

Numerous problems associated with the misuse of pesticides and agricultural chemicals could be eliminated by adherence to safe, approved methods of handling and application. Regulations establish the format for pesticide labels and prescribe what information they must contain. The pesticide applicator is the key to preventing pesticide accidents. First aid is the help given to a person exposed to pesticides before professional help is available. First aid is not a substitute for professional medical care.

Resources

Free complementary PowerPoint:
http://www.tagmydoc.com/dl/1E2qcg/gk8q

National Pesticide Information Center
http://npic.orst.edu/index.html

Human Health Issues
http://www.epa.gov/pesticides/health/human.htm

Signs and Symptoms of Pesticide Poisoning
http://www.rst2.edu/ties/DDTS/university/docs/toxic.pdf

Toxicity of Pesticides
http://edis.ifas.ufl.edu/pi008

Assessment

1. T or F? One of the potential human health hazards of pesticide use are absorption through the skin.

2. T or F? Pesticide labels contain some very specific information, but it is up to the company whether or not they choose to include each item.

3. T or F? Pesticide poisoning can only occur if pesticides are splashed onto skin or into eyes.

4. Applicators who handle pesticides on a regular basis should have a periodic _____ test.
    a.) cholinesterase   b.) health   c.) breathing   d.) vision

5. T or F? Never induce vomiting if you suspect the swallowed pesticide to be corrosive or petroleum-based.

Take assessment online here:

http://tinyurl.com/PlntSci-14low

Hint: When the answer is incorrect, you will see: "Wrong answer! Go Back!"

Notes

37 Insect Collections

Major Concept

Collecting insects helps in identification.

Objectives

- Collect and mount 15 insect specimens

Link to Standards

PS.03. Propagate, culture and harvest plants and plant products based on current industry standards.

Key Terms

- Entomology
- Ethyl acetate

Insect Collecting

- Entomology – study of insects

    o Insects have been on this earth for over 250 million years.

    o Insects may be helpful, neutral or harmful to humans.

    o Collecting, identifying and preserving insects aids in learning Integrated Pest Management (IPM)

- Collection

    o Insects can be found almost everywhere - under logs, rocks and debris.

    o A butterfly net can be swept through grasses and branches to dislodge and collect insects.

    o Light attracts insects at night.

- Killing insects is easily done with simple equipment.
  - A killing jar can be constructed quickly, using a wide mouth glass jar, absorbent material like cotton or sawdust and addition of **ethyl acetate** (finger nail polish remover) as the killing agent.

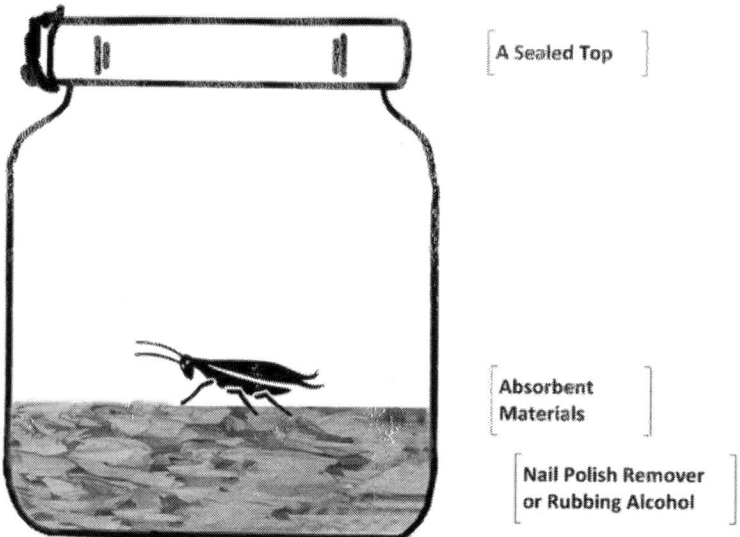

A Simple Killing Jar for Insect Collection

  - Soft bodied insects can be preserved in glass vials containing 70% alcohol solution.
  - Hard bodied insects can be mounted on a pin.
- Mounting insects
  - Large-winged insects are best preserved by placing them on a spreading board.
  - Insects can be pinned, labeled and placed into a display box.
  - Neat labels and an orderly display will last for years and will be an excellent reference for further insect study and identification.

Summary

The study of insects is called entomology Killing insects is easily done with simple equipment. Mounting insects provides a reference for insect identification

Resources

Free complementary PowerPoint:
http://www.tagmydoc.com/dl/Kwlxj/gk7O

Collecting and Preserving Insects
http://tinyurl.com/collectinginsects

Making an Insect Collection
http://www.uaex.edu/other_areas/publications/pdf/mp-83.pdf

Assessment

1. Insects have been on this earth for over _____ million years.
   a.) 300   b.) 250   c.) 275   d.) 225

2. T or F? Insects may be helpful, neutral or harmful to humans.

3. _____ attracts insects at night.
   a.) Sound   b.) Smell   c.) Light   d.) Humans

4. Soft bodied insects can be preserved in glass vials containing 70% _____ solution.
   a.) ethyl acetate   b.) alcohol   c.) peroxide   d.) Clorox

5. T or F? Insects can be pinned, labeled and placed into a display box.

Take assessment online here:

http://tinyurl.com/PlntSci-14collect

Hint: When the answer is incorrect, you will see: "Wrong answer! Go Back!"

Notes

38 Weed Identification

Major Concept

Common weeds can be visually identified.

Objectives

- Identify two ways weeds are harmful to crops
- List three resources that can be used for help in identifying plant species
- Name three life cycles of weeds
- List two common weeds along with their scientific names

Link to Standards

PS.03. Propagate, culture and harvest plants and plant products based on current industry standards.

Key Terms

- Broad-leafed
- Catkin
- Cotyledon
- Head
- Inflorescence
- Narrow-leafed
- Panicle
- Raceme
- Spike
- Umbel

Weeds

- Weeds are controversial plants that are neither all good nor all bad, depending on one's outlook.

- Many weeds can be enjoyed for their attractive flowers and interesting seed pods.

- Weeds quickly grow to cover unsightly scars made to the landscape by man or nature.

- Weeds reduce crop yields and increase the cost of producing crops.

- Some weeds are poisonous and others may cause allergies.

- Controlling troublesome weeds effectively requires exact identification.
- The selection of the most effective control method depends on the ability to properly identify the problem pest species.

Some common weeds and their scientific names

Common Name	Scientific Name	Common Name	Scientific Name
Barnyard grass	Echinochloa crusgalli	Henbit	Lamium amplexicaule
Bermuda grass	Cynodon dactylon	Horse nettle	Solanum carolinense
Bindweed	Conuolvulus sp.	Jimsonweed	Datura stramonium
Bitterweed (sneezeweed)	Helenium tenuifolium	Johnsongrass	Sorghum halepense
Black-eyed Susan	Rudbeckia huta	Lamb's-quarter	Chenopodium album
Broadleaf plantain	Plantago major	Little barley	Hordeum sp.
Broomsedge	Andropogon virginicus	Morning glory	Ipomoea sp.
Buckhorn plantain	Plantago lanceolata	Mouse-ear chickweed	Cerastium vulgatum
Buttercup	Ranunculus sp.	Nutsedge (nut grass)	Cyperus sp.
Cocklebur	Xanthium strumariun	Peppergrass	Lepidium virginicum
Common chickweed	Stellaria media	Pigweed (redroot)	Amaranthus retroflexu
Common milkweed	Asclepias syriaca	Pigweed (spiny)	Amaranthus spinosus
Common ragweed	Ambrosia artemisiifoli	Purslane	Portulaca oleracea
Crabgrass	Digitaria sp	Red sorrel	Rumex acetosella
Curly dock	Rumex crispus	Shepherd's purse	Capsella bursa-pastoris
Daisy fleabane	Erigeron strigosus	Smartweed	Polygonum sp.
Dandelion	Taraxacum officinale	Thistle	Cirsium sp.
Foxtail	Setaria sp.	Three-seeded mercury	Acalypha virginica
Goldenrod	Solidago sp.	Wild carrot	Daucus carota
Goose grass	Eleusine indica	Wild garlic	Allium vineale

Weed Collections

- Weed collections help the collector in identifying weeds.

- Collected specimens can be compared to drawings and colored photographs using references.

    o Use of weed keys such as those found in field guides and references do require specialized knowledge of weeds.

    o Specialists such as farm advisors, extension agents, or college or university agricultural staffs can be contacted for help in identifying plant species.

- Classification of weeds is achieved by grouping together those weeds whose similarities are greater than their differences.

    o Most weeds can be placed into two convenient groups, narrow-leafed and broad-leafed.

        ✓ **Narrow-leafed** weeds include grasses, sedges, rushes and cattails, which all have parallel veins in their leaves.

        ✓ **Broad-leafed** weeds include most others such as mustards, dock, pigweed, purslane and morning glory, all having a net-like pattern of veins in the leaves.

Life Cycles of Weeds

- Annual weeds live for one year or less.

- Biennial weeds live for two growing seasons.

- Perennial weeds live for three or more years.

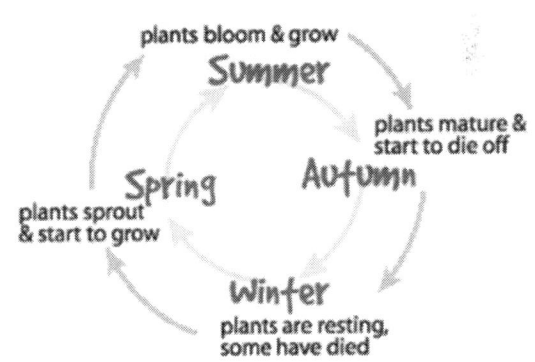

Identification

- Weeds and most other plants have unique physical features which can be used for identification.

    o Identifying weeds while they are in the **cotyledon** (one of a pair of the first leaves from a sprouting seed also called a "seed leaf") stage is helpful.

    o Weeds can be controlled before they compete with crop plants.

- Control measures are more effective and less costly when weeds are treated at an immature stage of their life cycle.

- Flowers and certain sexual reproductive organs and vary among species.

- To use flowers as an aid to identification, you need to be familiar with the different flower parts.

- Flowers appear singly or as compound inflorescence (e.g. groups of flowers arising from a single stem)

- Different names describe how flowers are arranged in an **inflorescence**:

  - ✓ **Catkin** - slim, cylindrical flower cluster, with inconspicuous or no petals, usually wind-pollinated

  - ✓ **Head** - a compact mass of flowers at the top of a stem

  - ✓ **Panicle** - loose, branching cluster of flowers, as in oats

- ✓ **Raceme** - a flower cluster with the separate flowers attached by short equal stalks at equal distances along a central stem.

- ✓ **Spike** - A flower head made up of a central stem with the flowers growing directly on it.

- ✓ **Umbel** - a flower cluster in which stalks of nearly equal length spring from a common center and form a flat or curved surface, as in parsley.

- o The arrangement, shape, vein patterns and presence of hairs or spines are noted differences in leaves.

- Stem variations such as rhizomes, stolons and tubers are helpful to help identify some species.

- Taproots of the broad-leafed weeds will separate them from the fibrous roots of grasses.

- Fruits and seeds are all unique in their shape, size, markings and color.

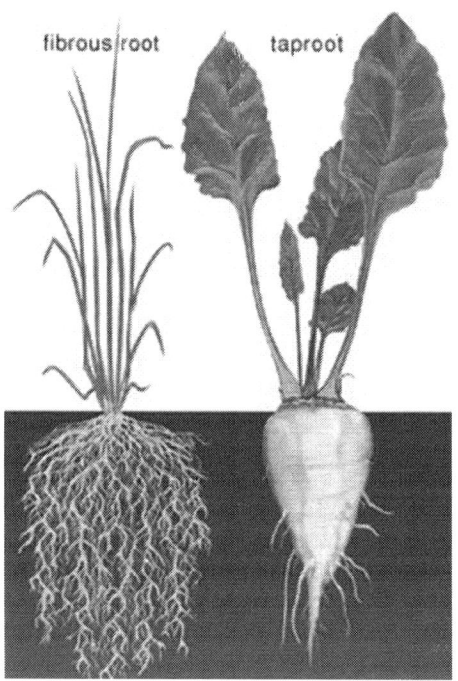

Summary

Weeds are controversial plants that are neither all good nor all bad, depending on one's outlook. Many weeds possess attractive flowers and interesting seed pods. Weeds quickly grow to cover unsightly scars made to the landscape by man or nature. The purpose of a weed collection is to help the person making the collection more adept at identifying weeds. The classification of weeds is achieved by grouping together those weeds whose similarities are greater than their differences.

Resources

Free complementary PowerPoint:
http://www.tagmydoc.com/dl/25wRE0/gk8v

Parker, R. 2010. Plant and soil science: Fundamentals and applications. (pg. 393) Clifton Park, NY: Delmar Cengage Learning.

Weed Identification
http://weeds.cropsci.illinois.edu/weedid.htm
Weed Photo Gallery
http://www.ipm.ucdavis.edu/PMG/weeds_intro.html

Weed Identification & Management
http://weedid.wisc.edu/

Assessment

1. T or F? Weeds reduce crop yields and increase the cost of producing crops.

2. T or F? Broad-leafed weeds include grasses, sedges, rushes and cattails, which all have parallel veins in their leaves.

3. A simple way to begin identifying some common weeds is to compare your specimens with _____.
   a.) crops b.) photographs c.) grasses d.) roots

4. T or F? An Agricultural Commissioner can be contacted for help in identifying plant species.

5. _____ weeds live for one year or less.
   a.) Poisonous b.) Annual c.) Biennial d.) Perennial

Take assessment online here:

http://tinyurl.com/PlntSci-14id

Hint: When the answer is incorrect, you will see: "Wrong answer! Go Back!"

Notes

39 Weed Control

Major Concept
Weed control is essential to crop production.

Objectives
- List two mechanical and two cultural weed control methods
- Define biological and chemical weed control

Link to Standards
PS.03. Propagate, culture and harvest plants and plant products based on current industry standards.

Key Terms
- Herbicides
- Post-emergent
- Pre-emergent
- Pre-plant

Importance of Weed Control
- Ideal method of weed control is to prevent them from becoming established.
  - Once established growers must rely on mechanical, cultural, biological and chemical methods to control them.

Weed Control
- Methods of controlling weeds include: mechanical, cultural, biological and chemical.
  - Mechanical methods
    - ✓ Hand pulling
    - ✓ Hoeing
    - ✓ Cultivation (includes plowing & clean tillage)
    - ✓ Burning

- Mowing
- Smothering with plastic mulches
  - Cultural methods
    - Crop rotation
    - Crop competition
    - Weed-free crop seed
    - Smother crops
  - Biological methods
    - Involves the use of natural enemies for the control of certain weeds.
    - Objective of biological control is reduction of the weed population, not eradication.
    - Examples include use of the Klamath Weed Beetle to control Klamath Weed, use of the Puncture Vine Beetles and Weevils to control Puncture Vine; or domestic geese to control a variety of weed seedlings.
  - Chemical methods
    - Chemical weed killers (**herbicides**) used because they are economical and effective when properly used.
    - Herbicides must be used carefully, always following label directions exactly.
    - Intelligent use of herbicides requires positive identification of weeds and recognizing their stage of growth.

Controlling Weeds with Herbicides

- Broadcast treatment
- Band treatment
- Spot treatment
- Direct spray (in direct contact with the target weed).

- Herbicides may be applied **pre-plant**, **pre-emergent**, or **post-emergent** (before planting, before the weed grows, or after the weed grows).

* For annual, biennial, and simple perennial weeds, almost any control method is satisfactory before the plant forms seeds.

  - Perennials that spread by rhizomes, stolon's or bulbs require special methods.

  - Weed seeds remain viable for varying periods of time, depending on species.

    - Many common weed seeds will remain viable in the soil for 20 years or longer.

  - Good for growers to remember the adage, "One year of seeds equals seven years of weeds."

Summary

The ideal method of weed control is to prevent them from becoming established. Once established we must rely on mechanical, cultural, biological and chemical methods to control them. For annual, biennial and simple perennial weeds, almost any control method is satisfactory before the plant forms seeds.

Resources

Free complementary PowerPoint:
http://www.tagmydoc.com/dl/2JUF3y/gk8m

Parker, R. 2010. Plant and soil science: Fundamentals and applications. (pgs. 389-393) Clifton Park, NY: Delmar Cengage Learning.

Methods of Weed Control
http://www.co.larimer.co.us/weeds/control.htm

Weed Control Using Herbicides
http://www.ipm.ucdavis.edu/QT/weedcontrolcard.html

Assessment

1. T or F? Controlling weeds by cultivation includes plowing and tillage.

2. Biological weed control involves the utilization of natural _____ for the control of certain weeds.
    a.) chemicals   b.) herbicides   c.) enemies   d.) seeds

3. T or F? The objective of biological control is eradication.

4. T or F? Intelligent use of herbicides requires positive identification of weeds and recognizing their stage of growth.

5. Many common weed seeds will remain viable in the soil for _____ years or longer.
    a.) 10   b.) 5   c.) 20   d.) 15

Take assessment online here:

http://tinyurl.com/PlntSci-14weed

Hint: When the answer is incorrect, you will see: "Wrong answer! Go Back!"

Notes

40 Workplace Safety

Major Concept

Workplace safety and procedures are essential to keeping employees safe.

Objectives

- List general rules for safety for lifting, using a ladder, or power tools
- Provide three reasons why safety is so important
- Identify the four major classifications of fire extinguishers

Link to Standards

CRP.08. Utilize critical thinking to make sense of problems and persevere in solving them.

CRP.11. Use technology to enhance productivity.

CRP.05. Consider the environmental, social and economic impacts of decisions.

Key Terms

- Chemical
- Hazard
- Inspection

Workplace Safety

- Safety is worth practicing.

- Agriculturalists work in a variety of situations where accidents may occur hurting the worker or a bystander.

- Awareness of the likely causes of accidents for prevention.

- Six reasons for working safely:

    1. Protect life

    2. Avoid injury

3. Avoid loss of time on the job
4. Avoid costly material loss
5. Avoid loss of time in getting the job done
6. Avoid inconvenience

Common Accidents and Identifying Prevention Procedures

- Lifting
    - Evaluate lifting projects to determine whether or not help is needed.
    - Lifting heavy objects improperly can injure the back.
    - Keep back upright when lifting objects.
    - Keep at least an 18 inch stance.
    - Let the legs do ALL the work.
    - Pivot with feet when moving object from one side to the other; don't twist at the waist.
    - Carry objects close to the body.
    - Use mechanical aids whenever available and practical.
- Ladders
    - Only buy ladders with non-skid footing (for use in and around structures).
    - Set straight ladders are set at 75 degrees (distance from base of ladder to the support is 1/4 the horizontal distance).

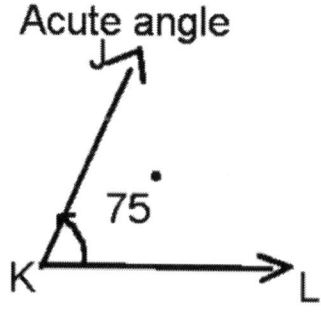

- Set ladder on firm level ground; do not lean it sideways.
- Never use ladder on snow or ice.
- Keep rungs free from slippery materials (plant materials, grease and snow).
- Never walk or jog ladder while standing on it.
- Never place ladder in front of a door without locking door.
- Never stand above third rung from the top.
- Only one person on a ladder at a time.

Safety

- General Tool Safety
    - Always respect the cutting edge of tools for the potential hazard they are.
    - Keep all cutting tools sharpened.
    - Always be prepared for the unexpected, especially when using power tools.
- Electrical Safety
    - Electricity is an unseen force which can be misdirected in many ways.
    - Main hazards of electricity are electrocution and overheating, which may cause a fire.
    - Make periodic electrical inspections of all electrical appliances and power tools used for home maintenance.
    - Look for unsafe electrical conditions and broken or exposed wires.
    - Never operate electrical tools near water or moist areas.
    - Make sure power tools are double-insulated and properly grounded.
    - Tool must have a three-prong plug if it is not double insulated.
    - Always keep the work area clean.
    - Overloading circuits can cause fire and damage appliances.

- Fire Safety

  - Sources of heat in the home or shop must all be maintained in safe working order and used properly to prevent fires.

  - Avoid improper storage of combustibles such as solvents paints cleaning and cooking oils and keep them away from flames (gas furnace, hot water heater).

  - Piles of waste oily rags can spontaneously ignite and burst into fire.

  - Fire extinguishers should be kept in every home.

  - Fires are classified as follows:

    - Class A - Fires of ordinary combustible materials such as wood, paper, cloth and rubber.

    - Class B - Fires of flammable liquids, gases and grease.

    - Class C - Electrical fires.

    - Class D - Fires of combustible materials such as magnesium, titanium, zirconium, sodium, and potassium (not likely to be found in normal households).

  - Correct class of fire for each extinguisher is on the label.

  - Follow directions on the extinguisher.

- Shop and Household **Chemical Safety**

  - Pesticide and cleaning agents must be properly stored and used according to label directions.

  - Keep them out of reach of children.

  - Always keep chemicals in their original container.

- Safe Clothing

  - Remove rings from fingers before working with power tools or electricity.

  - Never wear torn clothing or ties when working with power tools.

  - Keep hair short or out of the way.

- Wear safety glasses when the job dictates this protection.
- Ear plugs or muffs must be worn in loud noise areas.

- General Safety Tips
  - Know individual limitations.
  - Never try to do more than can be done safely.
  - Asking for help is no disgrace.
  - Always have a first aid kit in a convenient, specified place in the shop and home.
  - Take time to learn some of the simple and most important first aid procedures.

Summary

Safety is worth practicing. A general review of safe practices is important to prevention. Agriculturalists will work in a variety of situations where accidents may occur. Accidents may hurt the worker or the bystander. Understand the likely causes of accidents and the remedial aids in prevention. Common accidents involve lifting, ladders, electricity, fire hazards, chemicals and power tools.

Resources

Free complementary PowerPoint:
http://www.tagmydoc.com/dl/1ku0Ba/gk8k

OSHA
http://www.entomology.wisc.edu/mbcn/fea102.html

Workplace Safety & Health
http://www.dol.gov/dol/topic/safety-health/

Workplace Safety & Health Law
http://www.sba.gov/content/workplace-safety-health

Assessment

1. T or F? The most important reason for workplace safety is so you don't have to carry insurance.

2. The main hazards of electricity are electrocution and overheating, which may cause a/an _____.
    a.) argument   b.) wreck   c.) fire   d.) fall

3. T or F? You should never have more than one person on a ladder at one time.

4. Fires of flammable liquids, gases and grease are classified as Class_____.
    a.) A   b.) B   c.) C   d.) D

5. T or F? Always keep chemicals in the original container.

Take assessment online here:

http://tinyurl.com/PlntSci-14safety

Hint: When the answer is incorrect, you will see: "Wrong answer! Go Back!"

Notes

41 Genetic Engineering and Biotechnology

Major Concept

Biotechnology and genetic engineering improve plants and plant production.

Objectives

- Define the following: biotechnology, bioengineering, bioinformatics, genetic engineering, genomics, proteomics and plant tissue culture
- Identify the differences and similarities of traditional plant breeding and genetic engineering of plants
- List advantages and disadvantages of tissue culture
- Identify the steps in tissue culture
- Provide examples of genetic engineering in crop plants

Link to Standards

BS.01. NCAE Standard: Assess factors that have influenced the evolution of biotechnology in agriculture.

Key Terms

- Acclimation
- Bioinformatics
- Biotechnology
- Callus
- Clones
- Explants
- Genetic engineering
- Genomics
- GMO
- Proteomics
- Tissue culture

Biotechnology

- Application of molecular biology and genetic engineering for industrial, medical and agricultural advances or improvements or to solve problems.

- Management of biological systems for the benefit of humanity.

- Using living organisms or their products for commercial purposes.

- Practiced by human society since the beginning of recorded history in such activities as baking bread, making wine, or breeding food crops or domestic animals.

Genetic Engineering of Plants

- Relies on the manipulation of genes without depending on sexual reproduction for transferring genes and generating new genotypes.

- Advanced form of **biotechnology**, techniques involve gene splicing, replication and transfer of genes to other organisms.

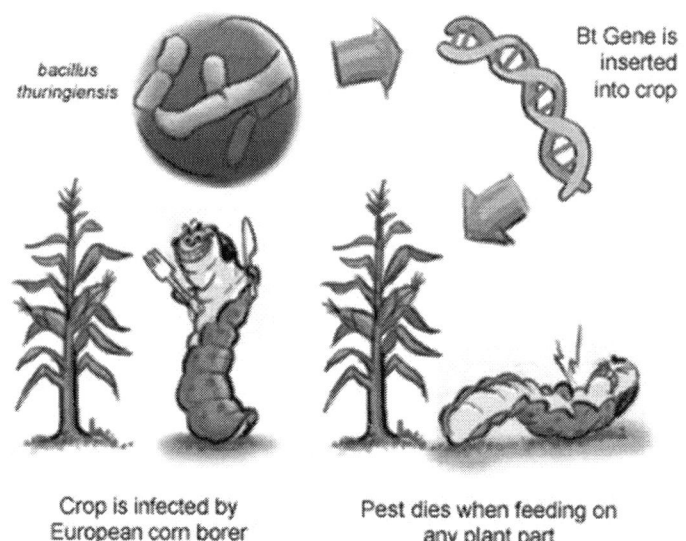

Purposes of Biotechnology

- Improve crop productivity

  o Increase yield

- Improve plant quality

  o Enhance nutritional quality.

    ✓ Ex: Change the amount and kind of amino acids in seed proteins.

  o Change plant products for new uses.

    ✓ Ex: Develop oil products that can be used for fuels or lubricants.

- Improve plant performance.

  o Increase plant disease/insect resistance.

  o Extend range of climate that plants can tolerate.

- Develop plants resistant to specific herbicides.
  - ✓ Ex: Roundup Ready Soybeans.
- Specific examples of **genetic engineering**:
  - Engineering to increase the efficiency of nitrogen fixation.
    - ✓ Ex: Transfer nitrogen-fixing genes from bacteria to plants.
  - Engineering organisms to combat plant diseases.
    - ✓ Ex: Breeding resistant varieties to control diseases.
  - Engineering for insect control.
    - ✓ Ex: Transfer genes for natural insect resistance from one plant to another.
  - Engineering to prevent forest damage.
    - ✓ Ex: Add genes from frost-resistant to frost-susceptible plants.
  - Engineering plants to tolerate environmental stress.
    - ✓ Ex: Add genes from desert plants to crop plants to increase their heat tolerance.

Examples of Biotechnology on Production Agriculture

- Scientists have been able to adjust the nutritional content of plants and produce disease-resistant and herbicide-resistant crops; produce plants that withstand drought, extreme cold or hot or salty soils, enabling producers to use land that is currently useless.
- Availability of Roundup-Ready Soybeans
  - The new soybeans were created with biotechnology that allowed a glyphosate-resistant gene to be inserted into a soybean cell.
  - The result was a genetically altered crop that stands up to glyphosate.
    - ✓ The same biotechnology is being used to make corn and soybeans that resist glufosinate, another nonselective herbicide.
- Tobacco, tomatoes, and other plants have had genes introduced to make them immune to tobacco mosaic virus.

- Engineered bacteria that prevent ice formation and frost damage to plants.

- Potato tubers in tissue culture systems to provide disease-free seed stock.

- Soybean plants and bacteria that will fix nitrogen more efficiently.

- A virus diagnostic kit to monitor the spread of viral disease in corn fields.

Tissue Culture, a Biotechnology – Advantages and Disadvantages

- Advantages

  - **Tissue culture** plants are genetically uniform and physiologically juvenile, which promotes vigorous growth and more branching, resulting in better finished plants.

  - Uniform maturity of plants, with fewer culls and relatively disease free population.

  - Lower shipping costs.

  - Increased availability of plants - production is not subject to season, weather conditions, or sudden disease or insect outbreaks.

  - Few quarantine restrictions.

  - Allows for more efficient space management for growers since propagation areas can now be used for finishing plants.

- Disadvantages

  - High lab costs - Labs may not be adaptable to seasonal needs of growers, since tissue culture provides a steady stream of plant material.

  - Long range planning is required by growers - labs require a commitment of need for up to one year by growers.

  - Cost effectiveness - growers often pay the same price for a smaller tissue culture plant than one conventionally propagated.

How Tissue Culture Works

- Each plant cell has all the genetic information it needs to reproduce and develop into an entire plant.

  - Tissue culture is a method of growing tiny pieces of plants called **explants** on artificial medium under sterile conditions.

- Plants regenerated through tissue culture are called **clones**, because they have the same origin and are identical to the parent plant.

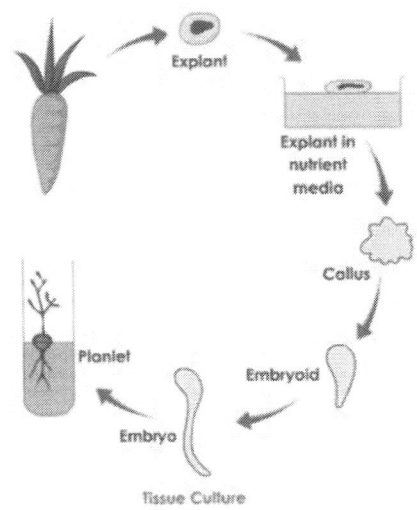

- Actively growing plant parts (root and shoot tips, developing leaves, lateral shoots, seed embryos) work best for tissue culture.

  - Although most any plant tissue can be used, cells from young tissue have been found to reproduce and grow better.

- Tissue taken from a plant should be small to ensure fairly homogeneous cells.

  - First form of growth of the tissue culture is called a **callus**, which is generally formed by placing the tissue in contact with a selected culture medium.

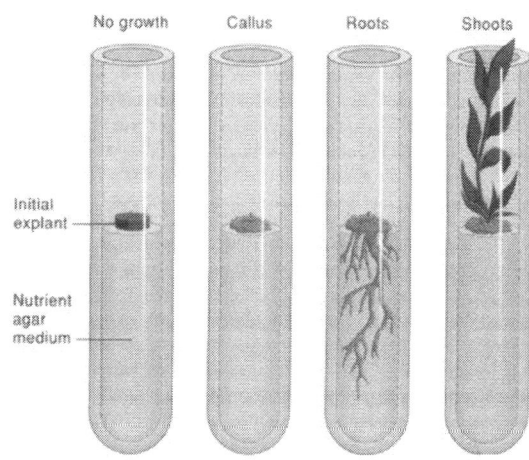

  - Important characteristics of the growing medium include salt mixture, solidity, pH, and hormone concentration.

  - Optimum growth occurs at cool temperatures.

  - Growth and differentiation depend primarily on the quality of the growth medium.

- Plant growth hormones promote cell division.

  - Proportions of shoot hormones in relation to root hormones determine whether the callus develops more roots or shoot development.

Steps in Tissue Culture

- Establishment of an aseptic culture (explant).

- Multiplication of cells in the starting tissue (proliferation).

- Preparation of the new plant for existence outside of the culture (**acclimation**).

  o Plants possess a unique capability to regenerate not only tissues and organs, but also entire plants.

  o New growth is usually initiated in meristematic tissue, where new tissue growth occurs.

    ✓ Cells in this tissue have not yet been programmed to differentiate into leaves, stems, roots, etc.

  o Differentiation occurs because of genetic makeup, environmental conditions, nutrients, hormone levels, and other factors.

  o Some differentiated cells are able to revert back to a meristematic (undifferentiated) state and to initiate growth of new and different tissue.

    ✓ Plant tissues normally respond to a wound by producing a mass of parenchyma cells (a callus). These cells often account for adventitious growth.

- New plant material started from tissue culture develops smaller than normal leaves, but produces normal size leaves after the tissue culture plantlets are rooted and have grown in soil for a short time.

New Words from Biotechnology

- **Genomics**

  o Operationally defined as investigations into the structure and function of very large numbers of genes undertaken in simultaneous fashion.

  o Study of all the nucleotide sequences, including structural genes, regulatory sequences and noncoding DNA segments, in the chromosome of an organism plant or animal is called genomics.

- **Bioinfomatics**

  o Study of the inherent structure of biological information and biological systems.

    ✓ Putting together the systematic biological data with analytic theory and practical tools of computer science and mathematics.

  o Part of "omics" revolution that has made it possible to analyze and interpret all of the genomics data is bioinformatics.

✓ For example, genomics generates data and bioinformatics provides the analytical tools enabling those data to be interpreted.

- **Proteomics**

    o Aimed to identify and characterize the expression pattern, cellular location, activity, regulation, post-transitional modifications, molecular interactions, three-dimensional structures and functions of each protein in a biological system.

Public Awareness

- Concern that widespread use of plants and animals with altered genetic characteristics may threaten the environment by disturbing the existing balance between or among organisms.

    o Gene mutation and changes in gene position within chromosomes are normal events in all living organisms; organisms with new properties are constantly emerging.

    o Transgenic technology expands the scope of these events.

- Careful examination of the properties of the transgenic organism is essential before it is studied outside the closed environment of the laboratory.

- Transgenic crops approved and found harmless.

- Some groups against genetically modified organisms (**GMO**).

- Labeling of GMO products.

Summary

Biotechnology is the application of knowledge for practical use in life in which molecular biology and genetic engineering can be applied to industrial, medical, and agricultural problems. Genetic engineering of plants relies on the manipulation of genes without depending on sexual reproduction for transferring genes and generating new genotypes. Scientists use genetic engineering to adjust the nutritional content of plants, produce disease-resistant and herbicide-resistant crops, produce plants that withstand drought, extreme cold or hot or salty soils. The purpose of plant tissue culture is a method of growing tiny pieces of plants called explants on artificial medium under sterile conditions. Genomics, bioinfomatics and proteomics are new words introduce by biotechnology.

Resources

Free complementary PowerPoint:
http://www.tagmydoc.com/dl/1eUkrm/gk8i

Parker, R. 2010. Plant and soil science: Fundamentals and applications. (Ch. 19) Clifton Park, NY: Delmar Cengage Learning.

Genetic Engineering of Crop Plants
http://www.yale.edu/ynhti/curriculum/units/2000/7/00.07.02.x.html

Biotechnology: Is the Science of the Future
http://www.acs.org/content/acs/en/careers/whatchemistsdo/careers/biotechnology.html

Assessment

1. T or F? Biotechnology uses living organisms or their products for commercial purposes.

2. Genetic engineering of plants relies on the manipulation of genes without depending on _____.
    a.) DNA segments   b.) public awareness   c.) sexual reproduction
    d.) tissue culture

3. T or F? Biotechnology in tissue culture decreases the availability of plants.

4. T or F? Plants regenerated through tissue culture are called clones, because they have the same origin and are identical to the parent plant.

5. Genomics is the study of all the _____, including structural genes, regulatory sequences and noncoding DNA segments, in the chromosome of an organism plant or animal.
    a.) sexual reproduction   b.) tissue culture   c.) molecular interactions
    d.) nucleotide sequences

Take assessment online here:

http://tinyurl.com/PlntSci-15

Hint: When the answer is incorrect, you will see: "Wrong answer! Go Back!"

Notes

42 Fiber Crops

Major Concept

Fiber crops generate jobs and provide important textile products.

Objectives

- Name five fiber crops
- Identify the cultural requirements of cotton
- Recognize the steps in harvesting cotton
- List steps in the processing of cotton
- Identify insect pests of cotton

Link to Standards

PS.02. Apply principles of classification, plant anatomy, and plant physiology to plant production and management.

PS.03. Propagate, culture and harvest plants and plant products based on current industry standards.

Key Terms

- Boll
- Defoliated
- Micronaire

Fiber Crops

- Grown mostly for textile cloth.

- Plant fiber crops include: cotton, flax, hemp, jute, sisal and kenaf.

- Cotton is a major fiber crop in the U.S.

Cotton

- A warm season perennial that is grown in the U.S. as an annual.

- Requires 180 frost free days.

- Cotton belongs to the Mallow Family.
- American Upland Cotton scientific name: *Gossypium hirsutum*

Cotton Description and Growth

- Two to six feet in height.
- Flower buds (squares)
    - White - first day
    - Pink - second day
    - Red - late second day
    - **Boll** - fruit of the plant
- Each pollinated blossom develops into a structure called a boll.
- Fibrous material is known as lint.

Adaptation and Distribution

- Requires a long growing warm season and adequate moisture (rainfall/irrigation).
- Primarily adapted to Southern and Southwestern States.
- Texas is the state with the greatest production but it is grown from coast to coast, south of the 37th parallel in the following states:

    - Texas
    - Mississippi
    - California
    - Arkansas
    - Louisiana
    - Tennessee
    - Georgia
    - Alabama

USDA Cotton Overview from the Economic Research Service
http://www.ers.usda.gov/topics/crops/cotton-wool.aspx#.UouyC8Ry2So

Management

- Production practices are similar to corn and soybean.
- All are planted in spring.
- Produce best on fertile soil, planted in rows and protected from weeds and pests.

Planting

- Planted in well-tilled seed beds in April and May.
- Rows are usually 30-38 inches apart.
- Usually 3-4 seeds per row foot (30,000-40,000 plants per acre).
- Usually planted, depending upon the moisture, from ½ to 1 inch deep.
- Usually safe to plant when the soil temperature reaches 65°F for 3 days.
- Some genetically modified cotton includes: Bt7 and Roundup Ready7

Pest Management

- Probably the most difficult part of cotton production.
- Major Insect Pests of Cotton (see table below)

Pests	Damage	Control
Boll weevil	feeds on deposits and eggs in squares and bolls	chemical; cultural; plant resistant varieties
Bollworm	bores into squares and bolls	chemical; cultural
Tobacco budworm	bores into squares and bolls	chemical; cultural
Pink bollworm	bores into bolls and eats developing seeds	chemical; quarantine
Plant bug	feeds on squares and destroys squares	chemical
Fleahopper	feeds on squares	chemical
Thrips	sucks sap from young plants	chemical; cultural
Spider mites	destroys leaves by creating massive webs on underside of leaves	biological; chemical
Aphids	feeds on underside of leaves and squares	beneficial insects; chemical

Pests	Damage	Control
Whitefly	feeds on underside of leaves; reducing plant growth efficiency	chemical; control host plants

Weed Management

- Cultivation

- Many new herbicides have been introduced allowing producers more flexibility in management.
  - Pre-plant incorporate
  - Post-plant
  - Use of Roundup Ready7 cotton

Protection from Insects and Fungal Diseases

- Usually apply fungicides and insecticides at planting.

- Most cotton is routinely checked for insects once or twice a week – scouted.

- As various plant pests reach economic thresholds, decisions to control with spray are made (Integrated Pest Management; IPM).
  - Given the Boll Weevil Eradication has been incorporated it is not a significant pest.

Fertilization

- Returns are usually adequate to provide a well-rounded nutrient program.

- Soil testing recommended every year on high value crops like cotton.

- Pre-plant- Most producers will apply fertilizer pre-plant as recommended by soil test results.

Tissue Analysis

- Some producers rely on tissue analysis to provide optimum fertility for the crop.

- Many producers will apply nitrogen, boron, potassium or minor nutrients as recommended by tissue analysis.

Irrigation

- Although considered an excellent dryland crop, cotton responds well to irrigation, often giving high return on investment as compound to soybean and corn.

- Specific irrigation and water use tables have been developed for optimum efficiency and production.

Harvesting

- All cotton harvesting is now done mechanically with 2 to 6 row cotton pickers.
    - Given all bolls do not ripen at the same time it is difficult to harvest.

- Most cotton must be **defoliated** to remove green leaves to prevent staining during harvest.

- Stained cotton is graded lower in quality and paid for at a reduced price.

- As the season progresses, it may become necessary to apply boll opening or ripening chemicals to fields to maximize picker efficiency.

Grading and Processing Cotton

- Cotton gin – removes trash and seeds from cotton fiber.

- Cotton is packed into bales weighing 500 lbs.

- Grading – based on fiber length, color and presence of trash.

- **Micronaire** – a measure of fiber fineness and maturity.
    - An airflow instrument is used to measure the air permeability of a constant mass of cotton fibers compressed to a fixed volume.
    - A micronaire of 3.4 or below is considered low micronaire, and 5.0 and above is considered high micronaire. Micronaire values of 3.5 to 3.6 and those from 4.3 to 4.9 are considered in the base range.
    - Premium range is 3.7 to 4.2.

Summary

Fiber crops are grown mostly for textile cloth. Crops include: cotton, flax, hemp, jute, sisal, and kenaf. Cotton is a major crop in the U.S. Cotton requires a long growing warm season and adequate moisture and is primarily adapted to Southern and Southwestern States. Weed management and fertilization must be taken into consideration when growing fiber crops. Some producers rely on tissue analysis to provide optimum fertility for the crop. Specific irrigation and water use tables have been developed for optimum efficiency and production. All harvesting is now done mechanically with 2 to 6 row cotton pickers. Grading is based on fiber length, color and presence of trash.

Resources

Free complementary PowerPoint:
http://www.tagmydoc.com/dl/1D11oW/gk8d

Parker, R. 2010. Plant and soil science: Fundamentals and applications. (p. 449-453) Clifton Park, NY: Delmar Cengage Learning.

University of Florida IFAS Extension - Cotton Cultural Practices and Fertility Management
http://edis.ifas.ufl.edu/ag200

Cotton and other Fiber Crops
http://www.dpi.nsw.gov.au/agriculture/broadacre/summer-crops/fibres

Assessment

1. Each pollinated cotton blossom develops into a structure called a _____.
    a.) boll   b.) lint   c.) ball   d.) plume

2. _____ is the state with the greatest cotton production but it is grown from coast to coast.
    a.) Mississippi   b.) Arkansas   c.) California   d.) Texas

3. T or F? Cotton is usually safe to plant when the soil temperature reaches 50°F for 3 days.

4. T or F? Soil testing is recommended every two years on high value crops like cotton.

5. T or F? Boll weevils are one of the major pests that feed on deposits and eggs in squares and bolls of cotton.

Take assessment online here:

http://tinyurl.com/PlntSci-16

Hint: When the answer is incorrect, you will see: "Wrong answer! Go Back!"

Notes

43 Cereal Grains

Major Concept

Important components of a grain production system include timely planting, disease control, proper fertilization, variety selection, timely harvesting and proper storage.

Objectives

- Identify four major grain crops
- List five criteria in selecting a grain crop
- List three cultural practices each for corn, wheat, and rice
- Name six cereal grain crops

Link to Standards

PS.01. Develop and implement a crop management plan for a given production goal that accounts for environmental factors.

PS.03. Propagate, culture and harvest plants and plant products based on current industry standards.

Key Terms

- Aflatoxin
- Degree day

Five Criteria for Selecting a Grain Crop

- Five criteria for selecting a grain crop are climate, soil and water needs, market availability, technology, personal skills and preference.

    1. Climate - must fill the needs of the crop.

    2. Soil and water - must be within the requirements of the selected crop.

    3. Market - availability of market is critical to success.

    4. Technology - includes use of improved seed, pest control, equipment, fertilizer.

5. Personnel skill and preference - experience in growing a particular crop, current with crop developments, skilled work force availability.

Cultural Practices for Major Grain Crops

- Corn

  - Variety- bred for local conditions.

  - Planting- should occur after the danger of frost.

  - Temperature is an important factor throughout the growing season.

  - General rule is to plant after the soil temperature is above 50° F at a soil depth of 2 inches; seed germination is affected by the temperature of the soil.

  - Stages of growth are related to growing degree days.

    - ✓ **Degree day** is maximum temperature + minimum temperature in a day divided by 2 minus 50.

  - Fertilization tends to need more fertilizer than most crops.

    - ✓ Soil test should be made prior to seedbed preparation to determine the needed soil amendments.

    - ✓ 150 bushels of corn per acre will require 170 pounds of nitrogen (N), 35 pounds of phosphorus (P_2O_5) and 175 of potassium (K_2O).

    - ✓ Soil with a pH of 5-8 is recommended.

  - Pest /weed control- weeds, insects, nematodes and some diseases.

    - ✓ Recommendations on pest control should be obtained at a university or through a local agricultural consultant.

    - ✓ Integrated Pest Management (IPM) is increasingly used to control pests.

    - ✓ Weeds are typically controlled with cultivation and chemicals.

    - ✓ Crop is targeted by bud worms and ear worms.

  - Harvesting - moisture content of 20 to 28%.

    - ✓ Higher moisture content increases the need for artificial drying.

- ✓ Grain with high moisture content will promote the development of **aflatoxin**, a highly poisonous substance produced by fungi in grain.

- ✓ Corn harvesting equipment must be properly set to avoid grain loss.

- ✓ Irrigation may be needed.

- ✓ Timing of harvest is important for maximum yield.

- Wheat

  - Seasonal plantings

    - ✓ Spring wheat (warm season) planted in northern states in spring; harvested in fall.

    - ✓ Winter wheat - grown in southern U.S.; planted in fall and harvested in spring.

  - Color - red or white? Most in U.S. is red.

  - Hardness - soft or hard? Some of each in U.S - depends on local markets; used for different products (hard- bread, soft- cakes).

  - Practices

    - ✓ Varieties – recommendations for local areas.

    - ✓ Planting - prepared seed bed; date based on type; narrow row (4-6") 12,000-20,000 seed/acre (+/- 14 seed per foot of row; at about 1" depth).

    - ✓ Fertilizers - high nitrogen (N) based on soil test data.

    - ✓ Pests - insects/diseases- based on local problems/recommendations.

    - ✓ Harvesting - when mature and below 12.5% moisture.

  - Fertilizer – based on a soil test.

  - Pest/Weed Control – a comprehensive disease/pest management program is recommended.

  - Harvesting – winter wheat is harvested early summer, spring varieties are harvested late summer.

- Rice
    - Planting – with a drill or may be broadcast by airplanes.
    - Fertilizer – based on soil test.
    - Pest/weed control – integrating cultural practices and herbicides.
    - Harvesting – depending on location, when mature, usually in July, September or October with combines.
    - Grown on large farms.
        - ✓ Can be seeded in a dry or wet bed.
        - ✓ Water management is necessary.
        - ✓ Water level of field kept between 2 – 4 inches.
        - ✓ Mechanization used extensively.
- Minor Grain Crops
    - Amaranth
    - Buckwheat
    - Millet
    - Quinoa
    - Teff
    - Triticale
    - Wild Rice
- Other Grain Crops
    - Oats - similar to wheat.
    - Sorghum - similar to corn.
    - Barley - similar to wheat.
    - Rye - similar to wheat.

Note: Soil fertility, plant nutrients and pest control are unique for each cereal grain but a general discussion of these items can be found in Topics 4, 6 and 14.

Summary

Five criteria for selecting a grain crop are climate, soil and water needs, market availability, technology, personal skills and preference. Cultural practices for corn, wheat and rice are included in this outline. Other grain crops, not covered, include oats, sorghum, barley and rye. Minor grain crops, not covered, include amaranth, buckwheat, millet, quinoa, teff, triticale and wild rice.

Resources

Free complementary PowerPoint:
http://www.tagmydoc.com/dl/F4R9j/gk8a

Parker, R. 2010. Plant and soil science: Fundamentals and applications. Clifton Park, NY: Delmar Cengage Learning.

Cereal Grain Crops
http://pnwhandbooks.org/weed/agronomic/cereal-grain-crops

Informed Farmers: Cereal Grain Crops
http://informedfarmers.com/crops/cereal-grain-crops/

Assessment

1. T or F? Corn, wheat, rice and teff are all major grain crops.

2. Five criteria for selecting a grain crop are climate, soil and water needs, market availability, _____, personal skills and preference.
   a.) recommendations on pest control   b.) stages of growth   c.) technology
   d.) ease of growth

3. T or F? Water levels on fields of growing rice should be kept at 4 to 5 inches.

4. T or F? Amaranth, buckwheat, millet and quinoa are minor grain crops in the U.S.
5. _____ may be planted with a drill or broadcast by airplanes.
   a.) Rice   b.) Sorghum   c.) Corn   d.) Wheat

Take assessment online here:

http://tinyurl.com/PlntSci-17

Hint: When the answer is incorrect, you will see: "Wrong answer! Go Back!"

Notes

44 Forage Crops

Major Concept

Forage crops provide feed and nutrients for livestock.

Objectives

- Identify the difference among hay, silage and pasture
- Explain the difference between grasses and legumes
- Identify five common forage crops
- Define four ways forage crops are grouped

Link to Standards

PS.01. Develop and implement a crop management plan for a given production goal that accounts for environmental factors.

PS.02. Apply principles of classification, plant anatomy, and plant physiology to plant production and management.

Key Terms

- Forage crops
- Grasses
- Hay
- Legumes
- Pasture
- Silage

Forage Crops

- A crop that contains leaves or plants which are usually eaten by animals.
    - Hay, silage, or pasture.
        - ✓ **Hay** - Cut and dried to contain a low level of moisture.
        - ✓ **Silage** - Chopped green forage that has been allowed to ferment in the absence of air.
        - ✓ **Pasture** - Forage harvested by livestock itself.

- Importance of Forage Crops
    - Allows farmers to grow feed for animals on land that is not suitable for cultivation.
    - Usually the least expensive source of nutrients available for feeding livestock.
- Grasses and Legume Differences
    - **Grasses** are hardier plants but require nitrogen fertilizer.
    - **Legumes** produce their own nitrogen and are higher quality plants.
- Common Forage Crops
    - Kentucky bluegrass
    - Timothy
    - Johnson
    - Brome
    - Fescue
    - Legumes
    - Clover
    - Kudzu
    - Alfalfa
    - Bermuda
- Forage Crop Groups
    - Cold or warm climate
    - Area grown in country
    - General use and nutritional value
    - Expected life cycle of crop
    - Maintenance required
    - Harvesting methods

Summary

Forage production deals with growing plants for livestock feed. The major forage crops are grasses and legumes and are grown for pasture, hay or silage. Land not suitable for cultivation can be used as forage and the cost of feed is reduced. There are many varieties of forage crops and they can be grouped by climate, where they are grown, nutritional value and maintenance.

Resources

Free complementary PowerPoint:
http://www.tagmydoc.com/dl/19rjAN/gk8Y

Parker, R. 2010. Plant and soil science: Fundamentals and applications. Clifton Park, NY: Delmar Cengage Learning.
Alternate Forage Crops
http://www.uwex.edu/ces/forage/pubs/altcrp.pdf

Forage Grasses and Legumes
http://www.hort.purdue.edu/newcrop/cropmap/indiana/crop/forage.html

Assessment

1. T or F? Forage crops contain leaves or plants which are usually eaten by animals.

2. _____ is chopped green forage that has been allowed to ferment in the absence of air.
   a.) Hay   b.) Pasture   c.) Straw   d.) Silage

3. T or F? Forage allows farmers to grow feed for animals on land that is not suitable for cultivation.

4. Legumes produce their own _____ and are higher quality plants.
   a.) nitrogen   b.) energy   c.) oxygen   d.) offspring

5. T or F? Forage crops can be grouped by climate, where they are grown, nutritional value and maintenance.

Take assessment online here:

http://tinyurl.com/PlntSci-18

Hint: When the answer is incorrect, you will see: "Wrong answer! Go Back!"

Notes

45 Oilseeds

Major Concept
Oilseeds are an important crop in the United States providing food, industrial products and income.

Objectives
- Identify five oil crops
- Describe how oil crops are harvested to maximize quality

Link to Standards

PS.02. Apply principles of classification, plant anatomy, and plant physiology to plant production and management.

PS.03. Propagate, culture and harvest plants and plant products based on current industry standards.

Key Terms
- Blight

Oil Crops
- Seeds of oil crops are extracted for oil to be used in cooking and for other purposes such as lubricants, paints and cosmetics.

- Oil Crops Grown
    - Peanuts
    - Cotton
    - Corn
    - Soybeans
    - Sunflowers
    - Canola (Rape)
    - Linseed
    - Tung seeds
    - Coconut
    - Olive
    - Peppermint
    - Spearmint

- Uses of Vegetable Oils
    - Cooking
    - Ethanol: gasoline

- o Biodiesel
- o Flavorings
- Byproducts of Oil Crops
  - o Starch by-products are used to make:
    - ✓ Chewing gum
    - ✓ Plywood
    - ✓ Crayons
    - ✓ Biodegradable plastics
  - o Meal by-products are used to make:
    - ✓ Animal feed
    - ✓ Fertilizer
    - ✓ Industrial processes

Soybeans - Most Important Oil Crop in the United States

- Common cultural practices affecting a soybean crop: climate, planting practices, controlling pests/weeds, nutrient needs and timing of harvest.
- Climate
  - o Ideal temperature for germination and growth is 86°F.
  - o Development occurs more slowly at higher or lower temperatures.
  - o Temperature below 75°F delays flowering.
  - o Varieties are developed to fit various climates and photo periods.
- Planting practices
  - o Rows
  - o Drilled
  - o Broadcast

- Soybeans begin blooming 6-8 weeks after planting.
- First blooms produce mature beans 12-15 weeks.
- Moisture is critical especially at blooming and bean development time; low moisture can result in lower yields.

- Common Problems Affecting Soybeans
  - Insects
    - Wireworms
    - White grubs
    - Bean leaf beetle
    - Grasshopper
    - Mexican bean beetle
    - Fall army worm
  - Diseases – **blight** is a disease or injury of plants marked by the formation of lesions, withering and death of parts.
    - Bacterial Blight
    - Brown Spot
    - Downy Mildew
    - Pod and Stem Blight
    - Soybean Cyst Nematode
    - Soybean Rust
  - Weeds
    - Control with a pre-emergence herbicide
    - Control with tilling

- Nutrient Requirements
    - Soybeans are a legume, thus the plant forms nitrogen nodules on the roots.
    - Seed must be inoculated at time of planting to assure maximum nitrogen fixation.
    - Require relatively high amounts of potassium and phosphorus.
    - pH range of 5.8-7.0
- Harvesting
    - Beans are harvested with 14% moisture content, if higher then must be artificially dried.
    - A combine is used to harvest.
    - Good yields are 60 or more bushels per acre.
    - Approximately 60 million acres of soybeans have a yield of 1.5 billion bushels.
    - Approximate 1/3 of soybean crop is exported.

Summary

Seeds of oil crops are extracted for oil to be used in cooking and for other purposes such as lubricants, paints, and cosmetics. Soybeans are one of the most important oil crops in the United States. One–third of the soy bean crop is exported. Soybeans can be affected by planting procedures, climate, pests and nutrient needs.

Resources

Free complementary PowerPoint:
http://www.tagmydoc.com/dl/QhRs4/gk8U

Parker, R. 2010. Plant and soil science: Fundamentals and applications. (pgs. 523-529) Clifton Park, NY: Delmar Cengage Learning.

Oil Seed Crops
http://www.bioenergy.wa.gov/OilSeed.aspx

Oilseeds Information
http://www.fas.usda.gov/oilseeds/default.asp

Crop Diseases
http://www.btny.purdue.edu/extension/pathology/cropdiseases/soybean/Soybean.html

Assessment

1. T or F? Plywood is made from the starch by-products of oil crops.

2. _____ is/are a disease or injury of plants marked by the formation of lesions, withering, and death of parts.
 a.) Wire worms   b.) Broadcasting   c.) Fall army worm   d.) Blight

3. T or F? Biodegradable plastics can be made from the meal by-products of oil crops.

4. T or F? Soybeans are harvested with 14% moisture content, if lower then must be artificially dried.

5. Soybeans are a legume, thus the plant forms _____ nodules on the roots.
 a.) phosphorus   b.) nitrogen   c.) potassium   d.) moisture

Take assessment online here:

http://tinyurl.com/PlntSci-19

Hint: When the answer is incorrect, you will see: "Wrong answer! Go Back!"

Notes

46 Sugar Crops

Major Concept

Sugar crops are important in the United States providing food, industrial products and income.

Objectives

- Classify important sugar crops according to production location
- Compare cultural practices for sugar cane and sugar beets
- Identify steps in harvesting sugar cane and sugar beets and their conversion to sugar
- Name the by-products of sugar cane and sugar beets

Link to Standards

PS.03. Propagate, culture and harvest plants and plant products based on current industry standards.

Key Terms

- Bagasse
- Blackstrap molasses
- Molasses
- Pulp
- Ratoon
- Vegetative

Sugar Crops

- Sugar is any food product used as a sweetener.
  - Sugar beets and sugar cane are the two most important sugar crops.
  - Corn syrup, maple syrup, and few other sources are used.
- Major Sugar Crops
  - Sugar cane (*Saccharum officinarum*)

- Sugar beets (*Beta vulgaris*)
- States leading in sugar beet and sugar cane production:
    - Sugar beets
        - ✓ Minnesota
        - ✓ Idaho
        - ✓ North Dakota
        - ✓ Michigan
        - ✓ California
    - Sugar cane
        - ✓ Florida
        - ✓ Louisiana
        - ✓ Hawaii
        - ✓ Texas
- U.S. sugar production statistics: http://www.ers.usda.gov/topics/crops/sugar-sweeteners/background.aspx#.UoKPVfmsim4

Growing and Harvesting Sugar Cane

- Sugar is extracted from the stalk.
- Leaves and roots are left in the field.
- Member of the grass family.
- Stalk is jointed and resembles a corn stalk.
    - As a tropical climate crop the stalk may grow 7-15 feet tall.
- Propagated **vegetatively** (asexual) - Stalks are cut into sections that range from 18-36 inches long.
    - These are laid end to end in a furrow and covered with soil 2-3 inches deep.
    - The nodes then grow tiny shoots that develop into mature stalks.
        - ✓ Roots also grow this way.

- Eight to thirty months are needed from planting to harvest.
  - At maturity it will produce seeds in tropical climates, so the cane is usually harvested by then, or the seeds are infertile.
- Forty five to fifty inches of rainfall or irrigation is required during growing season.
- Stalk reaches harvest size in one spring season or maturity in two years.
  - Cut sprouts will re-sprout and produce what is known as a **ratoon** (uncut or leftover) crop.
- Harvested in the fall in the U.S., and year round in Hawaii.
  - Two ways to harvest:
    1. Mechanical Harvester- cuts stalks, removes leaves and loads stalks.
    2. Field is burned to remove leaves before cutting, stalks are then raked into piles.

Extracting Sugar from Cane

- Sugar is extracted at a sugar refinery.
- Harvested stalks are crushed, which squeezes out the sugar juice.
- Clarification of the sugar solution accomplished by the application of lime.
- Sugar solution filtered several times to remove sediments (non-sugar substances).
- This juice is heated to get rid of moisture, which is released as a vapor.
- Juice concentrated by boiling, which promotes crystallization of the sucrose.
- Centrifuges separate the sugar crystals from the liquid portion or **molasses**.
- Molasses is produced if the heating process is stopped before brown crystals begin to form or if the sweet liquid is removed during the process.
- Brown raw sugar undergoes additional processing to become pure white sucrose.
- A Modern Sugar Factory http://www3.wooster.edu/stkitts/factory.htm#

By-products of Sugar Cane

- Syrup that remains after as much sugar as possible has been extracted is called **blackstrap molasses**; used in cattle feed, sold for human consumption, alcohol production.

- **Bagasse** – the fiber of the cane plant after crushing and extraction; used as a biofuel, and in the manufacture of pulp and building materials.

Growing and Harvesting Sugar Beets

- Biennial plant but is treated like an annual for production of sugar (if allowed the plants produce seeds the second year).

- Seeds are planted in spring using high speed precision equipment.

- One growing season the roots reach weight of 2 oz to 4.4 lbs.

- Sugar formation increases rapidly in late summer as nights get cooler and nitrogen sources are diminished in the soil.

- Harvesting is delayed as long as possible in the growing season to assure maximum sugar content.
    - Harvested with a machine that cuts off the tops, lifts the roots, and loads them onto a truck.
    - They are hauled into processing plants or beet piling stations.

- Most grown under contract with a processor.
    - Contract specifies:
        - ✓ When planted
        - ✓ Cultural practices used
        - ✓ When to harvest

Extracting Sugar from Beets

- Processing is a single, continuous process.

- Upon arrival at a sugar factory the beets are thoroughly washed and then shredded.

- Shreds are soaked in tanks of circulating hot water, allowing the diffusion of about 97% of the soluble sugar into the water.

- Next the shreds are pressed to squeeze out all of the sugary water.
    - Squeezed shreds are called **pulp**, which is a by-product.

- Sugar solution or "raw juice" contains about 10 to 15% sugar and many non-sugar substances.

- Clarification of the sugar solution accomplished by the application of lime, carbon dioxide and eventually sulfur dioxide.

- Sugar solution filtered several times to remove sediments (non-sugar substances).

- Juice is concentrated by boiling, which promotes crystallization of the sucrose.

- Centrifuges separate the sugar crystals from the liquid portion or molasses.

- Molasses is subjected to additional crystallizations, but eventually becomes a byproduct.

- Sugar at this point is raw sugar and is subjected to further refining which involves repeated washings and recrystallizations and de-colorization until it is pure white and nearly 100% sucrose.
    - At this stage beet sugar and cane sugar are identical.

By-Products of Sugarbeets

- Molasses and pulp - both used for livestock feed.

Summary

Sugar is any food product used as a sweetener. Sugar beets and sugar cane are the two most important sugar crops. Sugarcane is extracted from the stalk at a sugar refinery. Syrup that remains after as much sugar as possible has been extracted is called blackstrap molasses; used in cattle feed, sold for human consumption, alcohol production. The fiber of the cane plant after crushing and extraction is used as a biofuel, and in the manufacture of pulp and building materials. Sugar beets are a biennial plant but are treated as an annual for sugar production. Extracting sugar from beets is a continuous process. Most are grown under contract with a processor that specifies when planted, cultural practices used and when to harvest.

Resources

Free complementary PowerPoint:
http://www.tagmydoc.com/dl/DQRnx/gk8R

Parker, R. 2010. Plant and soil science: Fundamentals and applications. (pgs. 466-474) Clifton Park, NY: Delmar Cengage Learning.

Sugarcane Profile
http://www.agmrc.org/commodities__products/grains__oilseeds/sugarcane-profile/

Sugarbeet Profile
http://www.agmrc.org/commodities__products/grains__oilseeds/sugarbeet-profile/

Assessment

1. T or F? Sugar beet stalks are jointed and resemble a corn stalk.

2. Cut sugarcane stalk sprouts will re-sprout and produce what is known as a _____ crop.
    a.) biennial   b.) ratoon   c.) bagasse   d.) mature

3. T or F? During the refining process of sugarcane, molasses is produced if the heating process is stopped before brown crystals begin to form.

4. Harvesting sugar beets is delayed as long as possible in the growing season to assure maximum _____ content.
    a.) nitrogen   b.) root   c.) byproduct   d.) sugar

5. T or F? There comes a stage in the process of extraction that beet sugar and cane sugar are identical.

Take assessment online here:

http://tinyurl.com/PlntSci-20

Hint: When the answer is incorrect, you will see: "Wrong answer! Go Back!"

Notes

47 Vegetable Crops

Major Concept

A wide variety of vegetable crops important to human nutrition are grown commercially.

Objectives

- List ten vegetable crops by their botanical name and common name
- Identify importance of vegetables to U.S. Agriculture and human nutrition
- Classify vegetables based on edible parts
- Explain how the environment affects vegetable growth
- List the important soil factors that influence vegetable growth and production
- Name ways pests affect vegetable growth and production
- Identify how biotechnological advances can aid in increasing vegetable production
- Identify the methods of growing and marketing processes of vegetables
- List the intensive management requirements of vegetables

Link to Standards

PS.01. Develop and implement a crop management plan for a given production goal that accounts for environmental factors.

PS.03. Propagate, culture and harvest plants and plant products based on current industry standards.

Key Terms

- Fruit
- Marketing
- Vegetable

Economic Importance of Vegetables to U.S. Agriculture

- USDA National Agricultural Statistics Service – Vegetables:
  http://usda.mannlib.cornell.edu/MannUsda/viewDocumentInfo.do?documentID=1177

Botanical Names, Common Names and Edible Parts of Vegetables

Botanical Name	Common Name	Edible Plant Part
Allium cepa L. Cepa group	Onion	Bulb, leaf
Allium sativum L.	Garlic	Bulb
Allium schoenoprasum L.	Chive	Leaf
Zea mays var. *praecox* Bonaf.	Popcorn	Mature seed
Zea mays var. *rugosa* Bonaf.	Sweet corn	Immature seed
Asparagus officinalis L.	Asparagus	Shoot
Beta vulgaris L. Crassa group	Beet	Root, leaf
Spinacia oleracea L.	Spinach	Leaf
Lactuca sativa L.	Lettuce	Leaf
Taraxacum officinale Wiggers	Dandelion	Leaf
Ipomoea batatas (L.) Lam.	Sweet potato	Root, leaf
Armoracia rusticana P. Gaertn., B. Mey & Scherb	Horseradish	Root
Brassica juncea (L.) Czerniak.	Mustard greens	Leaf
Brassica napus L. Napobrassica group	Rutabaga	Root
Brassica oleracea L. Acephala group	Kale, collard	Leaf
Brassica oleracea L. Botrytis group	Cauliflower	Immature flower
Brassica oleracea L. Capitata group	Cabbage	Leaf
Brassica oleracea L. Gemmifera group	Brussels sprouts	Axillary bud
Brassica oleracea L. Italica group	Broccoli	Immature flower
Brassica rapa L. Rapifera group	Turnip	Root, leaf
Raphanus sativus L.	Radish	Root
Citrullus lanatus (Thund.) Matsum. & Nakai	Watermelon	Fruit
Citrullus lanatus var. *citroides*	Citron	Fruit
Cucumis melo L. Inodorous group	Honeydew melon	Fruit
Cucumis melo L. Reticulatus group	Muskmelon, Persian melon	Fruit
Cucumis sativus L.	Cucumber	Fruit
Cucurbita pepo L. var. *pepo*	Pumpkin, acorn squash	Fruit
Cucurbita pepo var. *melopepo* (L.) Alef.	Bush summer squash	Fruit
Glycine max (L.) Merrill	Soybean	Seed
Phaseolus limensis Macfady.	Lima bean	Seed
Phaseolus vulgaris L.	Snap bean	Fruit, seed

Botanical Name	Common Name	Edible Plant Part
Pisum sativum L.	Pea	Seed
Pisum sativum var. *arvense* (L.) Poir.	Field pea	Seed
Vigna unguiculata (L.) Walp.	Southern pea	Fruit, seed
Abelmoschus esculentus (L.) Moench	Okra	Fruit
Capsicum annuum var. *annuum* L.	Pepper: Bell, cayenne, chili, cone, red cluster	Fruit
Lycopersicon esculentum Mill.	Tomato	Fruit
Solanum melongena L.	Eggplant	Fruit
Solanum tuberosum L.	Potato	Tuber
Apium graveolens L. var. *dulce* (Mill.) Pers.	Celery	Petiole
Daucus carota L.	Carrot	Root

Importance of Vegetables in Human Nutrition

- Vegetable consumption and availability in the U.S. is tracked by the USDA and includes:

    - Artichokes
    - Asparagus
    - Snap beans
    - Broccoli
    - Cabbage
    - Carrots
    - Cauliflower
    - Celery
    - Sweet corn
    - Cucumbers
    - Eggplant
    - Endive
    - Escarole
    - Garlic
    - Romaine and leaf lettuce
    - Mushrooms
    - Onions
    - Bell peppers
    - Potatoes
    - Radishes
    - Spinach
    - Sweet potatoes
    - Tomatoes
    - Lima beans
    - Beets

- Depending on the vegetable, these are available fresh, dried, frozen or processed.

- Top five vegetable crops in the U.S.
    - Sweet corn
    - Onions
    - Lettuce
    - Broccoli
    - Tomatoes
- Top five vegetable producing states:
    - California
    - Florida
    - Arizona
    - Georgia
    - New York
- USDA Vegetables Summary provides statistics on vegetable production
  http://usda01.library.cornell.edu/usda/current/VegeSumm/VegeSumm-01-29-2013.pdf

Environment Affects Growth

- Require the proper amount of water, nutrients and sunlight.
- Important soil factors influence vegetable growth.
    - Soil needs the following components:
        - ✓ 25% H_2O
        - ✓ 25% O_2
        - ✓ 50% inorganic matter (containing nutrient elements)
- Sandy loamy (fertile soil of clay and sand containing humus) soil provides the best conditions for superior vegetable production.

Important Techniques in Producing a Vegetable Crop

- Appropriate soil type and fertility (quality)
- Water source
- Space
- Sufficient sunlight or other light source.
- Protection from animals.
- Lack of plant root competition from trees.

Pests Negatively Affect Growth and Production

- Pest can destroy or severely affect a plant's growth in numerous ways.
    - Destroy the vegetable portion of vegetable plants
    - Defoliate leaves
    - Bore into stalks
    - Destroy the fruiting structure
    - Eat the **fruit** (the sweet and flesh product of a plant that contains seed).
    - Lay eggs in fruit

Biotechnological Advances Can Aid in Increasing Vegetable Production

- Reducing costs of chemicals purchased.
- Reducing the number of times to spray.
    - Plants resistant to certain insects can help overall production.
    - Plants resistant to certain fungi, bacteria, viruses and other diseases can affect the overall production.

Marketing of Commercially Grown Vegetables

- Involves growers, buyers, shippers, wholesalers, brokers, chemical and seed industry, researchers, consultants and consumers.

- General **marketing** (the act or business of promoting and selling products) factors

  - High supply lowers price and increases quality required.

  - Low supply increase prices and lowers quality required.

- Reasons for commercial production in top five states

  - Warm temperatures

  - Well-suited soil types

  - Available water

- Intensive management requirements for **vegetable** (plant or part of a plant used as food) crops include:

  - Production factors

    - Irrigation

    - Disease, insects and weeds control

    - Temperature/growing season

    - Tillage maybe specialized

  - Labor requirements

    - Many crops are transplanted by hand.

    - Most crops are harvested by hand.

  - Economic factors to consider

    - Cost of planting

    - Cost of growing

    - Cost of harvesting

- Trend: Many growers opt to commercially produce vegetables instead of traditional agronomic crops.
    - Return on traditional crops declining.
    - Vegetables have the potential for greater return.

Summary

Vegetable consumption and availability in the U.S. is tracked by the USDA. The environment affects the growth of vegetables which require the proper amount of water, nutrients, and sunlight. Important techniques in producing a vegetable crop include the appropriate soil type and quality, water source and space. Pests can destroy or severely affect a plant's growth in numerous ways. Biotechnological advances can aid in increasing vegetable production. Marketing of commercially grown vegetables involves growers, buyers, shippers, wholesalers, brokers, chemical and seed industry, researchers, consultants and consumers.

Resources

Free complementary PowerPoint:
http://www.tagmydoc.com/dl/uS5xd/gk8O

Parker, R. 2010. Plant and soil science: Fundamentals and applications. (p.577-601) Clifton Park, NY: Delmar Cengage Learning.

USDA Economic Research Service – Vegetables and Pulses
http://www.ers.usda.gov/topics/crops/vegetables-pulses.aspx#.Uo5uKsRy2So

USDA Agricultural Research Service – Vegetable Crops Research
http://www.ars.usda.gov/main/site_main.htm?modecode=36-55-20-00

Assessment

1. Vegetable consumption and availability in the U.S. is tracked by the _____.
   a) FDA   b) CIA   c) USDA   d) FBI

2. In order to be a proper media for growth, soil needs water, oxygen and _____.
   a.) vegetable seeds   b.) organic matter   c.) inorganic matter   d.) bacterial resistance

3. T or F? Plant pests can potentially destroy the vegetable portion of vegetable plants.

4. T or F? Marketing factors excluded for commercially grown vegetables include researchers and brokers.

5. T or F? Some intensive management requirements for vegetable crops include irrigation, disease, insect and weed control, temperature and tillage.

6. The edible part of sweet corn is the _____.
   a.) fruit seed   b.) immature seed   c.) immature flower   d.) mature seed

Take assessment online here:

http://tinyurl.com/PlntSci-21

Hint: When the answer is incorrect, you will see: "Wrong answer! Go Back!"

Notes

48 Specialty Crops

Major Concept

Specialty crops for food, medicinal products and beautification create income as niche markets.

Objectives

- Identify the general categories and specific specialty crops
- Provide the USDA definition of a specialty crop
- List factors affecting the cultural requirements of various specialty crops
- Identify some specialty crop harvest techniques and processing

Link to Standards

PS.01. Develop and implement a crop management plan for a given production goal that accounts for environmental factors.

PS.02. Apply principles of classification, plant anatomy, and plant physiology to plant production and management.

PS.03. Propagate, culture and harvest plants and plant products based on current industry standards.

Key Terms

- Banding
- Broadcast
- Conifers
- Green initiatives

Specialty Crops

- Grown for a special purpose.

- Grown only in certain sections of the country.

- Defined by the USDA as:

  o The Specialty Crop Competitiveness Act of 2004 and the Food, Conservation, and Energy Act of 2008 have defined specialty crops as "fruits and vegetables, tree nuts, dried fruits, horticulture, and nursery crops (including floriculture)."

- Eligible plants must be intensively cultivated and used by people for food, medicinal purposes, and/or aesthetic gratification to be considered specialty crops.

- Processed products shall constitute greater than 50% of the specialty crop by weight, exclusive of added water.

- Accordingly the USDA definition specialty crops includes these general categories:

    - ✓ Fruits and Tree Nuts
    - ✓ Vegetables
    - ✓ Culinary Herbs and Spices
    - ✓ Medicinal Herbs
    - ✓ Horticulture
    - ✓ Annual Bedding Plants
    - ✓ Potted Flowering Plants
    - ✓ Potted Herbaceous Perennials
    - ✓ Cut Cultivated Greens
    - ✓ Cut Flowers
    - ✓ Foliage Plants
    - ✓ Christmas Trees
    - ✓ Deciduous Flowering Trees
    - ✓ Broadleaf Evergreens
    - ✓ Deciduous Shade Trees
    - ✓ Landscape Conifers (a tree that bears cones and evergreen needlelike or scale-like leaves)
    - ✓ Deciduous Shrubs

Specific specialty crop plants are identified in the following table (2013)

Fruits and Tree Nuts	
Almond	Grape (including raisin)
Apple	Guava
Apricot	Kiwi
Avocado	Litchi
Banana	Macadamia
Blackberry	Mango
Blueberry	Nectarine
Breadfruit	Olive
Cacao	Papaya
Cashew	Passion fruit
Citrus	Peach
Cherimoya	Pear
Cherry	Pecan
Chestnut (for nuts)	Persimmon
Coconut	Pineapple
Coffee	Pistachio
Cranberry	Plum (including prune)
Currant	Pomegranate
Date	Quince
Feijou	Raspberry
Fig	Strawberry
Filbert (hazelnut)	Suriname cherry
Gooseberry	Walnut

Vegetables	
Artichoke	Mustard and other greens
Asparagus	Okra
Bean, snap or green Lima, dry, edible	Pea Garden, English or edible pod
Beet, table	Onion
Broccoli (including broccoli raab)	Opuntia
Brussels sprouts	Parsley
Cabbage (including Chinese)	Parsnip
Carrot	Pepper
Cauliflower	Potato
Celeriac	Pumpkin
Celery	Radish (all types)
Chive	Rhubarb
Collards (including kale)	Rutabaga
Cucumber	Salsify
Edamame	Spinach
Eggplant	Squash (summer and winter)

Vegetables	
Endive	Sweet corn
Garlic	Sweet potato
Horseradish	Swiss chard
Kohlrabi	Taro
Leek	Tomato (including tomatillo)
Lettuce	Turnip
Melon (all types)	Watermelon
Mushroom (cultivated)	

Culinary Herbs and Spices		
Ajwain	Clary	Malabathrum
Allspice	Cloves	Marjoram
Angelica	Comfrey	Mint (all types)
Anise	Common rue	Nutmeg
Annatto	Coriander	Oregano
Artemisia (all types)	Cress	Orris root
Asafetida	Cumin	Paprika
Basil (all types)	Curry	Parsley
Bay (cultivated)	Dill	Pepper
Bladder wrack	Fennel	Rocket (arugula)
Bolivian coriander	Fenugreek	Rosemary
Borage	Filé (gumbo, cultivated)	Rue

Culinary Herbs and Spices		
Ajwain	Clary	Malabathrum
Allspice	Cloves	Marjoram
Angelica	Comfrey	Mint (all types)
Anise	Common rue	Nutmeg
Annatto	Coriander	Oregano
Artemisia (all types)	Cress	Orris root
Asafetida	Cumin	Paprika
Basil (all types)	Curry	Parsley
Bay (cultivated)	Dill	Pepper
Bladder wrack	Fennel	Rocket (arugula)
Bolivian coriander	Fenugreek	Rosemary
Borage	Filé (gumbo, cultivated)	Rue
Calendula	Fingerroot	Saffron
Chamomile	French sorrel	Sage (all types)
Candle nut	Galangal	Savory (all types)
Caper	Ginger	Tarragon
Caraway	Hops	Thyme

Culinary Herbs and Spices		
Cardamom	Horehound	Turmeric
Cassia	Hyssop	Vanilla
Catnip	Lavender	Wasabi
Chervil	Lemon balm	Water cress
Chicory	Lemon thyme	
Cicely	Lovage	
Cilantro	Mace	
Cinnamon	Mahlab	

Medicinal Herbs	
Artemisia	Marshmallow
Arum	Mullein
Astragalus	Passion flower
Boldo	Patchouli
Cananga	Pennyroyal
Comfrey	Pokeweed
Coneflower	St. John's wort
Fenugreek	Senna
Feverfew	Skullcap
Foxglove	Sonchus
Ginkgo biloba	Sorrel
Ginseng	Stevia
Goat's rue	Tansy
Goldenseal	Urtica
Gypsywort	Witch hazel
Horehound	Wood betony
Horsetail	Wormwood
Lavender	Yarrow
Liquorice	Yerba buena

Nursery, Floriculture, and Horticulture Crops

Horticulture	
Honey	Tea Leaves
Turfgrass	Maple Syrup
Hops	

Annual Bedding Plants	
Begonia	Coleus
Dahlia	Geranium
Impatiens	Marigold
Pansy	Petunia
Snapdragon	Vegetable Transplants

Potted Flowering Plants

African Violet	Azalea
Flowering Bulbs	Poinsettia

Potted Herbaceous Perennials

Astilbe	Columbine
Coreopsis	Daylily
Dianthus	Heuchera
Hosta	Ornamental Grasses
Peony	Phlox
Rudbeckia	Salvia
Vinca	

Cut Flowers

Carnation	Chrysanthemum
Delphinium	Gladiolus
Iris	Lily
Orchid	Rose
Tulip	

Cut Cultivated Greens

Asparagus Fern	Coniferous Evergreens
Eucalyptus	Leatherleaf Fern
Pittosporum	

Foliage Plants

Anthurium	Bromeliad
Cacti	Dieffenbachia
Dracaena	Fern
Ficus	Ivy
Palm	Philodendron
Spathipyllum	

Christmas Trees

Balsam Fir	Blue Spruce
Douglas Fir	Fraser Fir
Noble Fir	Scots Pine
White Pine	

Deciduous Flowering Trees	
Crabapple	Dogwood
Crepe Myrtle	Flowering Pear
Flowering Cherry	Flowering Plum
Hawthorn	Magnolia
Redbud	Service Berry

Broadleaf Evergreens	
Azalea	Boxwood
Cotoneaster	Euonymus
Holly	Pieris
Rhododendron	Viburnum

Deciduous Shade Trees	
Ash	Elm
Honey Locust	Linden
Maple	Oak
Poplar	Sweetgum
Sycamore	

Landscape Conifers	
Aborvitae	Chamaecyparis
Hemlock	Juniper
Pine	Spruce
Yew	

Deciduous Shrubs	
Barberry	Bubbleia
Hibiscus	Hydrangea
Rose	Spirea
Viburnum	Weigela

USDA Involvement

- Makes available USDA Specialty Crop Block Grants for specialty crops to create new economic opportunities and grow markets in local communities.

- Funding supports initiatives nationwide.

- Designed to assist producers of fresh fruits and vegetables and help strengthen markets for specialty crops such as fruits, vegetables, tree nuts, dried fruits, horticulture, and nursery crops, including floriculture.

- Hopefully these investments will strengthen rural American communities by supporting local and regional markets and improving access to fresh, high quality fruits and vegetables.

- Designed to help growers make food safety enhancements, solve research needs, and make better informed decisions to increase profitability and sustainability including:

    - Increase nutritional knowledge and specialty crop consumption.

    - Improve efficiency within the distribution system and reduce costs.

    - Promote the development of good agricultural, handling and manufacturing practices while encouraging audit fund cost-sharing for small farmers, packers and processors.

    - Support research through standard and **green initiatives** (to reduce energy use or support the use of alternative energy sources, reduce greenhouse gas emissions and global warming or to minimize the environmental impact of a business).

    - Enhance food safety.

    - Develop new/improved seed varieties and specialty crops.

    - Control pests and diseases.

    - Create organic and sustainable production practices.

    - Establish local and regional fresh food systems.

    - Increasing healthy food access to all individuals.

- Progress of this initiative, Know Your Farmer Know Your Food (KYF Compass), can be tracked on this website:
  http://www.usda.gov/wps/portal/usda/usdahome?navid=KYF_COMPASS

Production Practices to Successfully Grow These Crops

- Selection of varieties to plant for climate and market.

- Yields of the variety.

- Quality of the variety.
- Review of the variety test information.
- Disease resistance
- Maturity dates
- Demand

Soil Tillage Requirements

- Varies with crop
- Aids in the control of insect and diseases
- Incorporates fertilizer into the soil
- Breaks up layers of compacted soil

Crop Fertilization

- Soil test land to determine soil fertility and soil pH.
- Growers interpret soil test recommendations for the crop to determine the amount and kind of fertilizer.
- Nutrient needs similar to other crops:
  - Nitrogen (N)
  - Phosphorus (P)
  - Potassium (K)
  - Liming requirements to adjust soil to optimum pH for growing the crop.
- Secondary nutrients
  - Calcium (Ca)
  - Sulfur (S)
  - Magnesium (Mg)
- Micro nutrients
  - Boron (B)
  - Chlorine (Cl)

- Copper (Cu)
- Iron (Fe)
- Manganese (Mn)
- Zinc (Zn)
- Molybdenum (Mo)
- Sodium (Na)
- Cobalt (Co)

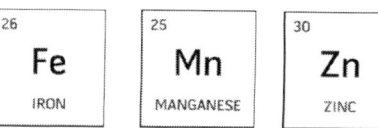

- Forms of Fertilizers
    - Granular
    - Liquid
    - Foliar

- Three methods of applying fertilizers

    1. Banding – material applied in a row.

    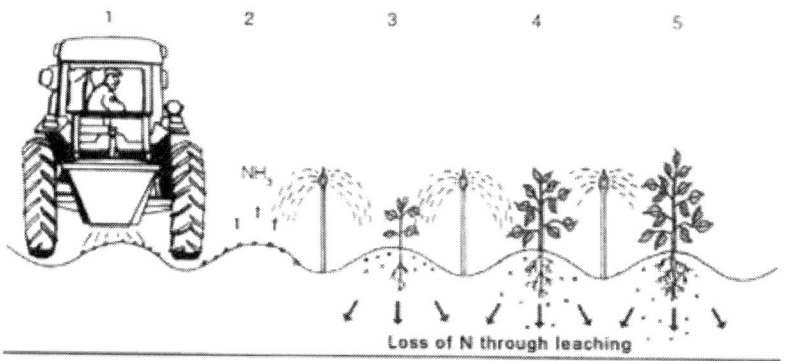

    2. Broadcast – material distributed uniformly over the field.

3. Applied through the irrigation system.

Pest Management

- Grower knowledge of the pests required.
- Use of Integrated Pest Management (IPM).
- Crop rotation practices
- Control methods
    - Tillage and cultivation
    - Chemical

Disease Control

- Unique for each crop
- Crop rotation
- Plant spacing
- Nutrient management
- Unique to varieties planted
- Chemicals to control

Specialty Crops Harvested to Maximize Quality

- Harvest crop when it matures or ripens.
- Methods of harvesting
  - Hand labor
    - ✓ Amount of labor available.
    - ✓ Length of time in which crop has to be harvested.
    - ✓ Can only harvest fruit that is mature or ripe.
  - Mechanical
    - ✓ High investment in the beginning.
    - ✓ Harvests the crop at one time.
    - ✓ Less labor required.

Post-Harvest Treatments

- Depends on the crop
- Dried or cooled depending on the crop
- Graded
- Additional processing
- Grading of products
- Packaging
- Marketing

Summary

A specialty crop is grown for a special purpose and grown only in certain sections of the country. Defined by the USDA, the Specialty Crop Competitiveness Act of 2004 and the Food, Conservation, and Energy Act of 2008 have defined specialty crops as "fruits and vegetables, tree nuts, dried fruits, horticulture, and nursery crops (including floriculture)." The USDA makes available Specialty Crop Block Grants for specialty crops to create new economic opportunities and grow markets in local communities and funds initiatives nationwide. Production practices to grow specialty crops are similar to other non-specialty crops such as tillage, irrigation, disease and pest management, harvesting, grading and marketing.

Resources

Free complementary PowerPoint:
http://www.tagmydoc.com/dl/13roD8/gk8l

USDA Farm Bill Forum Comment Summary and Background – Specialty Crops
http://www.usda.gov/documents/SPECIALTY_CROPS.pdf

Agricultural Marketing Resource Center – Specialty Crops
http://www.agmrc.org/commodities__products/specialty_crops/

Assessment

1. T or F? Eligible specialty plants must be intensively cultivated and used by people for food, medicinal purposes, and/or aesthetic gratification to be considered specialty crops.

2. T or F? Soil tillage requirements have nothing to do with the control of insects and diseases.

3. _____ a fertilizer causes the material to be distributed uniformly over the field.
    a.) Banding   b.) Mixing   c.) Broadcasting   d.) Irrigating

4. Secondary nutrients include calcium, sulfur and _____.
    a.) molybdenum   b.) manganese   c.) magnesium   d.) iron

5. T or F? Christmas trees are a specialty crop.

Take assessment online here:

http://tinyurl.com/PlntSci-22

Hint: When the answer is incorrect, you will see: "Wrong answer! Go Back!"

Notes

49 Fruits

Major Concept
Fruit crops are a very important source of food and income.

Objectives
- Classify vegetable fruit by use and climate requirements
- Identify fruit crops
- List harvesting and post-harvest management of fruit crops

Link to Standards

PS.01. Develop and implement a crop management plan for a given production goal that accounts for environmental factors.

PS.02. Apply principles of classification, plant anatomy, and plant physiology to plant production and management.

PS.03. Propagate, culture and harvest plants and plant products based on current industry standards.

PS.04. Apply principles of design in plant systems to enhance an environment (e.g. floral, forest landscape, and farm).

Key Terms
- Fruit
- Grafting

Cultural Practices for Fruit Crops
- **Fruit** – a fleshy, ripened ovary of a tree, shrub, or woody vine eaten raw or cooked.

- Many fruit trees require pollen from another tree in order to produce fruit.
    - Fruit trees must be **grafted** (insert a twig or shoot) and propagated asexually to produce the proper tree and rootstock of the selected variety.

✓ Examples of rootstocks are vigorous and dwarfing.

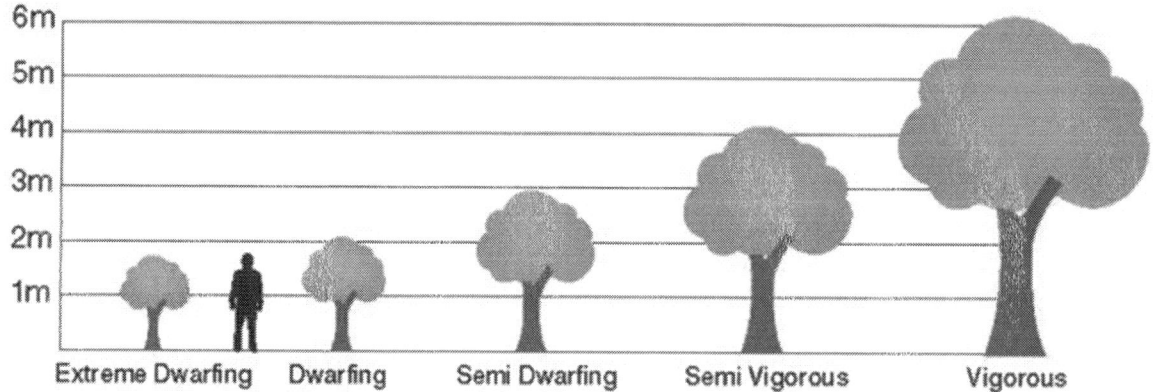

Extreme Dwarfing   Dwarfing   Semi Dwarfing   Semi Vigorous   Vigorous

- Fruit crops require proper spacing and pruning to receive the maximum sunlight, moisture and minerals they require.

- Producers use an (IPM) integrated pest management to carefully protect the consumers and the fruit from disease and pest infestation.

- Bush, cane, or vine fruit crops require mostly the same cultural practices as the tree fruits.
    - Bush or cane fruits are blueberries, strawberries and raspberries.
    - Vine fruit is grapes.

- Fruit flowers are damaged easily by frosts in the late spring.
    - Peaches, cherries and apricots are very sensitive to frost.
    - Citrus, oranges, lemons and grapefruits can only be grown in warm climates.

Harvest or Post-Harvest Methods for Fruit and Nut Crops

- Harvesting done by hand or machine depending on the fruit or producer.

- Producers are very careful not to bruise or damage fruits, unless they are used for processing.

- Some crops are stored in coolers which slows the ripening process.

- Some fruit crops are harvested by mechanical shakers, and then collected from the ground.

Summary

Fruit crops are a very important source of food and income. Like all crops, they require specific growing conditions, soil, fertilization and irrigation for proper growth and production. New technologies are being implemented for greater production and continue to improve for the future.

Resources

Free complementary PowerPoint:
http://www.tagmydoc.com/dl/m7IhS/gk8G

Parker, R. 2010. Plant and soil science: Fundamentals and applications. Clifton Park, NY: Delmar Cengage Learning.

For the Horticulturalist in all of us
http://www.fruit-crops.com/

Assessment

1. Bush, cane, or vine fruit crops require mostly the same cultural practices as the _____.
    a.) vegetable crops   b.) cereal grains   c.) tree fruits

2. T or F? Storing some unripened crops in coolers may quicken the ripening process.

3. T or F? Citrus, oranges, lemons and grapefruits can only be grown in warm climates.

4. Some fruit crops are harvested by _____, and then collected from the ground.
    a.) hand shakers   b.) mechanical shakers   c.) digital shakers   d.) movers and shakers

Take assessment online here:

http://tinyurl.com/PlntSci-23

Hint: When the answer is incorrect, you will see: "Wrong answer! Go Back!"

50 Nut Production

Major Concept

Nut crops are important in providing food and income.

Objectives

- Classify nut crops by use and climate requirements
- Identify nut crops
- List some harvesting and post-harvest management of nut crops

Link to Standards

PS.03. Propagate, culture and harvest plants and plant products based on current industry standards.

Key Terms

- Frost susceptibility
- Mechanical shaker
- Nut crop
- Rootstock

U.S. Nut Production

- **Nut crop** - Hard, bony, one-seeded fruit of a woody plant, includes:

  - Almonds
  - Hazelnuts
  - Macadamias
  - Pecans
  - Pistachios
  - Walnuts

Table provides the family, common and *scientific* name of the tree nuts:

Family	Common Name	Scientific Name
Rosaceae	Almond	*Prunus amygdalus*
Juglandaceae	English Walnut	*Juglans regia*
Juglandaceae	Pecan	*Carya illinoensis*
Betulaceae	Filbert	*Corylus avellana*
Proteaceae	Macadamia	*Macadamia ternifolia*

- Production and Value from the Agriculture Marketing Resource Center of the USDA: http://www.agmrc.org/commodities__products/nuts/

Selecting Nut Trees

- Proper climate

- Disease-free **rootstock** (part of a plant, often an underground part, from which new above-ground growth can be produced)

- **Frost susceptibility** (likely to be influenced or harmed by frost)

- Soil fertility and pH

- Pollination needs

- Growth patterns and production dates

Some Nut Varieties

- Almonds
  - Nonpareil
  - California
  - Carmel
  - Mission
- Chestnuts
  - Revival
  - Carolina
  - Layeroka
  - Chinese seedling
- Filberts
  - Barcelona
  - Davianna

- Black Walnut varieties
  - Thomas
  - Ohio
  - Myers
- English Walnut varieties
  - Franquette
  - Spurgeon
  - Chambers #9

Cultural Practices for Nut Crops

- Trees spaced far apart when planted due to large tree size, such as walnut, hickory and pecan.
- Fertilization based on soil tests
- Irrigation
- Pruning
- Winter cold, spring frosts, fall freezes, droughts, humid weather, and length of frost free growing season all affect how well a nut tree will produce.

Disease and Pest Control

- Many pests such as insects, birds and squirrels detract from the production of nut crops.
  - Pests need to be monitored and controlled.
- Some trees will need to be sprayed with insecticides and pesticides.
  - Some diseases and pests include:
    - ✓ Filbert moth
    - ✓ Bacterial blight

- ✓ Husk rot
- ✓ Husk fly
- ✓ Blight

Harvest or Post-Harvest Methods for Nut Crops

- Nuts fall to the ground when mature.
  - Some nut crops are harvested by **mechanical shakers** (shakes the tree causing nuts to fall off), and then are collected from the ground.
- Nuts may be dried and stored.
- Nuts may be shelled and packaged.

Summary

Nuts are the hard, bony, one-seeded fruit of a woody plant. When selecting a nut tree, it is important to consider the climate, disease-free rootstock, frost susceptibility, soil fertility and pH, pollination needs and growth patterns and production dates. A vast variety of nuts are grown in the U.S. Cultural practices for nut crops are location and season specific. Many pests such as insects, birds and squirrels detract from the production of nut crops.

References

Free complementary PowerPoint:
http://www.tagmydoc.com/dl/14cBf8/gk7g

Parker, R. 2010. Plant and soil science: Fundamentals and applications. (pgs.637-638) Clifton Park, NY: Delmar Cengage Learning.

Nut Production
http://www.agmrc.org/commodities__products/nuts/
Fruits and Nuts Research Information Center
http://fruitsandnuts.ucdavis.edu/

Growing Black Walnut for Nut Production
http://www.centerforagroforestry.org/pubs/walnutNuts.pdf

Assessment

1. T or F? Trees spaced far apart when planted due to large tree size, such as walnut, hickory and pecan.

2. T or F? Fertilization for nut crops is always based on soil test.

3. Some nut crops are harvested by mechanical shakers, and then are collected from the _____.
   a.) tree   b.) bin   c.) producer   d.) ground

4. T or F? Pests are beneficial to nut crops by keeping the bugs away.

5. T or F? All trees need to be sprayed with insecticides and pesticides.

Take assessment online here:

http://tinyurl.com/PlntSci-24

Hint: When the answer is incorrect, you will see: "Wrong answer! Go Back!"

Notes

51 Flowers and Foliage

Major Concept

Growing flowers and foliage contributes to U.S. agriculture by providing jobs and beautification.

Objectives

- Name four general categories of flowers or foliage
- Identify four types of flowering annuals, perennials and bulbs
- List five pests of bulbs

Link to Standards

PS.01. Develop and implement a crop management plan for a given production goal that accounts for environmental factors.

PS.02. Apply principles of classification, plant anatomy, and plant physiology to plant production and management.

PS.03. Propagate, culture and harvest plants and plant products based on current industry standards.

Key Terms

- Deadheading
- Dusting
- Harden off
- Media
- Rootbound

Value of Floriculture

- Floriculture Profile from the Agricultural Marketing Resource Center of the USDA
http://www.agmrc.org/commodities__products/specialty_crops/floriculture-profile/

- Components of the floriculture business:
  - Cut flowers and cut foliage or greens
  - Flowering potted plants
  - Tropical foliage plants
  - Hanging plants
  - Landscape plants
  - Annual bedding plants
  - Woody ornamentals
  - Herbaceous perennials

Flowering Herbaceous Perennials (common and *scientific* names)

- Yarrow, *Achillea mille folium*
- Gold dust, *Alyssum saxatile*
- Alkanet, *Anchusa italic*
- Windflower, *Anemone pulsatil la*
- Golden daisy, *Anthemis tinctoria*
- Rock cress, *Arabis alpine*
- Sea pink, *Ameria meritima alpine*
- Hardy aster, *Aster alpinus*
- False spirea, *Astilbe arendsii*
- Hardy begonia, *Begonia evansiana*
- Bergamot, *Bergenia purpurascens*

Growing Perennials

- Proper soil preparation.
- Some maintenance such as staking, pruning and weeding.
- Site selection determines species to grow.
- Most planted in spring.
- Water requirements depend on climate and plant species.
- Fertilization
    - Based on soil test.
    - Apply a complete fertilizer.
- Depending on climate winter protection may be needed.
- Dividing and transplanting
    - Periodic division to maintain vigor and maximum flow production.
    - Transplant soon after division.
- Insect and diseases specific for specific plants.
    - Correctly diagnose and treat.
- Propagation by tip and root cuttings.

Flowering Annuals (common and *scientific* name)

- Common flowering annuals include:
    - Ageratum (*Ageratum houstonianum*)
    - Amaranthus (*Amaranthus*)
    - Aster (*Aster amellus*)
    - Bachelor's Button (*Centaurea cyanus*)
    - Calendula (*Calendula officinilalis*)
    - Coreopsis (*Coreopsis gigantea*)
    - China Aster (*Callistephus chinensis*)
    - Cockscomb (*Celosia crista*)
    - Cosmos (*Cosmos* spp.)
    - Forget-me-not (*Myosotis sylvatica*)
    - Four-o'-clock (*Mirabilis jalapa*)
    - Gaillardia (*Gaillardia pulchella*)

- Lupine (*Lupinus*)
- Marigold (*Tagetes erecta, T. patula*)
- Morning Glory (*Ipomoea nil*)
- Nasturtium (*Tropaeolum majus*)
- Petunia (*Petunia x hybrida*)
- Phlox (*Phlox drummondi*)
- Portulaca (*Portulaca grandiflora*)
- Rudbeckia (*Rudbeckia hirta*)
- Scabiosa (*Scabiosa atropurpurea*)
- Sweet Alyssum (*Lobularia maritima*)
- Spiderflower (*Cleome hasslerana*)
- Strawflower (*Helichrysum bracteatum*)
- Sweetpea (*Lathyrus odoratus*)
- Zinnia (*Zinnia elegan*)

- Cultural Practices
    - Site selection and preparation.
    - Depending on annual; some need full sun, light shade, heavy shade.
    - Soil texture, pH and fertility considered.
    - Fertilizer often added, may need to soil test.
- Seed Selection
    - Viable seeds packaged for current year.
    - Consider use of hybrids.
- Considerations for starting indoors include:
    - **Media** – material plants grow in
    - Containers
    - Lighting
    - Transplanting
- Planting times
    - Depends on climate and date of last frost.
    - Seeds can be planted directly in the soil for some annuals.
    - For seeds started in greenhouse, transplant after date of last frost.

- - **Harden off** by setting outside during the day.
- Thinning
  - Directly seeded into soil, plants need thinning to recommended spacing.
- Water
  - Drip or sprinklers, depending on climate
  - Frequency depends on soil, climate and stage of growth.
- Mulching
  - Controls weeds and surface crusting of soil.
- Cultivation
  - Breaks surface crusting.
  - Controls weeds.
- **Deadheading**
  - Removal of old flowers maintains vigor and neatness.

- Staking
  - Tall species need stakes for support.

Annual Bulbs

- Refers to corms, tubers and rhizomes.

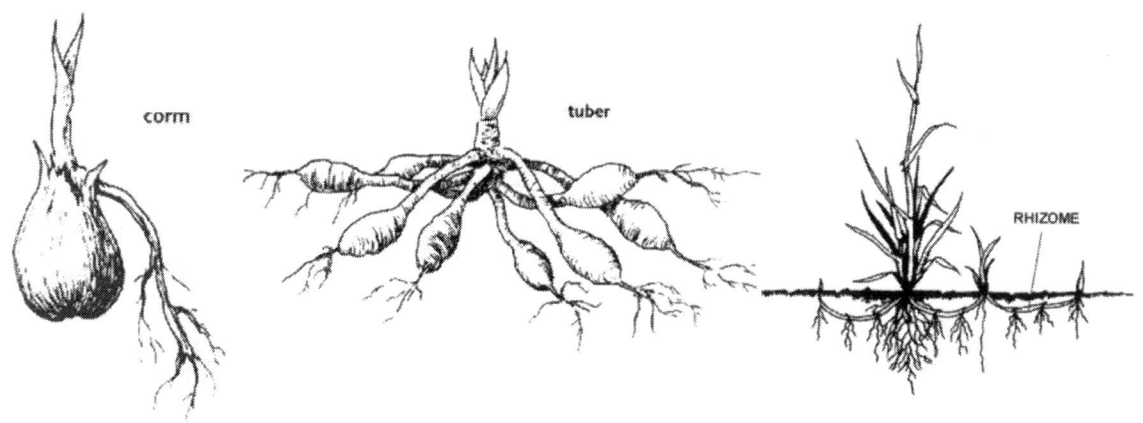

- Contain embryonic plant and stored food.
    - Spring planted bulbs
        - Begonia
        - Calla
        - Anemone
        - Ranunculus
        - Tigridia
        - Monbretia
        - Gladiolus
        - Amaryllis
        - Dahlia
        - Ismene
    - Fall planted bulbs
        - Muscari
        - Galanthus
        - Scilla
        - Crocus
        - Chionodoxa
        - Colchicum
        - Hyacinth
        - Iris
        - Lily
        - Tulip
        - Daffodil

- Cultural Practices
  - Site selection and soil.
    - ✓ Best in well-drained loam.
    - ✓ pH near 7
- Planting Bulbs
  - Bulb planter, spade or hand trowel.
  - Recommended depth and spacing depends on type of bulb.
- Fertilizing
  - Often small amount of NPK at planting.
  - Light application of NPK as plants start to grow.
- After flowering
  - Depending on the type bulb should be dug up each year or every three to five years after the foliage dies.
  - Replant to maintain high quality flowers.
  - **Dusting** bulbs during storage with a pesticide prevents insects and rodents from attacking the bulbs (see table below).
  - Disease or damaged bulbs removed.
  - Store in peat moss or sawdust.
- Forcing bulbs
  - Artificially breaks dormancy.
  - Store at 40 to 50°F for 10 to 12 weeks.
  - Bring into warm, lit area.

Common Bulb Pests and Diseases and their Control

Host, Pest, Disease	Damage	Control
Amaryllis		
Spotted cutworm	Feeds on flowers at night.	Scatter cutworm bait or spray with Sevin.
Bulb mites	Rotting bulbs. See *Hyacinth*.	Discard soft bulbs.
Narcissus bulb fly	Decaying bulbs. See *Narcissus*.	Discard soft bulbs.
Leaf scorch, Red blotch	Reddish spots on flowers, leaves, bulb scales; stalks deformed.	Discard bulbs or remove diseased leaves. Avoid heavy watering.
Gladiolus		
Thrips	Leaves silvered, flowers streaked, deformed.	Spray with lindane in spring. Dust corms before storing.
Botrytis and other flower blights	Flowers, leaves, stalks spotted, then blighted.	Spray with zineb (Dithane Z-78 or Parzate).
Corm rots, scab	Lesions on corms, spots on leaves.	Dust with Arasan before planting.
Yellows (due to a soil fungus)	Plants infected through roots, turn yellow and wilt.	Choose resistant varieties.
Hyacinth		
Bulb mites	Minute; less than 1/25 inch, white mites in rotting bulbs.	Discard infested bulbs.
Aphids, several species	Leaves are curled; virus diseases may be transmitted.	Spray with malathion, rotenone, or nicotine.
Bulb nematode	Dark rings in bulbs.	Discard.
Soft rot	Vile-smelling bacterial disease; often after mites.	Discard.
Iris (Bulbous)		
Tulip bulb aphid	See *Tulip*.	See *Tulip*.
Gladiolus, iris thrips	Leaves russeted or flecked, flowers speckled or distorted.	Spray or dust with malathion or lindane.
Leaf spot	Light brown foliage spots with reddish borders.	Spray with zineb or bordeaux mixture; clean up old leaves.
Lily		
Aphids (lily, bean, melon, peach, other species)	Curl leaves, transmit mosaic and other virus diseases.	Spray with malathion, being sure to cover underside of leaves.
Botrytis blight	Oval tan spots on leaves, which turn black, droop.	Spray with bordeaux mixture.
Mosaic and other virus diseases	Plants mottled, stunted.	Rogue infected plants. Start lilies from seed in isolated portion of

Host, Pest, Disease	Damage	Control
		garden.
Narcissus		
Narcissus bulb fly	Fly resembling bumblebee lays eggs on leaves near ground in early summer. Larva, fat, yellow maggot 1/2 to 3/4 inch long, tunnels in rotting bulb.	Sprinkle naphthalene flakes around plants to prevent egg-laying. Before planting, dust trench with 5% chlordane and dust over bulbs after setting.
Bulb nematode	Dark rings in bulb.	Discard bulbs. Commercial growers treat with hot water, adding formalin to prevent rot.
Basal rot	Chocolate-colored dry rot at base of bulbs.	Inspect bulbs before planting.
Smolder (botrytis rot)	Rots the foliage and flowers in cold, wet seasons; leaves stuck together when they emerge and infected bulbs rot in storage	Remove diseased plants. Put new bulbs in new location; Applications of fungicides such as chlorothalonil, thiophanate-methyl, iprodione, and mancozeb when new growth emerges in the spring.
Scorch	Affected plant parts often bent or deformed at the point of infection; brown spots or blotches with yellow borders develop.	Minimize moisture on the leaves and flower stalks by careful watering; provide good ventilation and plenty of light; discard heavily infected bulbs.
Tulip		
Tulip bulb aphid	Powdery white or grayish aphids common on stored bulbs.	Dust with 1% lindane before storing.
Green peach, tulip leaf, and other aphids	Transmit viruses to growing plants.	Spray or dust with malathion or lindane.
Botrytis blight, fire	Plants stunted, buds blasted, white patches on leaves, dark spots on white petals, white spots on colored petals, gray mold, general blighting. Small, shiny black sclerotia formed on petals, foliage rotting into soil and on bulbs.	Discard all infected bulbs. Plant new tulips in new location. Spray with ferbam or zineb, starting early spring. Remove flowers as they fade, remove all tops as they turn yellow.
Cucumber mosaic	Yellow streaking or flecking of	Do not grow near cucurbits or

Host, Pest, Disease	Damage	Control
	foliage.	gladiolus.
Lily mottle viruses	Cause broken flower colors, mottled foliage, in tulips.	Do not plant near lilies. Control aphids.

Courtesy of the Brooklyn Botanic Garden

Flowering Houseplants

- Considerations include light, temperature, water/humidity and maintenance.

    o Common indoor flowering plants:

    - African violets
    - Fuchsias
    - Gardenias
    - Geraniums
    - Impatiens
    - Wax begonias
    - Ageratums
    - Verbenas
    - Petunias

- Light

    o Depends on type of plant.

    o Full sun, direct sun, bright indirect, partial shade or shade.

- Temperature

    o Depends on type of plant.

    o Constant temperature best.

    o Usually 60 to 68°F.

- Water/humidity
    - Depends on type of plant.
    - Biggest danger is over-watering.
    - Good drainage essential.
- Maintenance
    - NPK fertilizer in slow-release form.
    - Dust, remove dead leaves and flowers, loosen soil.
    - Repot when roots become restricted – **root bound**.
    - Propagation depends on type; common asexual methods include: leaf and stem cuttings, removal of plantlets and air layering.

Summary

Growing perennials requires proper soil preparation, fertilization, dividing and transplanting, propagation by tip and root cuttings and depending on climate winter protection may be needed. Flowering annuals require specific practices such as seed selection, planting times, fertilizing, watering and thinning. Annual bulbs refer to corms, tubers and rhizomes which contain embryonic plat and stored food and require specific cultivation methods. Considerations for flowering house plants include light, temperature, water/humidity and maintenance.

Resources

Free complementary PowerPoint:
http://www.tagmydoc.com/dl/nFtys/gk7e

Parker, R. 2010. Plant and soil science: Fundamentals and applications. Clifton Park, NY: Delmar Cengage Learning.

Virginia Cooperative Extension - Flowering Bulbs: Culture and Maintenance
http://pubs.ext.vt.edu/426/426-201/426-201.html

North Carolina State University - Maintaining Perennials
http://www.ces.ncsu.edu/depts/hort/consumer/factsheets/perennials/text_maintaining.html

Cornell University - Introduction to Annuals
http://www.gardening.cornell.edu/homegardening/scenebd43.html

Assessment

1. T or F? Growing perennials requires periodic division to maintain vigor and maximum flow production.

2. T or F? Depending on the annual some need full sun, light shade or heavy shade.

3. Removal of old flowers is called _____.
   a.) dusting   b.) staking   c.) deadheading   d.) pruning

4. T or F? Perennials are insect and diseases specific for specific plants.

5. T or F? Annual bulbs contain embryonic plants and stored food.

Take assessment online here:

http://tinyurl.com/PlntSci-25

Hint: When the answer is incorrect, you will see: "Wrong answer! Go Back!"

Notes

52 Sod Production

Major Concept
Sod production involves growing a solid stand of a turfgrass species as a crop and harvesting it intact with a thin layer of soil and roots attached.

Objectives
- Define turf and sod
- List three functions of turf
- List four turf grass maintenance practices
- List four sod production practices
- Name four common turfgrasses

Link to Standards

PS.01. Develop and implement a crop management plan for a given production goal that accounts for environmental factors.

PS.02. Apply principles of classification, plant anatomy, and plant physiology to plant production and management.

PS.03. Propagate, culture and harvest plants and plant products based on current industry standards.

Key Terms
- Fumigation
- Sod
- Turf
- Turf grasses

Value of Turf
- Beautiful turf grass is appealing and useful in many ways.

  o For ballparks, football fields, parks, home and business landscapes, golf courses; success depends on turf itself.

  o **Turf** - Plants in the ground cover, the soil in which the roots grow.

- **Turf grasses** - Collection of grass plants that form a ground cover that requires regular maintenance; for example a golf course.
- **Sod** - Surface layer of the turf which includes the plants and a thin layer of soil.

Functions of Turf

- Utility: stabilizes the soil and reduces erosion.
- Ornamentation: enhances the surroundings.
- Sports: helps reduce injury and helps performance of the participants.

Turfgrass Maintenance Practices

- Type of soil important
- Addition of nutrients and fertilization for optimal growth
- Regular mowing
- Controlling weeds and pests to keep healthy
- Watering for deep health root growth
- Seasonal care

Turfgrasses (common and scientific names)

- Cool season

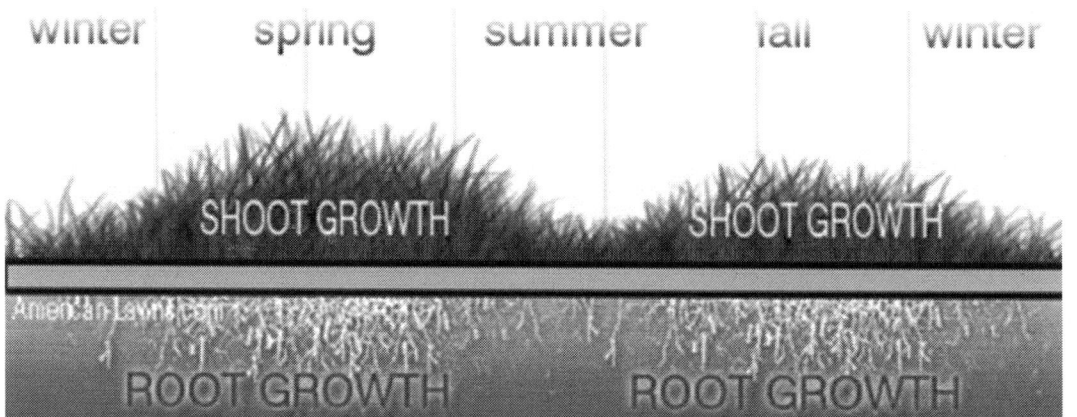

- - Colonial Bentgrass (*Agrostis tenuis*)
  - Creeping Bentgrass (*Agrostis palustris*)
  - Kentucky Bluegrass (*Poa pratensis*)
  - Tall Fescue (*Festuca arundinacea*)
  - Fine Fescue (various *Festuca* species)
  - Red Fescue (*Festuca rubra L*)
  - Perennial Ryegrass (*Lolium perenne*)
  - Crested Wheatgrass (*Agropyron cristatum*)
- Warm season

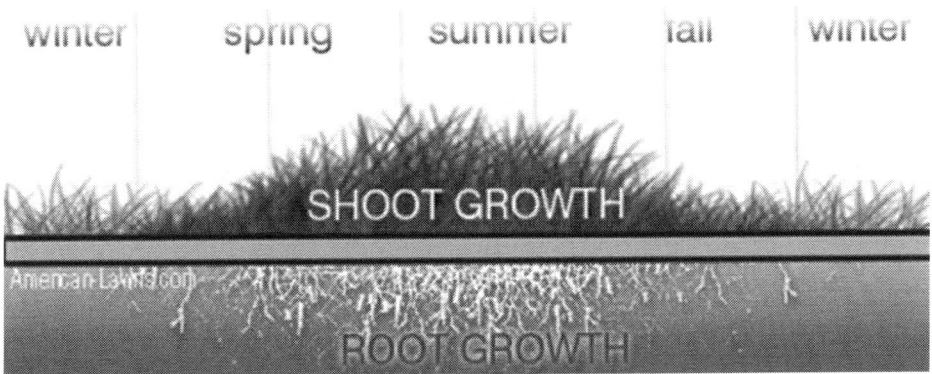

  - Bermuda grass (*Cynodon dactylon L*)
  - Zoysia grass (*Zoysia japonica Steud*)
  - Buffalo grass (*Buchloe dactyloides*)
  - Augustine grass (*Stenotaphrum secundatum*)

Sod Production Practices

- Growing a solid stand of a desirable turfgrass species and harvesting it, as a crop, intact with a thin layer of soil and roots attached.
- Located near targeted markets (reduces cost of shipping).

- Quantity and quality of water available needs consideration.
- Sandy-loam soil best but can be grown on a variety of soil types.
- Once established sod quality must continue to be maintained by mowing, periodic fertilization and weed control until sold and harvested.
- Preparation of Soil
    - Clearing, leveling, tilling and installation of drainage (if needed) and irrigation systems.
    - **Fumigation** (pest control through gaseous pesticides)
    - Rolling
- Fertilization practices
    - Soil test
    - Apply required nutrients.
    - Adjust pH if needed.
    - Frequency, nutrients and amounts depend on type of grass and growing conditions.
- Irrigation
    - Ample supply of quality water needed during planting stage.
    - Typically some type of a sprinkler irrigation system.
    - Soil moisture monitored closely to determine irrigation scheduling.
    - Single most important factor for a successful crop of sod.
- Pest management
    - Preplant fumigation or use of nonselective herbicide.
    - Once established, proper mowing and use of herbicides to control broadleaf weeds.
    - Maintain weed-free areas around the field.

- Insect pests of three categories:
    1. Shoot feeding
    2. Root feeding
    3. Burrowing
- Monitor and apply insecticide

• Diseases
  - Some environmental conditions favor incidence of diseases, such as: high humidity, rain, heavy dew or fog and possibly high temperatures.
  - Over fertilization can contribute.
  - Good management practices control incidence.
  - Treatment requires identification of disease.
  - Some diseases include:
    - ✓ Anthracnose
    - ✓ Brown patch
    - ✓ Copper spot
    - ✓ Dollar spot
    - ✓ Fairy ring
    - ✓ Fusarium blight
    - ✓ Leaf spots
    - ✓ Net blotch
    - ✓ Nematodes
    - ✓ Powdery mildew
    - ✓ Pythium blight
    - ✓ Red thread
    - ✓ Rots
    - ✓ Rusts
    - ✓ Slime molds
    - ✓ Smuts

• Other Problems
  - Dogs
  - Gophers
  - Ground squirrels

- Mice
- Moles
- Humans vandalism
- Vehicles and equipment

- Mowing
  - Important cultural practice
  - Regular schedule
  - Controls weeds and growth
  - Use of reel, rotary or flail depends on type of grass and use.

- Harvesting
  - When grass develops enough strength (root structure) to remain intact with minimum soil adhering when cut.
  - Depends on type of grass, soil type and growing conditions.
  - Conditioned just prior to harvest (mowing with reel mower, applying iron [Fe], no chemicals and removal of clippings).
  - Never cut under water stress.
  - Mechanical cutters cut and roll sod strips.
  - Rolled strips stacked on pallets for transport.

Marketing and Selling Sod

- Normally marketed by three methods each requiring different amounts of labor and equipment:

  1. Grower sells the sod to a sod broker at an agreed upon price per acre; then, over a period of time the grower continues to maintain the sod until the broker has harvested it.

  2. Grower purchases harvesting equipment and pallet loading equipment and upon receiving orders the grower then cuts and loads the customers' trucks.

3. Grower harvests, transports and installs the sod, excluding all middlemen.

Summary

Turf must have a good visual characteristic as well as be adapted to local climate and growing conditions. Turf maintenance requires mowing, watering, pest control and other practices that maintain a good environment, such as thatching, aeration and rolling. Common turf grasses include warm and cool season types. Pest management includes pre-plant fumigation or use of nonselective herbicide. Some environmental conditions favor incidence of diseases, such as high humidity, rain, heavy dew or fog and possibly high temperatures. Mowing is an important cultural practice. Harvest should take place when grass develops enough strength to remain intact with minimum soil adhering when cut.

Resources

Free complementary PowerPoint:
http://www.tagmydoc.com/dl/6rnTX/gk7c

Parker, R. 2010. Plant and soil science: Fundamentals and applications. Clifton Park, NY: Delmar Cengage Learning (pages 679-700).

Turfgrass Sod Production
http://www.uky.edu/Ag/CDBREC/introsheets/sod.pdf

Assessment

1. T or F? Sod plants in the ground cover, the soil in which the roots grow.

2. Functions of turf include sports, ornamentation and _____.
    a.) weed control   b.) utility   c.) pest control   d.) no maintenance

3. T or F? Turfgrass requires seasonal care.

4. T or F? Sod production does not require any preparation of the soil.

5. Bermuda grass, Zoysia grass, Buffalo grass and _____ grass are common warm season turfgrasses.
    a.) Colonial Bentgrass   b.) Augustine grass   c.) Creeping Bentgrass
    d.) Kentucky Bluegrass

Take assessment online here:

http://tinyurl.com/PlntSci-26

Hint: When the answer is incorrect, you will see: "Wrong answer! Go Back!"

Notes

53 Organic Production

Major Concept

Organic crop production relies on a number of methods not used by traditional agriculture.

Objectives

- Define organic and sustainable agriculture
- Identify reasons growers choose organic farming
- List the benefits of organic farming on the soil
- Identify the pros and cons of using manure to supply plant nutrients
- Define carbon: nitrogen ratio
- List the Best Management Practices (BMP) for using manure
- Identify the benefits of composting
- Define green manure and crop rotation
- Name the benefits of crop rotation to the organic grower
- Identify the weed, pest and disease control options used by organic growers

Link to Standards

PS.01. Develop and implement a crop management plan for a given production goal that accounts for environmental factors.

PS.02. Apply principles of classification, plant anatomy, and plant physiology to plant production and management.

PS.03. Propagate, culture and harvest plants and plant products based on current industry standards.

PS.04. Apply principles of design in plant systems to enhance an environment.

Key Terms

- Allelopathy
- Best Management Practices (BMP)
- Composting
- Cover crop
- Crop rotation
- Green manure
- Mesophilic
- Organic farming
- Organic standards
- Sustainable agriculture
- Thermophilic

Organic Farming

- A type of sustainable agriculture.

- Prohibits the use of synthetic substances, including inorganic fertilizers and pesticides.

- Major theme: promoting a healthy soil by controlling erosion and keeping organic matter levels high.

- Consumers believe organic products to be safer, more nutritious or flavorful or support the process of organic farming.

- Adds nitrogen by the use of manures, composts, legumes and organic nitrogen fertilizers.

- Phosphorus and potassium come from manures and mineral fertilizers such as rock phosphate.

- Tend to rely more on natural nutrient cycles.

- **Crop rotation** (growing a series of dissimilar/different types of crops in the same area in sequential seasons) is important.

- Weed control includes crop rotation, cultivation, and sometimes flaming or mulches.

- Farms of all sizes and crops.

- Benefits include reduced erosion, increased soil organic matter content, higher populations of earthworms, richer soil flora and others.

- Profitability tends to rely on the higher prices offered for organic produce.

- In 1990 the Organic Foods Production Act directed the USDA to set up a federal program.

    - Final rules for that program were published in 2000.

    - Rules set certain organic standards, prohibit the use of many substances on organic land including sewage sludge and provide a list of allowed and disallowed synthetic materials.

    - Also sets labeling requirements.

    - National and state standards define what can be sold as organic.

- Food to be sold as organic must bear a symbol that proves that it is truly organic.
- Obtained through a certification organization.
- Complex procedure and is potentially expensive.

International Organic Standards

- International Federation of Organic Agriculture Movements (IFOAM) produced a set of international organic standards, developed by individuals from many countries.

- Main principles of organic farming were developed by IFOAM in 1992, including:

  - Produce food of high nutritional quality in sufficient quantity.

  - Interact in a constructive and life enhancing way with all natural systems and cycles.

  - Encourage and enhance biological cycles within the farming system involving microorganisms, soil flora and fauna, plants and animals.

  - Maintain and increase long term fertility of soils.

  - Use, as far as possible, renewable resources in locally organized agricultural systems.

  - Work, as far as possible, within a closed system with regard to organic matter and nutrient elements, thus reducing external inputs.

  - Work, as far as possible, with materials and substances which can be reused or recycled, either on the farm or elsewhere.

  - Give all livestock living conditions which will allow them to perform the basic aspects of their natural behavior.

  - Minimize all forms of pollution that may result from agricultural practices.

  - Maintain the genetic diversity of the agricultural system and its surroundings, including the protection of plant and wildlife habitats.

  - Allow agricultural producers a living according to the United Nations human rights; to cover their basic needs and obtain an adequate return and satisfaction from their work, including a safe working environment.

  - Consider the wider social and ecological impact of the farming system.

Claims of Organic Production

- Provides long-term benefits to people and the environment.

- Aims to increase long-term soil fertility.

- Controls weeds, pests and diseases without harming the environment.

- Ensures water stays clean and safe.

- Uses resources which the farmer already possesses.

- Produces nutritious food, feed for animals and high quality crops to sell at a good price.

- Overcomes problems of modern, intensive agriculture, such as: artificial fertilizers and herbicides easily washed from the soil and pollute rivers, lakes and water courses; prevents prolonged use of artificial fertilizers resulting in soils with a low organic matter content which is easily eroded by wind and rain.

- Reduces dependency on artificial fertilizers.

- Artificial pesticides stay in the soil for a long time and enter the food chain where they build up in the bodies of animals and humans, causing health problems.

- Artificial chemicals destroy soil micro-organisms resulting in poor soil structure and aeration and decreasing nutrient availability.

- Pests and diseases become more difficult to control as they become resistant to artificial pesticides. The numbers of natural enemies decrease because of pesticide use and habitat loss.

- Control of pests and diseases

- Controlled by careful planning and crop choice, resistant crops, cultivation practice, crop rotation, useful predators, increasing genetic diversity, and natural pesticides.

- Combination of techniques that work together for the maximum benefit.

Crop Nutrition

- Organic farmer manages the soil.

- Consideration of soil life, soil nutrients and soil structure.

- Feeds the soil with manure or compost which feeds the variety of life in the soil, then turns this material into food for plant growth.

- Process also adds nutrients and organic matter to the soil.

- Green manures also provide nutrients and organic matter.

Manure

- Properly handled and applied correctly, manure benefits growers.

- Good amounts of nitrogen and potash.

- Phosphorus and calcium present and lesser amounts of sulfur and magnesium.

- Nutrient content of manures variable.

    - Table below shows the sample nutrient composition of several manures, on an as-is basis (not dried or composted), in pounds of nutrient per ton. Actual composition of manures varies widely and should be measured.

Pounds/Ton

Animal	N	P_2O_5	K_2O	S	Ca	Mg
Dairy Cattle	10	4	8	1	6	2
Beef Cattle	11	8	10	1	3	2
Poultry	23	11	10	3	36	6
Swine	10	3	8	3	11	2
Sheep	28	4	20	2	11	4
Horse	13	5	13	-	-	-

- Adds organic matter to the soil.

- Organic solids make up 20% - 40% of manure.

- Improved yields may continue years after manure stops being added to the soil.

- Problems of manure include:

    - Excessive application of phosphorus to land.

    - High soil-phosphate levels, runoff elevates phosphate levels in surface waters.

- Leaching of nitrates under animal confinement areas.
- Runoff of nitrates and organic materials into lakes and streams.
- Large spills from manure lagoons.
- Generation of gaseous air pollutants such as hydrogen sulfide (H_2S), which has human health effects, methane (CH_4), a greenhouse gas, and ammonia (NH_3), which can dissolve in local surface waters.

- Federal Clean Water Act of 1972
  - Concentrated Animal Feeding Operations (CAFOs) are Animal Feeding Operations (AFOs) that meet certain EPA criteria. CAFOs make up approximately 15% of total AFOs; these can be regulated.
  - Goal is to make the most efficient use of manures for profit while minimizing environmental problems.

- Content of Manure
  - Manure includes both solids and liquids, which, for the most part, are the feces and urine of the animal.
  - Solid part may also include bedding.
  - Solid part of the manure contains most of the phosphate.
  - Most of the potash is in the liquid part.

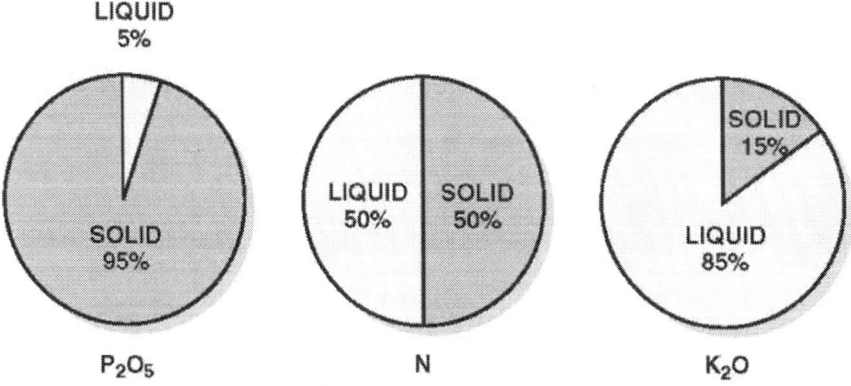

  - Urine holds about half the nitrogen in manure, primarily in the form of urea and similar compounds.
  - Rest of the nitrogen is contained in the animal feces.

- Factors determining the amount of nutrients in manure:

  o Type of animal

    ✓ Sheep and poultry manure have high nitrogen content; the manure of cattle, pigs, and horses has lower nitrogen content.

  o Amount and type of bedding.

    ✓ If high C:N ratio bedding, nitrogen tie-up can even occur in the soil for a time.

  o Amount and type of rations (feed).

  o Age and health of the animal.

  o NPK content of manure is much less than commercial fertilizer.

  o Manure is largely water and organic carbon.

  o Must be applied in quantities of tons per acre rather than pounds per acre.

  o Part of the secret to using manure is to keep its nutrient value intact and prevent large losses.

- Nutrient Losses from Manure

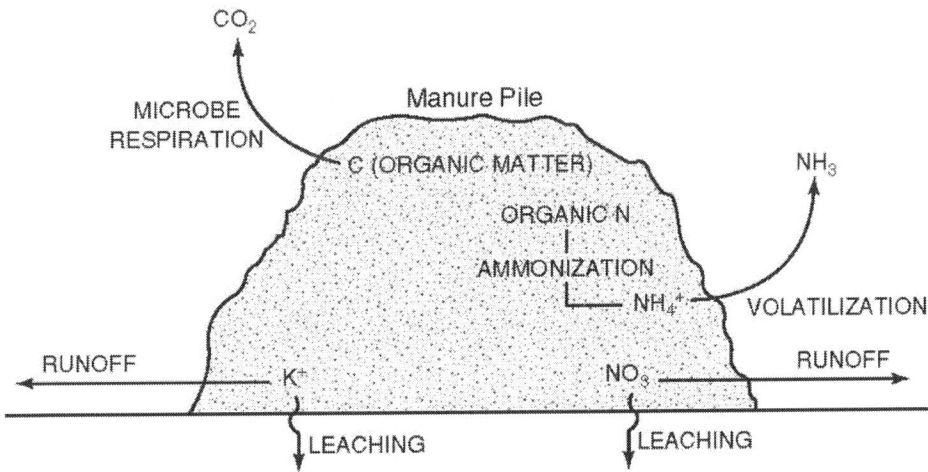

  o Urine contains about 50% of the nutrient value of manure.

  o Urine lost when it seeps into the ground through barn floors or in feedlots.

  o Sharp nitrogen losses occur if the manure begins to decay before it is spread.

- As much as 90% of the nitrogen can be lost within three weeks if manure is poorly handled.
- Losses occur when urea changes to ammonia gas during decay.

- Storage conditions promoting nitrogen loss.
  - High air temperatures.
  - Heat in a manure pile during decay.
  - As manure dries out during storage, ammonia enters the air rapidly.
  - Freezing also speeds up losses.

- Nutrient losses continue after manure is spread in the field.
  - Ammonia continues to escape unless the manure is mixed quickly into the soil.
  - Runoff and leaching increase the loss.
  - Spreading manure on frozen, sloping land increases the chances of manure being lost to runoff.

- Handling Manure
  - Spread it immediately on unfrozen ground and then plow it into the soil.
  - Technique is not always practical.
  - Needs to be stored properly and then applied when it can be plowed into the soil.
  - Loss of nitrogen varies with handling and storage systems.
  - Piles in an open lot, exposed to sun, rain, and air movement, will lose about half their nitrogen.
    - ✓ Long-term storage in lagoons even worse.
  - Short-term storage of solid or liquid manures in proper storage structures.
  - Good storage facilities have concrete floors and walls and a roof to stop drainage losses and slow down the drying of the manure.
  - Liquid manure handling systems, except for large lagoons, is the best way of saving nutrients.

- Growers store liquid animal wastes in concrete pits or tanks.
- Manure is about 90% or more liquid and can be handled by pumps.
- Freshly spread liquid manure should be plowed into the soil immediately.
- In warm weather, 20% of the nitrogen volatilizes within six hours.

Best Management Practices

- A grower's task is to make the most efficient use of animal manures without inflicting damage on the environment.
- Number of Best Management Practices (BMP) proposed:
  - Test manure and soil for nutrient levels.
  - Tests allow the grower to reduce fertilization by an amount equivalent to the nutrients in the manure.
  - Base manure application rates on phosphorus needs rather than nitrogen to avoid heavy phosphorus soil loading.
  - Incorporate all manures into the soil as soon as possible.
  - When land is insufficient for safe spreading of all the manure, a grower might compost the excess and sell it.

Composting

- Method of causing the decay of organic matter in a pile above the ground.
  - Household or garden scale, or larger-scale commercial, for example:
    - ✓ Yard wastes by cities and landscape companies.
    - ✓ Other municipal solid wastes, food processing wastes, or sewage sludge.
    - ✓ Nurseries and greenhouses compost organic materials like wood chips for use in potting soils.
    - ✓ Farmers may compost manure and bedding as well as animal carcasses.
  - Compost that results from these operations may be used as a soil amendment.

- Composting offers three benefits over simply spreading uncomposted organic matter:

    1. Reduces the weight and volume of organic material, making it easier to handle and ship.

    2. Reduces the carbon:nitrogen ratio of materials like woodchips or leaves, eliminating the problem of nitrogen tie-up when compost is added to soil.

    3. Heat generated in a compost pile kills most plant or human pathogens and weed seeds.

    ✓ Pile must be mixed a few times to ensure that the outer edges of the pile are pulled into the hot interior.

- Properly prepared compost pile mixes carbonaceous and nitrogenous materials to achieve a C:N ratio of about 30:1.

    o During the process the pile is kept moist but not wet, at a moisture level of about 50%.

    o Excess moisture creates anaerobic conditions, which causes very slowly decay, generates unpleasant odors, and produces "sour compost" containing organic acids and other chemicals that damage plants.

    o Process follows three stages:

        1. **Mesophilic** stage - organisms that prefer moderate temperatures begin the decay process and temperature begins to rise.

        2. **Thermophilic** stage - heat-loving microbes replace mesophilic ones, and temperature rises to around 150° F; temperatures are monitored and whenever it begins to drop, the pile is turned to bring in fresh oxygen and organic matter; bulk of decay occurs during the thermophilic stage.

        3. When temperatures drop for good, a second mesophilic stage takes a month or two, during which stabilization of the compost occurs.

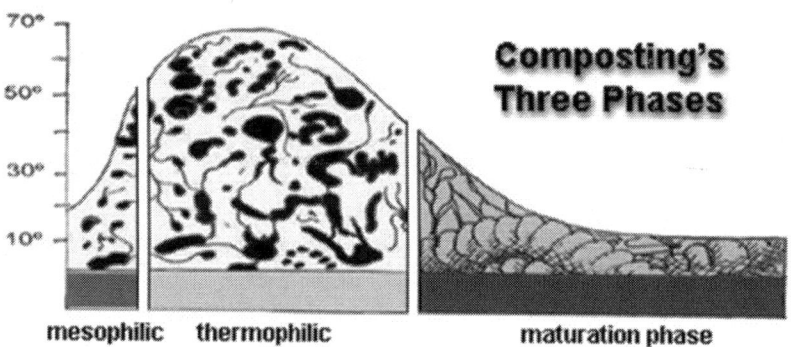

Characteristics of Well-prepared Compost

- Well decayed and stabilized

- Low in heavy metals and soluble salts

- pH between 5.0 and 8.0

- Particle size should be around a millimeter in size

- Little or no foreign matter, such as pop-can tabs

- C:N ratio should be between 15 to 25:1

- Free of the toxic residues of anaerobic decay

- Mostly organic matter, with little soil mixed in

Green Manures

- Crops planted to be turned into the soil rather than for harvest.

- Two types of plants grown as green manures.

    1. Legumes such as clover or vetch are useful because, in addition to the organic matter they leave behind, the nitrogen they fix supplies later crops.

    2. Grasses like oat or rye to provide a bulk of organic matter at the least cost if nitrogen additions are undesirable.

Cover Crops

- To prevent winter erosion, a **cover crop** is planted in the fall after the main crop is harvested.

    o Green cover protects soil during the fall, winter and early spring when it is most erosion prone.

    o Cover crop is then plowed down the following spring.

        ✓ Winter rye and other winter crops used for this purpose.

        ✓ May be planted immediately after harvest of a rapidly maturing crop, like oats following peas in the same season.

- Cover crop may be planted between rows of the main crop; sometimes called a companion crop or living mulch.

Choice of Crops

- Important to organic farmers.

- Each crop and crop variety has specific needs.

  - Crops are affected by:

    - ✓ Soil type

    - ✓ Rainfall

    - ✓ Altitude

    - ✓ Temperature

    - ✓ Type and amount of nutrients required

    - ✓ Amount of water needed

  - These factors affect how a crop grows and yields.

  - Crops grown in a climate to which it is not suited, are likely to produce low yields and be more susceptible to pest and diseases.

  - Success requires growing crops and varieties which are suited to the local conditions, geography, and climate.

Crop Rotations

- Growing the same crops in the same site year after year reduces soil fertility and can encourage a buildup of pests, diseases and weeds in the soil.

- Crops should be moved (rotated) to a different area of land each year and not returned to the original site for several years.

- Involve some combination of three kinds of crops: row crops, small grains, and forages.

- Typical four-year rotation could include a cycle with corn and beans, a root crop and cereals with either of the following:

1. Grass or bush fallow (a fallow period where no crops are grown).

2. A legume crop where a green manure, which is a plant grown mainly for the benefit of the soil, is grown.

- Benefits
    - Aids the control of diseases and insects that rely on one plant host, reducing a grower's pesticide bill.
    - Helps control weeds.
        - ✓ Some rotations suppress weeds by **allelopathy**, where one plant emits chemicals from the roots that suppress growth of other plants.
    - Supplies nitrogen if certain legumes like alfalfa are in the rotation.
    - Improves soil organic matter and tilth.
    - Reduces erosion compared with continuous row crops.

Weed Control

- Reducing the effects of weeds on crop growth and yield through one or more of the following methods:
    - Crop rotation
    - Hoeing
    - Mulches, which cover the soil and stop weed seeds from germinating.
    - Hand-weeding or the use of mechanical weeders.
    - Planting crops close together within each bed, to prevent space for weeds to emerge.
    - Green manures or cover crops to outcompete weeds.
    - Cultivation carried out at repeated intervals and at the appropriate time, when the soil is moist.
    - Animals (like goats) as weeders to graze on weeds.

- Mulching

  - Covering the ground with a layer of loose material such as compost, manure, straw, dry grass, leaves or crop residues.

    - ✓ Alternative mulching materials include black plastic sheeting or cardboard which do not add nutrients to the soil or improve its structure.

  - Always applied to a warm, wet soil.

  - Thick mulch prevents air flow and encourages pests.

  - For germination of planted seeds through the mulch, a layer of less than 4 inches should be used.

Pest and Disease Control

- Pests and diseases are part of nature.

  - Ideal system represents a natural balance which exists between predators and pests.

  - Imbalance allows one population to become dominant.

  - Aim of natural control in organic methods is to restore a natural balance between pest and predator and to keep pests and diseases down to an acceptable level.

- Organic growers avoid commercial pesticides.

  - Use of natural control based on three reasons:

    1. Safety for people
    2. Cost
    3. Safety for the environment

- Natural Control

  - Growing healthy crops that suffer less damage from pests and diseases.

  - Choosing crops with a natural resistance to specific pests and diseases.

  - Timely planting of crops to avoid the period when a pest does most damage.

- o Companion planting with other crops that pests will avoid, such as onion or garlic.

- o Trapping or picking pests from the crop.

- o Identifying pest and diseases correctly, preventing the grower from wasting time or accidentally eliminating beneficial insects.

- o Using crop rotations to help break pest cycles and prevent a carry over of pests to the next season.

- o Providing natural habitats to encourage natural predators that control pests.

- o Recognizing insects and other animals that eat and control pests.

    - ✓ When pests become a major problem organic growers use natural products like sprays made from chilies, onions, garlic or neem.

    - ✓ National and international **organic standards** provide information on which natural products are allowed or recommended.

Genetic Diversity

- Within a single crop many genetic differences may exist between plants; for example: variability in height or ability to resist diseases.

- Variation or "genetic diversity" between the plants within a crop is beneficial.

- Growing a number of different crops increases diversity and helps to protect against pests and diseases and acts as insurance against crop.

- Organic growers as a whole oppose genetically engineered plants.

- Recommendations for organic growers:

    - o Grow a mixture of crops in the same field (mixed cropping, intercropping, strip cropping).

    - o Grow different varieties of the same crop.

    - o Use as many local crop varieties as possible.

    - o Save the seed of local and improved crop varieties.

    - o Exchange seed with other farmers.

Use of Water

- Use water which is available locally.

- Avoid using water faster than it is replaced naturally.

- Methods practiced by organic growers to use water carefully include:

    - Use of terracing, rain water basins or catchments and careful irrigation.

    - Addition of organic matter to the soil to improve its ability to hold water.

    - Use of mulches to hold water in the soil by stopping the soil surface from drying out or becoming too hot.

Animals and Organic Growing

- Welfare of the animals is considered very important.

- Animals give space to carry out their natural behavior such as standing and moving.

- Confinement methods not used.

- Animals kept from damaging crops.

- Food for animals grown organically.

- Types and breeds of livestock chosen to suit local needs and local conditions and resources.

- Livestock provide manure used to maintain soil fertility.

Sustainable Agriculture

- Defined as "agriculture that, over the long-term, enhances environmental quality and the resource base on which agriculture depends; provides for basic human food and fiber needs; is economically viable; and enhances the quality of life for farmers and society as a whole." (American Society of Agronomy, 1989)

- Concerns include:

    - Depleting of agriculture's resource base.

    - Declining soil productivity due to erosion and loss of organic matter and nutrients.

- Depleting of fertilizer sources like phosphate rock.
- Increasing cost and declining availability of energy.
- Feared consequence of conventional agriculture is a degraded environment – pollution of water by agricultural chemicals, nutrients, and siltation.

- Additional definition
  - A philosophy and collection of practices that seeks to protect resources while ensuring adequate productivity.
  - Strives to minimize off-farm inputs like fertilizers and pesticides.
  - Maximizes on-farm resources like nitrogen fixation by legumes.
  - Top yields are less a goal than optimum and profitable yields based on reduced input costs.
  - Soil and water management are central components of sustainable agriculture.
  - Techniques include crop rotation, conservation tillage, cover cropping, nutrient management, and others.

Summary

Methods and materials used by organic farmers include: keeping and building good soil structure and fertility; using recycled and composted crop wastes and animal manures; correct soil cultivation at the right time, crop rotation, green manures and mulching. Additionally organic growers control diseases, pest, and weeds through careful planning and crop choice, resistant crops, cultivation practice, crop rotation, useful predators that eat pests, increasing genetic diversity and natural pesticides. Manure and compost provide a double benefit to growers—they contain nutrients to promote crop growth and organic matter to improve the soil. Applying these materials to land is a good alternative to other disposal methods. Proper handling of manure reduces nutrient losses and lowers the chance of polluting surface or groundwater. Composting is a way to reduce the C:N ratio of organic materials and to kill harmful organisms.

Resources

Free complementary PowerPoint:
http://www.tagmydoc.com/dl/1BR7t3/gk7a

Parker, R. 2010. Plant and soil science: Fundamentals and applications. (pgs. 220-236) Clifton Park, NY: Delmar Cengage Learning.

IFOAM website
http://www.ifoam.org

The National Organic Program (NOP) through the USDA AMS maintains a website:
http://www.ams.usda.gov/nop/NOP/NOPhome.html

Assessment

1. T or F? Composting increases the weight and volume of organic material used to make the compost.

2. _____ prohibit the use of many substances on organic land including sewage sludge, and provide a list of allowed and disallowed synthetic materials.
    a.) Biological cycles   b.) Organic standards   c.) Environmental qualities   d.) Improved crop varieties

3. T or F? Crop nutrition feeds the soil with manure or compost which feeds the variety of life in the soil, then turns this material into food for plant growth.

4. T or F? Heat generated during composting kills weed seeds.

5. Soil and water management are central components of _____.
    a.) genetic diversity   b.) natural control   c.) sustainable agriculture
       d.) integrated pest management

Take assessment online here:

http://tinyurl.com/PlntSci-27

Hint: When the answer is incorrect, you will see: "Wrong answer! Go Back!"

Notes

54 Hydroponics/Aquaponics

Major Concept

Hydroponics and aquaponics provide a soil-less system for growing crops.

Objectives

- Identify the difference between aeroponics and aquaponics
- List three advantages and three disadvantages of hydroponics
- Identify four plant growth requirements for hydroponics
- Name four vegetable crops suitable for hydroponics or aquaponics

Link to Standards

PS.01. Develop and implement a crop management plan for a given production goal that accounts for environmental factors.

PS.03. Propagate, culture and harvest plants and plant products based on current industry standards.

Key Terms

- Aeroponics
- Aggregate culture
- Aquaponics
- Continuous flow system
- Hydroponics

Hydroponics

- Growing plants without soil.

- Types of Hydroponics Systems

    o **Aggregate culture** - growing in sand, gravel, marbles.

    o Water – aquaculture

    o **Aeroponics** - roots hang in air and sprayed with nutrient solution.

- **Continuous Flow System** – nutrient solution flows constantly over plant roots; used mostly for commercial production.

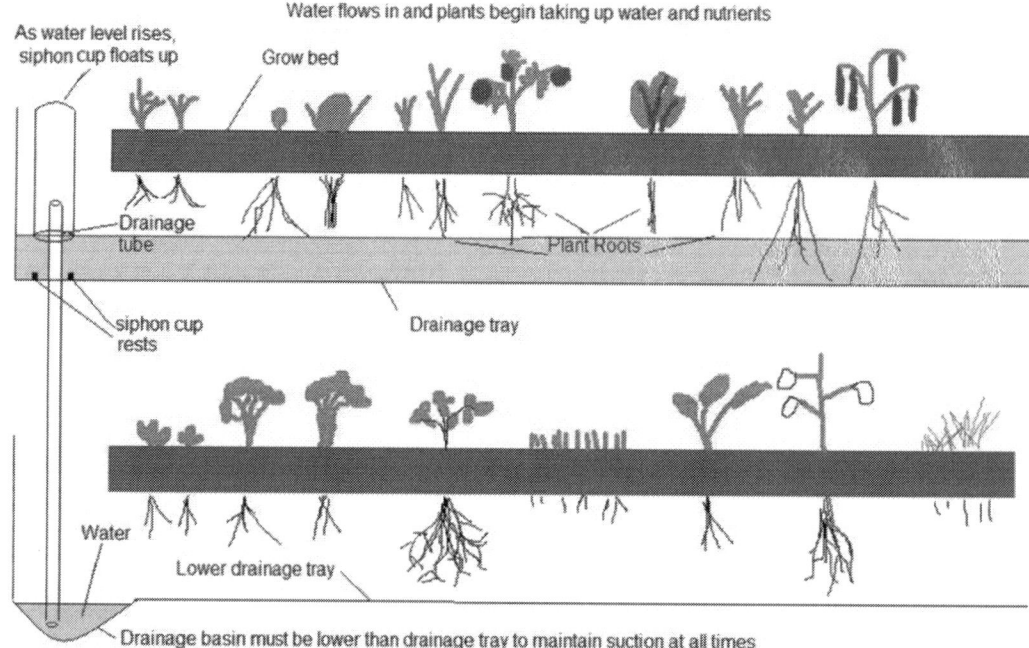

- **Aquaponics** – plants grown in water containing dissolved nutrients, often in combination with fish culture.

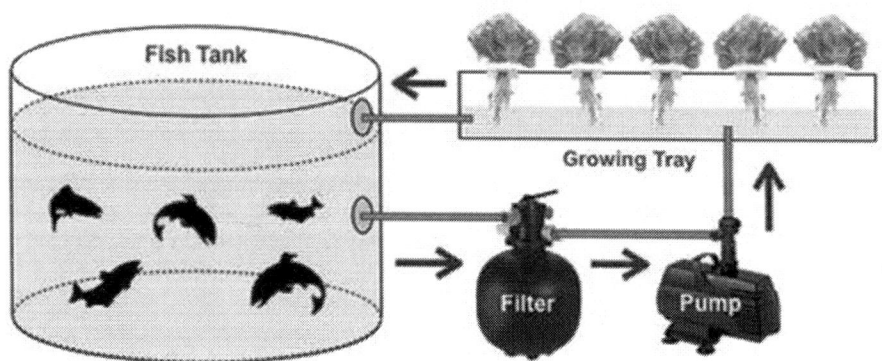

- Advantages of Hydroponics
  - Less pests
  - No weeds
  - Optimum nutrients
  - Higher yields

- Disadvantages of Hydroponics
    - High startup costs
    - High production costs
    - Rapid spread of disease
    - Difficult pollination in greenhouses

Plant Growth Requirements

- Water – very easy to supply.
    - Good water quality needed but requires constant management.
        - Alkalinity or salt content can cause nutrient imbalance.
        - Softened water can contain harmful amounts of sodium.
        - Water that has 320 parts per million of salts is likely to cause nutrient imbalance.
- Oxygen – required for respiration.
    - When plant roots are grown in water, the dissolved oxygen is soon depleted and it becomes necessary to bubble air through the water.
    - Not always necessary to provide supplemental oxygen in aeroponics or continuous flow systems.
- Mineral nutrients – plants absorb minerals through roots to survive.
    - Minerals needed in large quantity are nitrogen, phosphorus, potassium, calcium, magnesium and sulfur.
- Some nutrients are needed in very small amounts such as iron, manganese, boron, zinc, copper, molybdenum, and chlorine; oversupplying is toxic to plants.
- Light – all vegetable plants require large amounts of light.
    - Hydroponic vegetables require at least 8-10 hours of direct sunlight each day.
    - Artificial light is a poor substitute for sunlight and is too expensive for commercial operation.

- Spacing – adequate spacing permits plants to receive adequate sunlight.
    - Tomato plants trimmed to a single stem should be allowed four square feet per plant.
    - Seeded cucumbers need 7-9 square feet per plant.
- Temperature – plants grow well within a limited temperature range.
    - Warm season vegetables should be grown at 50-70°F.
- Support
    - Plants grown in the garden or field are supported by the soil.
    - Hydroponic plants must be supported by strings, staked, or by other means.

Common Vegetable Crops Suitable for Hydroponics or Aquaponics

- Artichokes
- Beans
- Broccoli
- Cabbage
- Carrots
- Celery
- Cucumbers
- Lettuce
- Onions
- Peas
- Peppers
- Potatoes
- Radishes
- Squash
- Tomatoes

Summary

Types of hydroponics include aggregate culture, aeroponics and aquaponics. The growth requirements specific to hydroponics includes water, oxygen, mineral nutrients, light, spacing, temperature and support.

Resources

Free complementary PowerPoint:
http://www.tagmydoc.com/dl/20gP4b/gk7Y

Parker, R. 2010. Plant and soil science: Fundamentals and applications. Clifton Park, NY: Delmar Cengage Learning.

What Hydroponics to Grow?
http://www.interiorgardens.com/grow-hydroponics.html

Assessment

1. Plants growing in water containing dissolved nutrients, often in combination with fish culture is called _____.
   a.) aeroponics   b.) aggregate culture   c.) aquaponics   d.) continuous flow

2. T or F? Disadvantages of hydroponics include less pests, no weeds and optimum nutrients.

3. Water that has 320 parts per million of _____ is likely to cause nutrient imbalance.
   a.) salts   b.) oxygen   c.) weeds   d.) light

4. T or F? It is always necessary to provide supplemental oxygen in aeroponics or continuous flow systems.

5. T or F? Adequate spacing permits plants to produce more vegetables.

Take assessment online here:

http://tinyurl.com/PlntSci-28

Hint: When the answer is incorrect, you will see: "Wrong answer! Go Back!"

Notes

Glossary

A

acclimation Preparation of the new plant for existence outside of the culture.

acre inch/feet Water is measured in acre feet.

adjuvant Herbicide performance enhancer

adenosine diphosphate (ADP) It is converted to ATP for the storage of energy during cell metabolism.

adenosine triphosphate (ATP) The universal energy-transfer molecule.

aeroponics Roots are hung in air and sprayed with nutrient solution.

aflatoxin Highly poisonous substance produced by fungi in grain.

aggregate culture Growing in sand, gravel, marbles.

aggregate fruit Developed from a single flower with many ovaries.

aggregation Mixture of first or primary soil particles into compound particles.

allelopathy One plant emits chemicals from the roots that suppress growth of other plants.

anaphase Mitosis continuing - where pairs of identical chromosomes separate from each other.

annuals Complete life/growing cycle in less than one year and must be planted again.

anther Holds pollen sacs.

apex Tip of the leaf.

aquaponics Plants grown in water containing dissolved nutrients, often in combination with fish culture.

asexual Without sexual means.

autotrophic Plants having the ability to "produce" their own energy directly, being self-sufficient.

B

bacteria Microscopic, single-celled organisms.

bactericides May inhibit bacterial multiplication, or cause their death.

bagasse Fiber of the cane plant after crushing and extraction.

banding Material applied in a row.

base Bottom of the leaf and attaches to the petiole.

beneficial insects Help man by pollinating, providing food and other helpful materials.

best management practices (bmp) Making the most efficient use of animal manures without inflicting damage on the environment.

biennials Complete growing cycle in two growing seasons, not necessarily two years but more than one year.

bioinformatics Study of the inherent structure of biological information and biological systems.

biotechnology Application of molecular biology and genetic engineering for industrial, medical and agricultural advances or improvements or to solve problems.

biplane Early type of aircraft with two pairs of wings, one above the other.

blackstrap molasses Syrup that remains after as much sugar as possible has been extracted from sugar cane.

blade Main body of a leaf.

blight Disease or injury of plants marked by the formation of lesions, withering and death of parts.

boll Fruit of the plant.

border Irrigation used where the land is level.

broadcast Material distributed uniformly over the field.

broad-leafed Having a net-like pattern of veins in the leaves.

budding A bud with bark is removed from the desired plant and placed on the rootstock.

byproduct An incidental or secondary product made in the manufacture or synthesis of something else.

C

calibrate Mark with a gauge or instrument with a standard scale of readings.

callus First form of growth of a tissue culture.

cambium Provides diameter growth in the stem.

capillary water Used by plants and moves freely in the soil.

catkin Slim, cylindrical flower cluster, with inconspicuous or no petals, usually wind-pollinated.

cell plate Forms the wall between the two new daughter cells in a dividing cell.

cell wall Made of hemicellulose and secondary cell walls made of cellulose, lignin, suberin and cutin.

cell Basic structural and physiological unit of crop plants, within which chemical reactions of life occur providing metabolites for plant life and for human use.

check Area bounded by levees [an embankment] running down slope.

chemical A compound or substance that has been purified or prepared, especially artificially.

chlorophyll A green pigment, present in all green plants and in cyanobacteria, responsible for the absorption of light to provide energy for photosynthesis.

chloroplast Double-membrane plastids with chlorophyll, used in photosynthesis, storing starch, and contain genetic information (DNA).

chlorosis Loss of normal green coloration of plant leaves.

chlorotic Lack green color; without chlorophyll.

cholinesterase Enzyme in the body that breaks down acetylcholine, which makes nerves fire, which makes the rest of the body work.

citric acid cycle Also known as the tricarboxylic acid cycle (TCA cycle) or the Krebs cycle; is a series of enzyme-catalysed chemical reactions, which is of central importance in all living cells, especially those that use oxygen as part of cellular respiration.

clay Soil separate consisting of particles less than .002 mm in diameter.

clones Plants regenerated through tissue culture.

combustion The release of energy all at one time, like a fire or an explosion.

complete flower Flower that contains both male and female structures.

compost Organic residues or a mixture of organic residues and soil that have been allowed to biologically decompose to increase plant nutrient availability from organic materials.

composting Piling organic materials under conditions that cause rapid decay. Reduces the carbon-nitrogen ratio and destroys many weed seeds and disease organisms.

compound leaf A leaf that consists of several leaflets.

conifer A tree that bears cones and evergreen needlelike or scale-like leaves.

continuous flow system A system where nutrient solution flows constantly over plant roots; used mostly for commercial production.

cotyledon Embryonic leaves that serve as foodstoring organs or develop into photosynthetic structure as the seed germinates.

cover crop A crop planted to prevent erosion on a soil. Cover crops can be planted on soils not currently being farmed, between crop rows, or after main crop harvest.

cristae Each of the partial partitions in a mitochondrion formed by infolding of the inner membrane.

crop rotation Practice of growing a series of dissimilar types of crops in the same space in sequential seasons for various benefits.

cuttings A portion of a plant that is removed and made to form roots.

cytoplasm Cell contents other than the nucleus.

D

damping-off Plant disease occurring in excessively damp conditions, in particular the collapse and death of young seedlings as a result of a fungal infection.

dark reaction A light independent process that occurs when the products of the light reaction are used to form carbon-to-carbon (C-C) covalent bonds of carbohydrates.

daughter cells Have the same genetic makeup as parent cells.

day-neutral A plant that may flower under any day length.

deadheading Removal of old blooms.

defoliate Removal of green leaves to prevent staining during harvest.

degree day Maximum temperature + minimum temperature in a day divided by 2 minus 50.

dehiscent Fruit that opens naturally and releases seeds when mature.

dicot A flowering plant with two-seed leaves or cotyledons, with xylem and phloem cells separated into zones and nonparallel venation in leaves.

distribution system Canals, ditches, pumps and pipelines that deliver water to an individual farm.

divisions How plants are ordered concerning their characteristics;

dormant Condition of live trees (or some plants) at rest in winter.

dose Refers to the dose (amount) in "milligrams per kilogram" that will kill 50% of a test group of animals.

drip irrigation A method of irrigation that conserves water by slowly releasing small amounts of water through emitters near the plant.

drop spreader An inverted triangle-shaped hopper is mounted between two wheels and usually pulled by a tractor or pickup truck.

drupe A fruit with a large hard seed called a stone.

dusting Sprinkling flowers or plants with pesticides to protect them from insects and rodents.

E

electrical conductivity Ability of the soil solution to conduct an electrical current.

element A simple form of matter that cannot be decomposed by ordinary chemical means. Nitrogen (N), phosphorus (P), potassium (K), carbon (C), and the like, are examples of elements.

emitters In drip or trickle irrigation systems, they are the water delivery mechanisms or outlets.

endoplasmic reticulum Structure extending throughout the cytoplasm of a cell. It functions in the transport of cell products and as a surface for protein synthesis by the ribosomes.

energy Capacity for doing work and for overcoming inertia.

entomology The study of insects.

enzyme A protein that catalyzes a specific chemical change without being used up in the reaction.

epicotyl The part of the axis of an embryo above the region of attachment of the cotyledons.

epidemic Any increase of disease in a population.

epidermis The outer layer of cells on all parts of a young plant and on some parts of older plants-for example, the leaves and fruits.

erosion The removal of soil material by wind or water moving over the land; erosion is a natural process. Most hills and valleys are the result of very slow erosion by water.

ethyl acetate Finger nail polish remover.

eukaryote Genetic information or DNA contained in the nucleus like most organisms.

explants Small pieces of plant tissue.

F

Fertilization (1) Practice of adding nutrients to soil or plants for use by plants (2) The union of the egg and sperm.

fertilizer grade Guaranteed minimum analysis (in percent) of the major plant nutrient elements contained in a fertilizer (refers to percent of N, P_2O_5, K_2O, and S).

fertilizer number Refers to a ratio of nitrogen (N) to phosphorus (P) to potassium (K) and reflects the percentage of nutrients in the material.

fibrous root A type of root system characterized by many branches of fine roots.

field capacity-Amount of water a soil can hold against gravity; expressed as a percentage of the dry weight of a soil.

filament The thin stalk that attaches the anther to the rest of the flower.

firming Once sown, seeds should be pressed into firm contact with the medium (soil) using a tamp.

first aid Assistance given to a person exposed to pesticides before professional help is available.

flood irrigation On level land, water enters through a head ditch or biplane and is released into the individual checks (areas bounded by levees running downslope) by siphons, gates, or valves.

forage crops Feedstuffs from the leaves and stocks of plants and usually eaten by animals. These could be grasses, legumes, or other cultivated crops.

frost susceptibility Likely to be influenced or harmed by frost.

fruit A fleshy, ripened ovary of a tree, shrub, or woody vine eaten raw or cooked.

fumigation Pest control through gaseous pesticides.

fungi Microscopic plants that lack chlorophyll and conductive tissues.

fungicide A chemical used for controlling fungi.

furrow irrigation Water runs down the furrows between plant rows. Water moves to all parts of the soil by capillary action or gravity.

G

gate Door or valve controlling water passage.

genetic engineering Alteration of the genetic components of organisms by human intervention.

genomics Study of an organism's entire genome. The field includes intensive efforts to determine the entire DNA sequence of organisms and fine-scale genetic mapping efforts.

glycolysis The breakdown of glucose by enzymes, releasing energy and pyruvic acid; part of the metabolic process.

GMO Genetically modified organisms.

golgi apparatus Cell organelle, important for glycosylation and secretion in cells.

grafting A shoot or scion is removed from the desired plant and grafted onto the cambium layers of the scion.

grasses Hardy plants that require nitrogen fertilizer.

gravity water Water in excess of capillary water.

green initiatives Actions taken to reduce energy use or support the use of alternative energy sources, reduce greenhouse gas emissions and global warming or to minimize the environmental impact of a business.

green manure A crop grown to be turned under while still green to improve the soil.

greensand Sandy rock or sediment containing a high percentage of the green mineral glauconite and has a very slow K release rate.

guaranteed analysis The nutrient content of commercially available fertilizer is expressed as a percent.

guard cell Openings in the stomata during the daylight hours to permit the free exchange and release of water vapor, and the release of oxygen (O_2).

H

hardening off Treatment of tender plants to enable them to survive a more adverse environment.

harmful insects Compete with man for food.

hay Cut and dried to contain a low level of moisture.

hazard A danger or risk.

head A compact mass of flowers at the top of a stem.

herbicide A phytotoxic chemical used for killing or preventing plant growth.

heterotrophic Organisms that derive their sustenance from other living creatures.

horizon Soil layer.

hydroponics Cultivation of plants in water.

hygroscopic water Water that bonds to the soil particles.

I

immobilization Converting an element from inorganic to organic forms in microbe or plant tissues, immediately rendering the nutrient temporarily unavailable. As nutrients recycle, elements may be released for plant uptake.

imperfect flower A flower missing the stamen or pistil.

incomplete flower Flowers that lack one or more of the four regular parts of a complete flower.

indehiscent Fruit that remains closed at maturity.

inflorescence Groups of flowers arising from a single stem.

insoluble A chemical compound that does not readily dissolve in water.

inspection Careful examination or scrutiny.

internode The region of the stem between any two nodes.

interphase The first step during mitosis called the Resting Stage - This is the period between one division and the next. Individual chromosomes are not visible but the nuclear membrane is visible.

invertebrate Signifies animals without backbones (no vertebrae).

irrigation Applying water to crops in such a way as to keep them wet but not too wet. Different irrigation methods depend on the land, sources of water, work involved and so on.

J-K-L

langbeinite Potassium-magnesium sulfate. This material ($K_2SO_4 \cdot MgSO_4$) is allowed as a nutrient source if it is used in the raw, crushed form without any further refinement or purification.

larvae The active immature form of an insect.

layering A vegetative method of propagating new plants by producing adventitious roots before the new plant is cut from the parent. A portion of an attached shoot is partially buried underground where roots develop.

LD50 Refers to the dose (amount) in "milligrams per kilogram" that will kill 50% of a test group of animals.

legume Plants with the characteristic of forming nitrogen-fixing nodules on their roots, in this way making use of atmospheric nitrogen.

leucoplasts Organelles in cells, used for the storage of oil. starch, and proteins.

levee Earthen dike used to enclose water.

light reaction Occurs in the grana when light strikes chlorophyll a in such a way as to excite electrons to a higher energy state. In a series of reactions, the energy is converted (along an electron transport-like process) into ATP and NADPH. Water is split in the process, releasing oxygen as a by-product of the reaction.

long-day Plants that require a day longer than its critical day length in order to flower; also called short-night plants.

M

macronutrient Chemical element necessary in relatively larger amounts (usually greater than 500 parts per million in the plant) for plant growth. These elements are C, H, O, N, P. K, S, Ca and Mg.

margin The edge of the leaf.

marketing The act or business of promoting and selling products.

mechanical shaker A machine designed to shake a tree causing fruit or nuts to fall off.

media Growing materials in which plants can be started that are loose, well drained, fine textured, low in nutrients, and free of diseases.

meristem A region of a plant where cells are not fully differentiated and are capable of repeated mitotic divisions.

mesophilic Oganisms whose optimum temperature for growth is an intermediate range, between 59 and 95 degrees Dominant microorganisms in early and late stages of composting.

metamorphosis In an insect or amphibian, the process of transformation from an immature form to an adult form in two or more distinct stages.

metaphase The third step during cell division, between prophase and anaphase, during which the chromosomes become attached to the spindle fibers.

micronaire A measure of fiber fineness and maturity.

micronutrient Chemical element necessary in relatively small amounts (usually less than 100 parts per million in the plant) for plant growth. These elements are B, Cl, Cu, Fe, Mn, Mo, and Zn.

microtubules Organelles made from tubulin which compose centrioles and cilia.

midrib The large central vein down the middle of the leaf.

mineralization Decomposition or oxidation of the chemical compounds in organic matter into plant-accessible forms.

mitochondria Cell organelles composed of an outer membrane and a winding inner membrane. A series of chemical reactions that occur on the inner membrane convert the energy of oxidation into the chemical energy of ATP.

mitosis The division of cells in which the genetic material of the cell is duplicated exactly.

molasses Syrup that remains after as much sugar as possible has been extracted from sugar cane.

mollusk An invertebrate of a large phylum that includes snails, slugs, mussels, and octopuses. They have a soft, unsegmented body and live in aquatic or damp habitats, and most kinds have an external calcareous shell.

molt Shed old feathers, hair, or skin, or an old shell, to make way for a new growth.

monocot A flowering plant with one seed leaf or cotyledon, xylem, and phloem contained within bundles, and parallel venation in leaves.

mottled Spotted or blotched leaves.

mulch Materials such as straw, sawdust, leaves, plastic film, and the like, spread upon the surface of the soil to protect the soil and plant roots from the effects of raindrops, soil crusting, freezing, evaporation, and so on. Apply protective materials to the soil surface.

multiple fruit A classification of fruit with flowers that are separated but closely clustered such as in mulberry, fig and pineapple.

N

narrow-leafed Grasses, sedges, rushes and cattails, which all have parallel veins in their leaves.

necrotic The death of most or all of the cells or tissue due to disease.

nematodes Microscopic roundworms, usually living in soil, many of which feed on plant roots. They cause galls on roots, cause root lesions, injure root tips, and sometimes cause excessive root branching. Nematodes reproduce by eggs.

neutron moisture probe Measures soil water content using a radioactive source.

nitrogen cycle Sequences of transformations in N forms among gaseous. inorganic. and organic compounds. These transformations occur in cycles and involve numerous compounds, organisms. or reactions.

node The region of the stem where one or more leaves are attached. Buds are commonly borne at the node.

no-till Planting a crop directly into an unprepared seedbed. The tillage involved in planting is nothing more than opening the soil for the purpose of placing seed at the intended depth. This usually involves opening a small slit or punching a hole into the soil. Usually no cultivation occurs during crop production. Weed control is achieved entirely by surface applied and contact herbicides. Also referred to as zero tillage or slot planting.

nucleus A membrane-bounded cellular body that contains the principal hereditary material.

nut crop Hard, bony, one-seeded fruit of a woody plant.

nutrient availability Amount of soil or fertilizer nutrient supply that can be immediately used by plants.

nutrients Fertilizer. particularly phosphorus and nitrogen-the two most common components that run off in sediment.

O

organelles The inside parts of a cell such as the golgi apparatus. nucleus. Ribosomes, microtubules and storage particles.

organic Chemical compounds of carbon combined with other chemical elements and generally manufactured in the life processes of plants and animals. Most organic compounds are a source of food for bacteria and are usually combustible; derived from living organisms (plants and animals).

organic farming Pest and nutrient management are achieved with nonchemical methods.

organic matter Partially decomposed plant and animal residues in soil and soil humus.

organic soil Soil that contains a high percentage of organic matter or materials (greater than 15-20 percent) throughout the soil profile.

organic standards A framework of guidelines and regulations that govern the production of organic crops.

ovary Enlarged. bulbous. basal part of the pistil that bears the ovules-the egg-containing units that. after fertilization. become the seeds attached either to its central axis or to its inner wall.

ovule Contains the female gametes.

oxidative phosphorylation A series of chemical reactions occurring on the inner membrane that convert the energy of oxidation into the chemical energy of ATP. In this process the predominant energy transfer molecule is ATP.

P-Q

palisade cells Cells within the leaf may be formed into two layers: the upper, tightly packed with elongated palisade cells; and the lower. loosely packed with spongy tissue.

palmate In leaves, the principal veins extend from the petiole near the base of the blade similar to the bones in the hand.

panicle Loose, branching cluster of flowers, as in oats.

parenchyma Cells with thin cell walls and with large vacuoles. In leaves. Parenchyma cells contain chloroplasts for photosynthesis.

parent cells Daughter cells having the same genetic makeup as parent cells.

parent material Unconsolidated and somewhat chemically weathered mineral or organic matter from which soils are derived by natural soil development processes.

parts per million (ppm) A ratio similar to percent, the number of parts in one million parts; percent is the number of parts in one hundred parts.

pasture Land covered with grass and other low plants suitable for grazing animals, especially cattle or sheep.

pathogens Disease-causing organisms.

perennial A plant or plant part that lives for more than two years.

permanent wilting point (PWP) Point at which no more water is available to the plant.

peroxisomes Organelles in the plant cell that use oxygen to carry out catabolic reactions.

pesticide A chemical substance used to kill or control pests such as weeds, insects, fungi, mites, algae, rodents, and other undesirable agents.

petiole Stalk of the leaf.

pH, soil Negative logarithm of the hydrogen ion concentration of a soil [pH = -log (W)]. Degree of acidity or alkalinity as determined by an electrode or indicator at a specified soil moisture content and expressed in terms of the pH scale (1-14); a low pH indicates acid soil, a pH of 7 is neutral, and a high pH indicates an alkaline soil.

phloem One of the two components of the vascular system whose primary function is the transport of manufactured products.

photoperiod Length of daylight.

photoperiodism Response of the plant to the length of daylight.

photosynthates Products of photosynthesis are carbohydrates such as sugars and starches (CHOs) and other complex compounds referred to collectively.

photosynthesis Process in a plant of making sugars for growth and respiration from the raw products of water, carbon dioxide, and, sunlight releasing oxygen.

phototropism Tendency of plants to "lean" in the direction of the greatest light intensity.

pinnate In the leaf, the secondary veins extend from the midrib, like the divisions of a feather.

pistil Female portion of the flower responsible for the formation of seeds.

plasmolemma Plasma membrane or cytoplasmic membrane.

plumule Young shoot.

pollen Contains the male gametes.

pollination Act of placing pollen from the male reproductive organ onto the female reproductive organ of a flower; often is carried out by bees or wind.

pome Fruits that have a core and embedded seeds.

post-emergence Application of an herbicide after weed or plant has emerged (and is usually visible) from the soil.

post-emergent Occurring or applied after emergence of a plant from the soil and before full growth.

pre-emergent Of or pertaining to seedlings before they emerge or appear above ground:

pre-plant Before planting.

prophase The second stage of cell division, before metaphase, during which the chromosomes become visible as paired chromatids and the nuclear envelope disappears.

protective equipment Must be worn when handling, mixing or applying the pesticide.

proteomics Study of genetics which refers to all the proteins expressed by a genome; involves the identification of proteins in an organism and the determination of their role in physiological functions.

protoplast Refers to the inside of the cell or the cellular contents.

pruning Removing all the old wood and leaving growth that will produce next year's crop.

pull-type spreader Consists of a bin mounted on a two- or four-wheeled trailer frame and pulled by a tractor or truck.

pulp Squeezed shreds.

pupa Inactive immature form of an insect.

R

raceme A flower cluster with the separate flowers attached by short equal stalks at equal distances along a central stem.

receptacle Where the apex of the pedicel upon which the organs of a flower are developed.

radicle Root.

ratoon Second harvest.

regulations Establish the format for pesticide labels and prescribe what information they must contain.

remote sensing Science of getting information about an object by acquiring data with a device not in contact with that object.

residues Crop materials, including roots and tops, that remain on the soil following harvest.

respiration Process of converting sugars into carbon dioxide, water, and energy. Often, the energy is in the form of heat.

rhizomes Underground stems.

ribosomes Where the RNA goes for translation into proteins.

root cap Conductive tissue involved in plant growth.

root hairs Specialized cell extensions that penetrate into the openings between soil particles.

rootbound Restricted roots.

rootstock That part of a tree that becomes the root system of a grafted or budded tree.

runners New plants are formed at nodes by runners, which are stems from old plants. The stems grow along the ground.

runoff That portion of precipitation or irrigation water that flows off a field and enters surface streams or water bodies; water that flows off the surface of the land without sinking into the soil.

S

sand Small coarse-grained pieces of rock.

saprophytes Organisms that live on dead or decaying matter.

saturation When all of the pore (voids) spaces in the soil are full of water.

scion A piece of last year's growth with three or four buds; the part inserted on the understock.

sclerenchyma cells Thick cell walls, which make plant fibers.

secondary growth Follows primary growth in some plants and results in an increased girth as layers of woody tissue are laid down. Monocots and herbaceous dicots typically exhibit only primary growth.

seed Unit of dispersal for the new plant. It provides some protection from injury and drying and some nourishment for the young plant until it can make its own food.

seed coat Ovule walls develop from the seed coat.

seedbed Soil prepared to receive seeds.

self-pollination Process by which pollen is transferred from an anther to a stigma of the same flower or another flower of the same plant or cultivar.

segmentation Parts of an insect body.

separation A form of propagation by which plants that produce bulbs or corms multiply.

shoot bud A bud on the aboveground portion of a plant.

short-day Plants requiring a day shorter than its critical day length or a night longer than its critical dark period in order to flower; also called long-night plants.

side dressing Apply fertilizer to the side of a row for best growth results.

sieve tube cells Long, slender tubes with porous ends (occur only in angiosperms).

signal word WARNING, DANGER, CAUTION, etc.

silage Chopped green forage that has been allowed to ferment in the absence of air.

silt A very soft and flour-like soil separate (particle size).

siphon Tube used to convey liquid upwards

slag A byproduct of steel manufacturing.

slow-release Slowly available: Do not go readily into solution in water but will release slowly with time.

sod Grass that has soil and roots attached.

sodic Containing excessive amounts of sodium. Sodic soil contains sufficient exchangeable sodium to interfere with plant growth (ESP greater than 15 percent).

soil The upper layer of earth in which plants grow, a black or dark brown material typically consisting of a mixture of organic remains, clay, and rock particles.

soil aeration Exchanges soil and atmospheric air to maintain adequate oxygen for plant roots.

soil air Underground, plant roots and soil organism's use up oxygen and emit carbon dioxide resulting in soil air that has less oxygen and more carbon dioxide than the atmosphere.

soil classification Soils based on three dimensional entities that can be grouped together according to their similar physical, chemical, and mineralogical properties.

soil conservation Protection of the soil from erosion or chemical deterioration. Prevention of excessive loss of fertility by either natural or artificial means. A combination of land use and management methods that safeguard the soil against depletion or deterioration by natural or human-induced factors. A division of soil science concerned with soil conservation by preventive action.

soil erosion The movement of soil particles from one place to another under the influence of water or wind.

soil profile Refers to the arrangement and properties of the various soil layers.

soil separates Mineral soil particles defined by specified size limits: sand (2.G-0.05 mm), silt (0.05 mm-D.002 mm), and clay (less than 0.002 mm).

soil solution Water held by soils and the nutrients it contains.

soil test Analysis of nutrient-supplying properties of a soil sample to determine the capacity of that soil to support crop growth.

soluble Able to be dissolved.

solvent A liquid capable of dissolving. Water is the universal solvent.

spike A flower head made up of a central stem with the flowers growing directly on it.

staking Keeping plants in the correct growing position by using wires, wooden posts, or similar supports.

stamen Male part of a flower; it produces pollen.

stem Forms the major aboveground structural part of the plant; also is the attachment point for leaves, flowers, and fruit. It also contains the water and food distribution system.

stigma Tip of the style or pistil, especially adapted to receive the pollen grains, which is expanded into a bulb or disk or divided into two or more slender parts.

stolons Above ground stems.

stomata Pores on the bottom of a leaf through which carbon dioxide enters the plant and water vapor exits.

strip cropping Practice of growing crops that require different types of tillage, such as row and sod, in alternate strips, along contours or across the prevailing direction of wind.

stuntiny A virus in leaves causing a yellow mosaic pattern.

style Elongated stalk or neck connecting the ovary with the stigma.

subsoil The layer of soil just under the topsoil.

sustainable agriculture Agriculture that, over the long-term, enhances environmental quality and the resource base on which agriculture depends; provides for basic human food and fiber needs; is economically viable; and enhances the quality of life for farmers and society as a whole.

T

taproots Prominent primary roots from which all other lateral rootlets or secondary roots grow. They may divide, become fleshy, and often penetrate deeply into the soil.

taxonomy Organizational system for descriptive classification of plants.

telophase The final phase of cell division, between anaphase and interphase, in which the chromatids or chromosomes move to opposite ends of the cell and two nuclei are formed.

tensiometer Consists of a porous cup filled with water that can be buried to a desired depth in the soil in the vicinity of roots.

terminal When fowers or clusters of flowers are carried on the ends of the axis or branches.

terraces Low dams or dikes built across slopes to catch runoff water and eroded soil before they leave the field.

thermophilic The description of an organism that thrives at high temperatures.

tillers First side shoots in small grains.

tilth Physical condition of soil related to its ease of tillage, fitness as a seedbed, and degree of impedance to seedling emergence and root penetration.

tissue Large groups of organized cells of similar structure to perform specific functions in the plant. The two generalized types of tissues are meristematic and permanent.

tissue culture Process or technique of making plant or animal tissue grow in a culture medium outside the organism.

tonoplast A membrane that bounds the chief vacuole of a plant cell.

top dressing Uniformly apply fertilizer over the field, generally with P on established forage and N on small grains during the growing season.

topography Slope of the land and the position on the landscape, such as the top of a hill, a hillside, or the foot of a slope.

top soil Layer of soil moved in normal cultivation.

toxic Poisonous.

tracheids Elongated, conductive cells, the contents of which are non-living.

translocation Movement of water and dissolved compounds through the plant.

transpiration Process of water exiting the plant through the stomata.

turf grasses Collection of grass plants that form a ground cover that requires regular maintenance; for example a golf course.

tuber Edible portion of the plant, and botanically, stems not roots. They are stems because they contain all the morphological features of stems.

turgid Condition in which a cell or plant is fully expanded by hydrostatic pressure exerted on the cell wall by the protoplast.

turgor Stiffness in the cells.

U

umbel Type of inflorescence

V

vacuole A space or vesicle within the cytoplasm of a cell, enclosed by a membrane and typically containing fluid.

variety A plant group different in the wild from the general species. It is often used for varieties named from the general species.

vector Carrier of disease.

vegetable A plant or part of a plant used as food.

vegetative Period when the plant grows vigorously and rapidly.

vertebrate Signifies animals without backbones (no vertebrae).

vesicle An air-filled swelling in a plant.

viruses pathogenic particles that infect cells of plants and animals.

volatile Evaporates rapidly, as in chemical.

volatilization Diffusion into the atmosphere.

volunteer plants Plants that may grow following harvest or the next season without being planted.

W

warm-season Refers to plants that are usually killed by frosts and require much warmer temperatures to grow properly. They are planted later in the spring.

water erosion Erosion by water is caused by raindrops, surface flow and gully flow. Water erosion is a selective process in which the organic matter and finer soil particles are removed first. This selective feature of soil erosion rapidly destroys productivity of cultivated lands.

water holding capacity Ability of a soil to hold water.

water-logged soil A condition of poor soil aeration with an oxygen level around zero.

watershed Surrounding land area that drains into a lake, river, or river system.

weed A plant growing where it is not wanted.

whorl Three or more leaves at each node.

wilt When plants lose water more rapidly than they take it up, they wilt. Life processes slow, and growth may even stop.

wilting point (WP) Plant will not revive unless immediately irrigated.

wind The perceptible natural movement of the air, especially in the form of a current of air blowing from a particular direction.

wind erosion Erosion by wind is common in dry areas where soils are often bare of vegetation and high wind velocities are common.

X

Xeric Referring to the tropical zone.

xylem One of two components of the vascular system whose primary function is to transport water and soil nutrients.

Y

yield Amount of crop produced in response to cultural practices.

yield potential Level of crop productivity that can be obtained under specific physical, chemical, and environmental conditions.

Z

zygote Cell formed by the union of the male and female gametes, the new organism developing from this cell.

Appendix

National Agriculture, Food and Natural Resources (AFNR) Career Cluster Content Standards

National AFNR Content Standards, Revised 2015

Source: https://www.ffa.org/thecouncil/afnr

Purpose

The AFNR Career Cluster Content Standards provide state agricultural education leaders and educators with a high-quality, rigorous set of standards to guide what students should know and be able to do after completing a program of study in each of the AFNR career pathways.

State leaders and local educators are encouraged to use the standards as a guide for the development of well-planned curriculum and assessments for AFNR-related CTE programs. These standards are intended to help shape the design of all components of an agricultural education program including:

- Classroom and laboratory instruction.
- Career and Technical Student Organization (CTSO) experiences through organizations such as the National FFA Organization and the Post-Secondary Agriculture Students Organization (PAS).
- Work-based learning experiences such as Supervised Agricultural Experience (SAE) Programs and internships.

Process

The 2015 revision focused on ensuring that the content standards:

- Reflect essential and up-to-date knowledge and skills that students need to be ready for early-career success in a variety of AFNR disciplines.
- Provide a sound basis upon which to design AFNR related Career and Technical Education (CTE) courses.
- Provide a sound basis for developing end of course/program assessments to measure students' attainment of essential disciplinary knowledge and skills.
- The multi-stage review and revision process began in 2014 and was informed by input and guidance from more than 270 secondary and post-secondary educators, business, industry and state leaders in career and technical education

Alignments and Crosswalks

The National Association of State Directors of Career and Technical Education/National Career Technical Education Foundation (NASDCTEc/NCTEF) have provided permission to use the Common Career and Technical Core (CCTC) Standards in support of this project. In addition, the standards have been reviewed to identify crosswalks to the following national academic standards:

- Common Core English Language Arts
- Common Core Mathematics
- Next generation Science Standards
- Green/Sustainability Knowledge and Skill Statements
- National Standards for Financial Literacy
- AFNR Documents AFNR Career Cluster Content Standards
- AFNR Career Cluster Content Standards CROSSWALKS
- AFNR Cluster Skills: Agribusiness Systems Career Pathway; Animal Systems Career Pathway; Biotechnology Systems Career Pathway; Career Ready Practices; Environmental Service Systems Career Pathway; Food Products and Processing Systems Career Pathway; Natural Resource Systems Career Pathway; Plant Systems Career Pathway and Power, Structural and Technical Systems Career Pathway

Availabiltiy

All of the National AFNR Content Standards and associated information are available online at the National FFA website or by following this link: https://www.ffa.org/thecouncil/afnr

Also, the complete document of the National AFNR Content Standard can be downloaded from the National Agricultural Institute's "TagMyDoc" site by following this URL: : http://www.tagmydoc.com/AFNRSTDS

Or by scanning this QR code:

Made in the USA
San Bernardino, CA
22 January 2018